RETHINKING MONEY AND FINANCE

*Economics, Morality
And Common Sense*

by Richard G. Patterson

© Richard G. Patterson 2023

Contents

Introduction 1
Money 7
Banks 23
Interest 31
Wealth and Growth 47
Finance 58
Risk Management and Liquidity 68
Investment, Capital and Property 84
Deficit Spending 96
Inflation and Recession 107
Employment and Work 123
Foreign Trade 136
Currency Exchange 158
Taxes 164
Markets 170
Appendix: What About Cryptocurrency 179
Endnotes 189
Bibliography 197
Name Index 217

*For my granddaughter
in the hope that her generation
can repair the damage done by mine.*

Join a discussion of some of these ideas on
www.RethinkingMoney.org

Introduction
"The Economy, Stupid"[1]

Presidential elections often involve debates about the economy – what ails it and how to fix it. Increasingly it seems to me that candidates exist in parallel universes in terms of economics. Each side bases its analysis and policy proposals on a set of certainties which seem hopelessly contradictory to the certainties of the other. Campaigns do not really permit candidates to explain the assumptions behind their economic proposals. Speeches tend to be peppered with buzzwords or references that will enable the "average American voter" to connect the proposals to some personal experience that shapes his or her ideas about "the economy."

Economics was the only course in my undergraduate education that I did not love, and I sampled a wide variety of courses. I did find a course in Marxism genuinely exciting, but it was a philosophy course about the nature of man and society that did not come anywhere near government publications about gross national product or inflation. Only later in life as I struggled to keep my head above water financially did it occur to me that I may have missed out on learning about how the world actually works. Knowing what it takes to get ahead in the world is, of course, very different from understanding why society works the way it does or whether it might be possible for it to work better. I may have resigned myself to my fairly limited ability to "get ahead," but I continue to ruminate on what is wrong with the way society works and whether it could be improved.

This book is the result of two things: a growing concern about the political divide in this country and the 2007-2008 financial crisis. My initial efforts to understand what really separates liberals and conservatives led me to embark on a sustained analysis of the thought of Thomas Sowell,[2] a conservative whose policy recommendations I found repugnant but whose books included attempts to explain the differences in "vision" or "ideology" at the root of all political debate. I wanted to find the most fundamental point where I parted company with him. My conclusion was that it lay somewhere in his conception of the relationship between individuals and society. Since Sowell is an economist, it is no surprise that his thought is built on the idea of the "market" as the glue which holds society together.

After the financial crisis as political debate became more and more unhinged, I became increasingly convinced that the root of most of the anger was economic insecurity. The reading I did in my efforts to understand the 2007-2008 financial crisis included *How Markets Fail* by John Cassidy and *The Big Short* by Michael Lewis. Cassidy's book seemed to confirm my skepticism about free market theory and to suggest that the best solution that could be hoped for was more vigilant regulation of financial markets.

Cassidy makes a distinction between "utopian economics" and "reality-based economics" where utopian economic theory is based on the idea that a market is a self-regulating system that tends towards equilibrium. Cassidy does not hesitate to call it an ideology which attempts to impose a system onto the messy realities of business and finance and which derives policy recommendations from models rather than empirical study of the real world. Reality-based economics is of course much less coherent because it is based on all kinds of phenomena studied from a variety of angles.

Cassidy's interpretation of the development of economic theory since Adam Smith is very persuasive, and one wants to hope that policy recommendations based on truly scientific analysis of real-world data can push us towards a more stable (and just?) economy. Nonetheless I think there is another dimension in the approach to economics that needs to be considered. I am all for vigilant regulation and incremental reform, but it needs to be guided by a vision of where we want to go. Real world data can tell us how the current system works. It may even reveal that the current system is inherently unstable. It cannot show us how it could be improved or even what "improvement" would be. The problem is that economics is dealing with social institutions and conventions. It is not a matter of physical or natural laws but of human choices. The way we live together is a political choice in the most fundamental sense.

The Big Short, of course, captured the absurdity of the events that precipitated the crisis, and, as much as I was repulsed in the abstract by the idea that anyone could profit from a catastrophe of this magnitude, I found myself rooting for the oddball characters who saw the writing on the wall despite the obstinate blindness of the rest of the financial community. I also read a paper Ben Bernanke wrote in response to the recommendations of "The Squam Lake Report."[3] I was encouraged by the idea that respected academic economists had specific suggestions for fixing problems with the system, even if I failed to see everyone rushing to implement the reforms they suggested.

Still there was something surreal about the whole context of these discussions. When I was reading *The Big Short*, I sent an email to my brother, who had given me the book, in which I said, "I do have one question. I can't figure out the concept of credit default swaps. The descriptions of it as insurance against default on a loan make sense except I have the impression people are buying insurance against loans in which they have no ownership stake at all. It strikes me as betting pure and simple, and I don't get why it has to be legal. This is probably the third time I've read an explanation of credit default swaps and I'm still not getting it."

The economists at Squam Lake, of course, had addressed this very question:

> Although credit default swaps can be used as insurance against a default, the buyer of protection is not required to own the named borrower's debt or to be otherwise exposed to the borrower's default. Both buyers and sellers may use credit default swaps to speculate on a firm's prospects. Some have suggested that investors should not be allowed to purchase CDS protection unless they are hedging exposure to the named borrower. This argument is flawed. Buying and selling credit default swaps without the underlying bond is like buying and selling equity or index options without the underlying security. The advantages of these activities are well understood. Eliminating this form of speculation would make CDS markets less liquid, increasing the cost of trading and making CDS rate quotes a less reliable source of information about the prospects of named borrowers.[4]

Since the advantages of buying and selling equity or index options were not well understood by me, I was disqualified from mounting a rebuttal to this argument. I did know the advantages of making quick money with options (as well as the disadvantages of losing money with the same), and I had heard an argument that derivatives help reduce market volatility; but I could not escape the feeling that there was something screwy with a system in which I can borrow money to sell something I do not own (i.e. a "put on margin").

A few months after I read *The Big Short*, I stumbled onto a translation of a book by two Italian academics, Massimo Amato and Luca Fantacci. It is called *The End of Finance*, and it was almost as much of an eye-opener for me as *The Big Short*. Needless to say it is an entirely different kind of book, but it seemed to me to offer a persuasive analysis of the real roots of the financial crisis and to suggest practical long-term solutions. You can still see my review of the book on Amazon, and I was surprised that virtually no one else in the U.S. seemed to pick up on the book. I never saw a review of it in a magazine or paper, although I gather it got a bit more attention in the U.K. I gave it to my brother, who had a career at the United Nations Industrial Development Organization and has taught economics. He found the philosophical style of it difficult reading and the proposals unconvincing. I tried to suggest it to a couple of friends, but they seemed too skeptical of my summary of the argument in the book to give it much thought.

Part of the reason I embarked on this attempt to explore my own "common sense" understanding of economics was that I hoped to present the ideas from *The End of Finance* in a way that is more accessible. The middle portion of that book is a history of finance since the Middle Ages, and I am not going to try to repeat that. Anyone trying to read the book should really stick with it until it gets to the historical survey. Even if one finds the attempt to analyze finance and credit "phenomenologically" off-putting, the description of the watershed moments in the history of finance is fascinating. The net effect of this history is the sense that there is nothing inevitable about the way finance currently works. It is a result of very specific decisions made in the past for a variety of reasons, and it can be altered.

The conclusions of their analysis of finance can be summed up in some seemingly radical statements about money, credit and financial markets. Amato and Fantacci argue that the ultimate cause of the last financial crisis is the confused notion that money is a commodity. They insist that a market economy can exist without financial markets or even interest-bearing loans. They are fully aware of the social, political and intellectual obstacles to implementing such an economy, and they do not have a fully developed plan for how to achieve it, but they do seem to think steps can be taken towards it. What is needed above all is an understanding of the goal. In their introduction to *Saving the*

Market from Capitalism they summarize in no uncertain terms their perspective:

> To begin with, we have to distinguish between markets for actual goods and services, which should be as free, integrated and extensive as possible, and financial markets, which shouldn't even exist…Market economy and capitalism are not synonymous. Actually, they are incompatible. Capitalism is a market economy with one market too many: the money and credit market…
>
> Above all, however, and at a more basic level, even people who don't invest in stocks and bonds, and possibly protest against the excessive power of Wall Street, are still hardly likely to call into question the underlying principle of the financial markets – the dogma of liquidity. This consists in the apparently natural idea that cash (liquidity, in other words) is the safest form of saving and, consequently, one will part with it only for an investment that is equally liquid or that yields sufficient interest to compensate for the lack of liquidity. …
>
> But there is still more to it. Independently of the financial markets, the idea that money is wealth and that the mere holding of it merits a reward is the root of an endemic evil that is both social and human. Call it as you will. Until a couple of centuries ago, it was called usury. Then the classical economists called it rent, and criticized it harshly. Today it's called rate of interest. In any case it is income obtained without working or running entrepreneurial risks and is thus quite distinct from both the worker's wage and the entrepreneur's profit.
>
> Now it may seem trite to point it out, but in times like these we'd better try to be basic: if somewhere someone is making money without working, somewhere else someone is working without making money.

Much of their argument is based on their analysis of "liquidity." The full implications of this analysis are by no means immediately obvious or intuitive, but it is clear that one factor in the 2007-2008 financial crisis was the way in which credit dried up, and they see this as a "liquidity trap" caused by a misconception of finance at the root of the system. They try to get at this misconception partially by their dissection of what is really involved in "credit." There was a long and winding road from my muddled common sense understanding of credit to the point where I was able see that the very existence of financial markets is the heart of the problem. To begin we must start with the idea of money.

Money

A feast is made for laughter, and wine maketh merry; but money answereth all things.[5]

Money doesn't grow on trees, but it is supposed to grow if it is put in the right place. Most people probably see no contradiction in these two ideas.

Everyone understands money. It's what makes the world go round. It is also, of course, the root of all evil. No one needs to understand modern monetary theory much less psychoanalytical or anthropological theories about money to pay his or her bills. While I am intrigued by the connection psychoanalysis sees between money and excrement, it has never seemed particularly relevant to my attempts to manage my finances. Like most people I understand money well enough to know I never have "enough."

There was a moment, however, when I felt my understanding of money changed as I was struggling to make ends meet. It struck me that money was really a kind of scorecard tracking my activities. Some things I did enabled me to win points; others involved losing them. Perhaps what triggered the thought was the realization that many of the things I most wanted to do seemed to have no effect on my "score" whatsoever. I could not pin down how my perception of money had changed, but something felt different. In retrospect I think what shifted was that I no longer thought of money as a tangible object. The coins and bills that had always been "money" in my imagination were replaced by a completely abstract accounting system. Somehow to me there seemed to be a difference between possessing something physical and simply having a credit balance on some set of books. It seems trivial, but I think it was a genuine intuition into something about money that has significant implications.

The most common definition of money is a functional one: money is what serves as a medium of exchange, a store of value, and a unit of account. Unit of account refers to the numerical metric used to assign values or prices to things and services. A medium of exchange may be physical coins and currency, or it may be entries in a bookkeeping system reflecting economic transactions. Being a store of value simply means that money may be held for a period of time without losing its value. It can be accumulated and used for future purchases. This seems innocuous and general enough to be devoid of controversy, but in fact it all depends on how it is interpreted. There are some who have said that the last financial crisis ultimately had its roots in the mistaken idea that money should be a store of value or a commodity whose price is set by a market. There are others, however, who start with this definition and proceed to demonstrate that the problem is rooted in the abandonment of the gold standard.

Alan Greenspan wrote a short essay in 1966 entitled "Gold and Economic Freedom." Most people might assume that an essay on gold and freedom would simply point out that the more money you have, the freer you are to do whatever you want, but this was not at all Greenspan's point. He claimed that only a society in which money is tied to a precious metal can hope to enjoy basic freedoms, or at least what he called "economic freedom."

It is mainly the notion of a medium of exchange that tempts us to think of money as a thing. While "store of value" may conjure up an image of Scrooge McDuck's money bin, most of us are perfectly comfortable with the idea that we do not physically possess the money we "have." A large figure on a bank statement is sufficient. Certainly "unit of account" does not imply anything physical. The dollar in this sense is like the inch. An inch can be represented by something physical like a ruler, but it is itself an abstract concept serving as a unit of measurement. It is not made of plastic or metal.

In an exchange, however, one feels that "things" are involved. I give you something (money) and you give me something (a car). To some extent the idea of "exchange" assumes things are involved, but we all know that physical money is involved in very few of our larger purchases, and "exchange" also covers payment for services where what is purchased is not an "object."

So what exactly is a "medium of exchange?" Money facilitates the exchange of goods. You want a car, and I want a boat. I can sell you a car; you give me money; I buy a boat from someone else (who does not need a car). Money enables us to keep track of the relative value we assign to things and to establish equivalences between the features and condition of a car and those of a boat.

Money as a "medium of exchange" is an abstract and completely rational concept. Nonetheless we all know that people are completely irrational when it comes to money. I grew up in a culture in which money was not really a polite topic of conversation. There was something "crass" about it, and even the concept of "commerce" still carried a very faint odor of disdain, as though one really ought to be able to live without having to buy and sell things. The idea that everything (and everyone) has its price was vaguely repugnant since things and people should be valued in ways that cannot be expressed numerically.

Note that there is nothing inherent in the idea of money as a medium of exchange that implies that money itself should be a commodity with a price. Years ago when someone told me he earned his living in money markets, I asked half-facetiously if that meant he bought and sold money. To me the idea of buying and selling money was circular to the point of absurdity, but clearly this was hardly the case with my acquaintance, who made a much better living than I by doing precisely that.

How can money be a commodity that is bought and sold (using money)? If I give you a five for five ones, that is hardly an economic transaction. The main reason "medium of exchange" seems to be associated with a commodity is because it is generally explained with the classical narrative about how money emerged from barter. If you base economics on a myth that starts with autonomous self-interested individuals trading, you end up with money as one commodity that is a convenient "medium of exchange." This is the basic assumption of what is probably the most popular analysis of money, *The Theory of Money and Credit* by Ludwig von Mises.

Mises starts with what seems to be an anthropological account of the origin of money using the concept of an economy based on barter between individuals. His crucial first step is to assume that money arose from the choice of some commodity among all those being traded that was sufficiently durable and universally valued to be held and exchanged later for other commodities. He then suggests that precious metals and jewels were logical candidates and that precious metals had the advantage of being homogenous and easily divisible. While there may have originally been several different commodities that functioned as intermediates in exchange, it is logical to assume that the convenience of having a single commodity serving this function led to the choice of the one best suited for this purpose, i.e. precious metal.

The second step in his argument builds on the notion that whatever is used as money has intrinsic worth. Even when gold coins were standardized and stamped with an indication of their value, the acid test was the weight and purity of the metal. Given this definition of money it follows that any attempt to substitute something else without intrinsic value for use as a medium of exchange is cheating in some way. The theory does allow for bank notes that are readily convertible to the specified amount of gold or silver, but if paper money proliferates in a way that it is no longer fully convertible, it has ceased to function properly as money, and it has lost value.

The principal underlying assumption in the argument is that the use of money emerges spontaneously from the development of trading. It is a convenience discovered and used by the individual traders, which gradually settles into a custom or convention. Note that neither a state nor any other kind of communal authority is required for its introduction. The implication seems to be that trading between individuals can arise without any degree of social organization. The first role that the state plays seems to be in the standardization of coinage. This again appears to be a matter of convenience, and there seems on the surface to be no necessity for the state to assume the role of the sole minter of legitimate coins. Any reputable firm could mint coins that contained the proper amount of gold and would be widely accepted.

When money is defined as a commodity with intrinsic worth which has been spontaneously adopted by traders in a market as a medium of exchange, the state appears to be just one agent participating in the market like any other merchant or consumer. If the state assumes sole responsibility for minting coins, it is put into a position of being able to exert an influence on the economy much greater than that of any other single participant. From Mises's perspective this is clearly a danger. The state already has the ability to siphon off money from the economy through enforced taxation, and it may have a disproportionate influence on the economy simply because of the amount of resources or money at its disposal. If it uses its monopoly on coinage to debase the currency, i.e. to issue coins that are actually worth less than their face value, it is essentially confiscating money from all the other participants in the market.

It is easy to see why this story about money is part of a libertarian worldview in which the state is a threat to the individual. It starts with individuals freely trading with each other to their mutual benefit and ends with an image of the state intervening in the "market" in ways that rob individuals in order to increase the power of the state. It is still widely accepted as a "common sense" explanation of money even though the gold standard has long since been abandoned. The result, of course, is that what functions as money in our society is not "really" money. It is a substitute for money that has been pawned off on an unsuspecting public.

The formulation of this theory kicks up a swarm of issues that beg to be explored. The first is the idea that an explanation of the nature of money begins with an historical account of how money originated. If the account is meant to be literal, it must incorporate genuine anthropological data. Even a cursory survey of 20th century anthropology reveals that what we think of as money emerged from objects endowed with ritualistic or even magical value in association with gift-giving customs that provided the initial forms of social solidarity. Seemingly useless objects like shells, animal teeth, or feathers were displayed and given away or even destroyed as signs of social prestige or power. The social bond was essentially one of debt or obligation – either a shared debt to ancestors or a reciprocal debt to contemporaries. In other words primitive societies do not consist of self-interested individuals trading commodities in a mutually beneficial way.

To explore the historical or anthropological origins of money one must first have some kind of definition of money, and given the threefold functional definition of money it can be argued that truly primitive societies simply did not have money. What they had were objects that functioned as a kind of store of value but not as a medium of exchange or unit of account. The value they stored was not an exchange value or a use value but a value in terms of social prestige or standing. The question then becomes how trading evolved and how these ritualistic objects came to play a role in trade. This is a very different and much more complex process than the selection of one commodity from among those traded to be an intermediate medium of exchange.

Does economic theory really depend on anthropology for its understanding of money? Anthropology can often shed revealing light on contemporary cultural practices. Things that seem completely "normal" or "inevitable" may be revealed to be contingent upon a host of other things. "Normal" patterns of thought or behavior take on a completely different cast when they are seen as remnants of archaic magic or ritual. Nonetheless the functional definition of money is based on an analysis of contemporary transactions without reference to anthropology.

The medium that facilitates economic transactions these days seems to be simply an accounting system for keeping track of transactions. One account is credited and another debited. A bookkeeping transaction is not a commodity – at least not on the surface. Only in the Wonderland of Finance can a bookkeeping entry become a tradable asset.

More likely the narrative used to describe the origin of money is not meant to be taken literally as anthropology, but is simply a convenient way of articulating the essential nature of money. It uses a narrative to lend credence to the idea that money must be essentially a commodity with intrinsic worth that is convenient to use as a medium of exchange even if the currency actually used is just pieces of paper referring to that commodity. The problem with this is that so many forms of primitive money seem to be useless objects. The oldest known form of money seems to be the cowrie shell. In fact the idea that "precious" metals are inherently valuable may involve a kind of circular reasoning or anachronistic projection of current convention.

Murray Rothbard states the classic case for the intrinsic value of gold or silver in terms of scarcity and aesthetic appeal in its refined form.

> In all countries and all civilizations, two commodities have been dominant whenever they were available to compete as moneys with other commodities: gold and silver.
>
> At first, gold and silver were highly prized only for their luster and ornamental value. They were always in great demand. Second, they were always relatively scarce, and hence valuable per unit of weight. And for that reason they were portable as well. They were also divisible, and could be sliced into thin segments without losing their pro rata value. Finally, silver or gold were blended with small amounts of alloy to harden them, and since they did not corrode, they would last almost forever.
>
> Thus, because gold and silver are supremely "moneylike" commodities, they are selected by markets as money if they are available. Proponents of the gold standard do not suffer from a mysterious "gold fetish." They simply recognize that gold has always been selected by the market as money throughout history.[6]

He seems to be basing his case on historical evidence, but some anthropology suggests that the importance of gold and silver is rooted in a symbolic relationship with the sun and the moon and even derives the ancient exchange ratio between the two from the ratio of solar and lunar periods. Valuing gold and silver because of they way they look does seem on some level to beg the question. Surely in a truly primitive barter objects that were useful for survival would be valued more than ornaments – unless one recognizes totemic use as necessary for survival in some sense.

As a kid in grammar school I was encouraged to think that it was a bit ridiculous of the Indians to sell Manhattan Island to the Dutch for $24 worth of beads and trinkets. Historical scholarship has revealed many aspects of this story to be completely fabricated and has even turned the tables a bit by revealing that the land purchased was actually inhabited by a different tribe from the one whom the Dutch initially paid for it. Although there is documentary evidence that the purchase was made with items worth 60 guilders, there is apparently no evidence the items consisted of "beads and trinkets." In the traditional story, however, the beads and trinkets were presented as virtually worthless. There was no suggestion that they may have represented something very different to the tribe accepting them, even though we were taught that Indians used "wampum" for money. There was also no indication that Native Americans did not believe it was possible to "own" land.

Another common argument in favor the gold standard is that tying the amount of money in circulation to some commodity like gold puts limits on the amount of money available and thereby serves to prevent inflation. Inflation is diagnosed primarily in terms of the supply of money in relation to the supply of goods. Such an argument is really an argument about limiting the amount of money in circulation and does not require that the money be tied to a commodity much less a precious metal.

There is, of course, a countervailing theory of money as a creation of the state, which facilitates commerce by declaring some form of currency to be "legal tender" for all debts and taxes. Something is "money" because it is designated as such by some political authority. This is termed "fiat money." While historical evidence may be cited to show that money as a unit of account for recording trading transactions may be at least as old as the use of gold or silver coins, this theory is not based on historical origins so much as functional analysis. The anthropological roots of money are less important than the functional analysis contained in a philosophical myth about the "creation" of money, although there are plenty of historical instances of governments declaring what is to be considered legal tender. The equation of money with gold or silver coins is a confusion based on outmoded conventions. "Fiat" paper money is every bit as "real" as gold coins.

I can remember as a kid wondering if there was really any difference between a dollar bill that was a "Silver Certificate" and one that was a "Federal Reserve Note" and wanting to go down to the bank to see how much silver I got in exchange for a one dollar silver certificate. A silver certificate said on it "This certifies that there is on deposit in the Treasury of the United States of America one dollar in silver payable to the bearer on demand." (I probably would have been given a silver dollar.) In its simplest form the gold standard requires that every paper dollar in circulation be backed by a fixed amount of gold on deposit with the government. The historical development of such a paper currency assumes that gold pieces of some sort were used for money and were purchased by the government using the new paper bills. The government could also purchase newly mined gold thereby increasing the amount of money in circulation. If gold is discovered in California, there may be a significant increase in the amount of money in circulation. (The enormous influx of gold and silver into Spain from their conquests in the New World may have been a major factor in the widespread inflation in Europe during the 15th and 16th centuries.) It seems strangely arbitrary to me that gold should be invested with this kind of significance. It is a "precious" metal which is mined from the earth and then buried again in government vaults in order to fix the "value" of the currency. The real debate about the gold standard seems to me to be a debate about the causes and cures of inflation rather than a debate about the "essence" of money.

The standard economics textbook summarizes the history of money in a way that implies that money evolved naturally from barter to commodity money to paper money to what it terms "bank money," which is money as we know it today.[7] Whether this means that money changed in some essential way is a matter of how you interpret evolutionary processes. The question is whether the logic derived from commodity money still applies to "bank money."

The difference between money as an object one possesses and money as an entry in a complex social accounting scheme becomes much clearer when you think about buying something on credit. Part of the reason that the classical concept of money as a commodity used as a medium of exchange has such a hold on our imagination or seems so self-evident by the standards of common sense is that we think of money as a "thing." Once I start to think about money as "purchasing power," it no longer seems to be a "thing" in quite the same way. Credit seems like something distinct from money because credit is clearly a relationship. Even if it is assigned a numerical value in a "credit limit," it is still a relationship of trust. Both credit and money, however, are purchasing power. Perhaps we should say that credit and "cash" are two forms of money. In terms of my scorecard it is possible to say that the main difference between them is that cash is based on past actions while credit is based on future actions. Cash is purchasing power I have because of things I have already done; credit is purchasing power based on things I am promising to do.

My first understanding of credit was "buy now, pay later." It meant that you could walk out of the store with something simply because you had given your word that you would pay for it when the bill arrived. This was expanded to include buying on time where the payment of the bill could be spread out over several months and made in "installments." At some point it became obvious to me that the store might charge you more for the item on the installment plan than if you paid cash up front. Nonetheless the notion of credit still seemed to be primarily its root sense of belief or trust.

As anyone who has filled out a credit application knows, the ability to purchase something is partially a function of one's social status, character, or history rather than just how much money one has in the bank or under the mattress. If money represents the power to acquire things, then clearly money is not just the cash that one possesses.

Excessive buying on credit, which used to be called living beyond your means, is often cited as one of the causes of the current economic mess. Everyone knows you can't go on forever running up debts. Sooner or later it will catch up with you, and

... What? You may have to declare bankruptcy in order to be forgiven for your debts without having to forgive your debtors. Does this tell us something about the nature of money?

The point here is simply that someone declaring bankruptcy probably got himself there by spending money he did not have. Credit means you can "spend" money you do not "have." If you spend money you do not have, someone else has money that no one had before. Does buying on credit increase the amount of money in circulation? Almost. The department store where I have a charge account is willing to let me walk out with a shirt because I have agreed to pay for it in the future. The store can record the "sale," but it does not actually have the money yet. However, if I draw on a credit line with a bank to pay a bill, the transaction does seem to "create" money. I pay the bill with money that exists only as a new entry in the bookkeeping for my account. Whomever I pay can use that money just as though I had paid them with cash I had stored under my mattress, and it continues to circulate through the economy.

If I "pay off" my credit line, then the money created by it seems to evaporate. I use money that has circulated through the economy to me, and by erasing the balance on my account the bank is siphoning money out of the economy and thereby reducing the "supply" of money.

Ann Pettifor, an economist who predicted the financial crisis and is, among other things, a member of the British Labour Party's Economic Advisory Committee, is fond of saying that money is created out of thin air by bank loans. In the introduction to her book, *Just Money: How Society Can Break the Despotic Power of Finance*, she says:

> I hope to shed some light on what Keynes called capitalism's "elastic production of money", and to indicate how monetary reform can restore oversight of the finance sector to democratic institutions.
>
> First, to challenge and nail the argument that 'there is no money' for society to address major threats, to fight poverty and to meet human needs. Money and monetary systems, I will argue, are social constructs, and can and must be managed, mobilised and deployed to serve the wider interests of society and the ecosystem.
>
> Second, I want to force into the open a subject that is taboo: the role of private, commercial banks in the creation of

money 'out of thin air'. For too long orthodox economists have misled politicians and others, and focussed only on central bank money creation. They have deliberately downplayed the role of the private sector: in credit creation or 'printing' money; in providing or denying finance to productive sectors; and in generating inflation.[8]

The problem with this metaphor is that "thin air" conjures up a magic trick in the way that money is "created." To the borrower there is no magic involved in the fact that he is obligated to pay back the bank eventually. This is true whether the borrower uses the money to start a dry cleaning business or to pay emergency medical expenses. When he "spends" the money, it circulates through the economy just like money withdrawn by depositors. Bank loans temporarily increase the "supply" of money.

If money is conceived in terms of purchasing power, the distinction between cash and credit begins to evaporate. The way in which I am endowed with purchasing power is obviously a "social construct." We may like to think that hard work, resourcefulness, innovation, creativity or perseverance have value in and of themselves, but they only have monetary value because of the social context in which they take place. The rules by which it is possible to "earn a living" or "retire" are social customs or institutions. They are not natural laws of the physical universe. Ultimately rules of this sort are rooted in the morality or values of the community or society.

Economists are fond of thinking in terms of supply and demand. In mainstream economics money is essentially a commodity which has a price and is subject to the "laws" of supply and demand. The "price" of money is an interest rate and theoretically as interest rates increase the demand for money declines. If demand declines then eventually the supply should decline to find an equilibrium point with the demand.

One of the ways in which the Federal Reserve has attempted to prevent inflation is manipulating interest rates to control the supply of money. Monetary theory analyzes the supply of money in terms of different categories of money. Depending on a country's banking system there may be as many as five different categories of money supply (M0, M1, M2, M3, M4), but the basic distinction is between money which is circulating (narrow money) and money which is being "saved" but readily available in liquid assets such as savings deposits, CDs, money market funds, etc. The amount of money circulating seems to correlate with inflation under certain conditions, but controlling inflation by attempting to control the amount of money in circulation has been an elusive goal.

The number of economic transactions taking place during any given time period is a function not only of the amount of money circulating, but also of how fast it circulates. Formulas in economics multiply the supply of money by its "velocity." Affecting or even monitoring the velocity of money is apparently a complicated task. It is generally calculated indirectly by just dividing the gross national product by the supply of money. Part of the difficulty in combating inflation by controlling the "supply" of money is the it can be hard to distinguish between money that is circulating and money that is not. There used to be a clear distinction between checking accounts and savings accounts, but the introduction of interest-bearing checking accounts muddied that up. Whether money is being "saved" is just a matter of how long I wait to spend it, and not all money is circulating at the same "velocity." Short term investing may also be a way of holding money until you need to spend it rather than saving for retirement. The supply of money is further complicated by the way in which bank loans "create" money.

In addition to bank loans there is another way in which credit can "create" money. One basic type of credit is the "terms" offered in the supply chains for businesses. Company A issues a purchase order to Company B and receives the goods with the understanding that they will pay for them within a certain amount of time. B trusts A to comply with the terms and may even have legal means to compel them to do so. If Company A is a start-up or is expanding, credit of this sort can be a powerful means to bootstrap the operation until sales revenue permit them to pay for their supplies.

One particularly revealing extension of this type of credit is the "commercial credit clearing exchange" or "local exchange trading system." Merchants in an area create a virtual local currency for doing business with each other by accepting payment in multilateral credit accounts. An interesting example is called Sardex. In 2008 when the ripple effect of the global financial crisis hit Italy, banks in Sardinia stopped making loans and local businesses began closing. A group of young Sardinians formed a bank of sorts using a local currency which existed only as bookkeeping entries for transactions between members of the exchange. The currency was not exchangeable with Euros and was meant to be complementary to it. The original members of the exchange all started with a zero balance and agreed to extend credit to others. When a transaction was recorded, the credit balance in an account could be used to settle debts with any member of the exchange. It took a while to get the ball rolling, but by 2105 the exchange had about 3,000 members, and it was expected that it would facilitate about 50 million Euros worth of transactions. Eventually they began charging annual membership fees and an initiation fee, but none of the loans involve interest. The effect was virtually to pull at least part of the local economy up by its own bootstraps. In his article about Sardex, Edward Posnett quotes one owner of a small business:

> The owner of a local store showed me her online Sardex account, indicating her balance and all the firms with whom she could potentially transact. She had sold lingerie to companies in the network, earning Sardex, which she then used to pay her accountant. "It's ingenious," she said. "It makes the money circulate here [and] doesn't allow it to leave the island. It creates a connection."[9]

This is by no means an oddball experiment. The idea of using a local currency to insulate an economy from global finance was first implemented in Switzerland in 1934 with the Swiss WIR, which is still being used by 45,000 members. There are some 300 local currencies or local exchange trading systems (LETS) all over the world, including many in the US.[10]

While there are various schools of monetary theory, the assumption underlying the concept of money in mainstream economics is that money itself is a commodity, some kind of "thing" which moves through the economy like particles of blood circulating in the body. We still seem to assume that all money is essentially tangible currency – coins and paper minted by the government. But purchasing power is not a tangible "thing." You may want to say, "Yes, credit is a relationship, but it is a relationship involving money which is still somehow tangible – even if it is represented only by bookkeeping entries."

We need a different metaphor for the circulation of money – an electrical circuit, perhaps, although it has never been clear to me whether an electrical connection actually involves the movement of individual ("physical") electrons through a length of wire or whether the "charge" consists of something else. A monetary transaction involves a transfer of power from one purchaser to another. Purchasing power is a kind of status in a society. It is a unique form of status in that it has a numerical value.

Sociology is generally the discipline that describes ways we confer status in society, and Geoffrey Ingham, a sociologist at Cambridge, insists that the nature of money can only be properly understood as a social relation.

> Obviously, money is socially produced in the sense that it does not occur naturally, and it also mediates and symbolizes social relations – for example, capital-wage labor. However, I wish to go further and argue that money itself is a social relation. By this I mean that "money" can only be sensibly seen as being constituted by social relations. I have already hinted that this claim is most obviously sustained in the case of credit-money as "promises" to pay; but I shall argue that all forms of money are social relations and consequently, for example, the conventional textbook distinction between "money" and "credit" is not merely anachronistic, but is based on a conceptual confusion.[11]

If money is essentially a bookkeeping entry recording social relationships, how does it become a commodity which can be bought and sold via a "financial market?" Credit is a promise to pay, an IOU. It is easy enough to see how IOUs can become "legal tender" for payment of debts. If I have a piece of paper that says someone will pay the bearer a certain amount of money, I can persuade someone else to accept that paper as payment for goods or services provided there is some legal framework for doing so. He will then receive the payment that I was originally owed. Note that the legal framework makes it possible for an IOU to be a document which specifies that the money is payable to the bearer rather than a specific person. It is the "pay to bearer" which makes an IOU into an something which can be sold. The need for this legal framework is an indication of the extent to which any economic system is based on social convention, cultural tradition or deliberate political choices.

Suppose the IOU has a due date some time in the future so that it cannot be redeemed immediately. If I need cash now, perhaps I can persuade you to buy it at a discount so that you pay me less than what you will be able to redeem it for on its due date. Now we have a "market" in which a price for the IOU can be negotiated. The debt that someone owes me becomes a marketable "instrument," i.e. an asset or a commodity. Have I performed some kind of sleight of hand? Is there anything suspect about the way in which I have transformed a creditor-debtor relationship into a marketable asset? Are there unexpected consequences of this convenience?

Suppose the loan in question is a mortgage and the bank is willing to cut the borrower some slack because the bank knows it can package the loan into some form of "security" and sell it to another investor. Perhaps the bank is primarily interested in pocketing the fees associated with originating the loan and wants to avoid any repercussions if the borrower is unable to make payments at some point down the road. Anyone vaguely familiar with the causes of the 2007 financial crisis will recognize the broad outlines of the sub-prime mortgage bubble. Aggressive lenders gave mortgages to people who really could not afford the house they were buying (unless the house's value continued to skyrocket so they could continually re-finance until they could eventually afford it or sell it for a profit). The lenders then took their "fees," sold the mortgage to some other bank or lender who then packaged a whole bunch of these "assets" and sold "bonds" or "securities" based on their value (with the help of the ratings agencies who were basically paid to declare these AAA-top-notch-super-safe investments). Similar deals continued to spread the risk far and wide until people began to default on their mortgages and housing prices declined. The devastating effect that this wheeling and dealing had on the global economy surely makes it worth taking a look at what is really driving the world of finance.

It is said that paper money originated with goldsmiths who would provide individuals with safe storage for gold their gold and give them a receipt that was a piece of paper indicating that they were entitled to redeem a certain amount of gold. People realized that these "notes" themselves could be used to settle debts rather than having to redeem them first with the goldsmith. The notes began to circulate as "money."

At some point the goldsmiths realized they could themselves pay for things with their own notes and that they could issue notes for more gold than they actually had on hand since it was unlikely that all their customers would need to redeem all their gold at once. I have no idea if this is historically accurate, but it is a nice myth to describe "fractional reserve banking" which developed after banks replaced goldsmiths as depositories for wealth. To understand what money is, it is necessary to understand how banks function.

Banks

When I was a kid I had a piggy bank. Fortunately mine had a plug in the bottom that allowed me to make withdrawals without destroying the bank. For most people I think the primary association with the idea of a bank is that of a safe place to store accumulated money. I can remember how much in awe I was of the door to the vault at the bank where my mother had accounts and a safe deposit box. Any place with a door like that had to be safe from robbers. The image of Brink's bullet-proof trucks carrying money to and from the bank also enhanced that image. By now I have seen enough movies about bank robbery to know that the real reason the depositors' money is safe is because it is "insured." I also know enough about the Depression to know this was not always the case. About 9,000 banks failed in the 1930s and in 1933 alone depositors lost something like $140 billion.

Most of us understand that banks don't just put their depositors' money in a vault. They use at least a portion of it to make loans. It is the proceeds from these loans which are supposed to finance the bank's operations. When the Dust Bowl wiped out farmers in the 1930s, they defaulted on their bank loans to the point where there was not enough money left in many banks to cover withdrawals. If enough depositors withdrew their money, a bank itself went bankrupt. In the initial years of the Depression the dollar was still tied to gold, so neither the bank nor the government could "print" more money. The bank would have had to borrow money to cover all the withdrawals. Eventually the government went off the gold standard and insured bank deposits, but banks could still fail. During the 80s and 90s about 1000 savings and loan associations failed as a result of their attempts to deal with volatile interest rates.

In classical economic theory banks have two functions. They facilitate economic transactions by "clearing" or settling through checking accounts, and they make loans to individuals or businesses. In theory when banks make loans they are lending money deposited by customers in their accounts. The idea is that depositors do not need all the money immediately, especially when it is deposited in "savings" accounts, so the bank can put some portion of it to work in loans.

This theory seems to imply that the banks deposits are all currency that is held in its vaults and that the loans are made by doling out some portion of that currency. Needless to say most banks deposits these days are bookkeeping entries rather than actual currency, and loans are made simply by crediting an account via another bookkeeping entry. In fact most of the "money" in circulation was "created" by similar bookkeeping entries somewhere in the financial system, and, once loans are repaid, the money that was created by them evaporates. Most people will probably balk at this idea initially, because they think of money as a physical thing – a limited resource that circulates through the economy and is not just some bookkeeping entry that can be erased or evaporate like fairy dust.

Creating money by loans seems like a self-contradiction when we think of loans as money accumulated by one individual or company which is then transferred to someone else with the provision that they will eventually give it back and perhaps even pay "rent" on it until it is returned. A loan between two individuals or businesses does not "create" money, but banks are in a special position due to their function as clearing houses for economic transactions. They can credit one account without any other customer's account being debited. The debit entry occurs somewhere else in the banks books.

When a bank "uses" some portion of the money deposited in various accounts to make loans, all of the account holders are still entitled to withdraw all their money. It is supposed to be available to them at any time, and it is in fact counted as part of the total money in circulation in the economy. But the credit which is extended in making the loan adds to an account an amount equal to the amount of the loan, and the borrower is free to withdraw that money to pay expenses. This money then can circulate through the economy just like the money in the original deposits, so in the official accounting of the amount of money circulating in the economy shows that it has increased as a result of the loan. When the loan is paid off, the total amount of money in circulation has decreased by the amount of the loan. The borrower pays money to the bank which is credited against the loan balance until the loan balance is zero. That money in some sense goes away since it no longer available to circulate in the economy.

In the traditional system a bank could "fail" if it lent money and all of its original depositors withdrew all of their money. In theory because the bank has lent some of the money to others, it does not have enough on hand to "cover" all the deposits. Banks were required to maintain a certain percentage of their deposits as "reserves" so that they could cover withdrawals up to a certain point. The National Bank Act of 1863 had set the reserve requirement at 25%, but when the Federal Reserve bank was created the requirements were lowered to 13%, 10% or 7% depending on the type of bank. Obviously this was not enough to save banks during the Depression when they were subject to "runs." As of March 2020 the reserve requirement has been reduced to zero, but deposits up to $250,000 are insured by the Federal Deposit Insurance Corporation.

The idea that a bank can go bankrupt if it cannot cover a run of withdrawals makes sense if all the depositors want currency and the currency in the vaults has been used to make the loans. However, if the loans and the bulk of the deposits are just bookkeeping entries, it might seem that the bank could just issue cashier's checks to be deposited elsewhere and honored by the bank with additional bookkeeping entries even if it meant that the books at the bank temporarily showed a "negative balance." How a bank "honors" a check it has issued when it has been deposited at another bank and submitted by that bank is part of the function of a central bank or the Federal Reserve bank in the US. Presumably having a "negative balance" even temporarily amounts to being "bankrupt."

Banks have changed radically over the past 50 years. In the classical model banks functioned as "intermediaries" channeling savings into investments via loans. The Banking Acts of 1933 and 1935 prohibited checking accounts from paying interest on their deposits and limited the interest that could be paid on time deposits or savings accounts. In 1970 two American businessmen invented the money market mutual fund which offered investors an alternative to bank deposit accounts. Since investors were buying shares of a fund rather than "depositing" the money in a bank account, the fund was not subject to the regulations regarding banks. It was able to offer higher returns than a savings account with minimal risk.

As the stock market flourished in the 60s and 70s, it began to compete for the funds that had previously been deposited in savings accounts or certificates of deposit. People wanted the greater returns that could be had with securities as opposed to a savings account, and it became increasingly difficult for banks to attract deposits and make a profit on its loans. They began to rely on fees for their services to bolster their income, and they began to lobby for the repeal of banking regulations in order to be able to make a profit. Gradually regulations on banks were scaled back until they were in effect completely eliminated in 1999.

Most banks are businesses run for profit, and they have increasingly been run like other businesses answerable to shareholders. Part of this has been the increased reliance on borrowed money. Banks can borrow money from the Federal Reserve at a low rate and lend it to businesses at a higher rate. Once they were no longer restricted in terms of the kinds of investments they could make (theoretically with their depositors funds), the banks began investing in securities of all sort. This eventually included the ability to originate loans and the get them off their books by "securitizing" them. The distinction between commercial banks and investment banks was all but eliminated in 1999, although some attempts to reintroduce regulations of banks have been made since the financial crisis.

After the invention of money market funds financiers found a host of other ways to channel investors' money into investments that competed with banks ability to finance via loans. What developed was termed a non-banking financial institution which was a financial institution without a banking license and not subject to the same regulations as banks but able to provide most of the services of a bank. It has also been called the "shadow banking system."

> The financial system is one of the most important and innovative sectors of a modern economy. It forms the vital circulatory system that channels resources from savers to investors. Whereas finance in an earlier era consisted of banks and the country store, finance today involves a vast, worldwide banking system, securities markets, pension funds, and a wide array of financial instruments.[12]

Theoretically the justification for this vast "financial system" is to channel savings into investment. People who are foregoing current consumption in order to accumulate funds for future expenses are making it possible for the economy to invest in enterprises and grow or at least prosper. A cynic might be inclined to point out that what the textbook actually says is "channels resources from savers to investors" without specifying exactly how these resources are used by those investors. "Investment," however, has a specific meaning in economics:

The Meaning of "Investment" in Economics

> Remember that macroeconomists use the term "investment" or "real investment" to mean additions to the stock of productive assets or capital goods like computers or trucks. When Amazon.com builds a new warehouse or when the Smiths build a new house, these activities represent investment.
>
> Many people speak of "investing" when buying a piece of land, an old security, or any title to property. In economics, these purchases are really financial transactions or "financial investments," because what one person is buying, someone else is selling, and the net effect is zero. There is investment only when real capital is produced.[13]

Note that "financial investments" are not "real investments." In other words "financial investments" have no direct impact on the "real" economy. The idea that financial markets channel funds from "savers" to "investors" seems to imply that investment in securities results at least indirectly in "real investment." In the classical model money is available for investment only because of "savings" accumulated by foregoing current consumption, but bank loans are one method of financing "investment," and as we have seen bank loans "create" money. Banks could conceivably lend money for investment purposes without any of their depositors foregoing current consumption to accumulate "savings." For this type of investment there seems to be no necessary connection to savings.

The other method for investment in the classic model is "equity" investment through the sale of "shares" in an enterprise, i.e. the stock market. This assumes that someone has money available to invest, i.e. some form of "savings," but what if the money they invest is "borrowed" from a bank or a brokerage house, i.e. newly created money. Equity investment seems to imply savings, but it hardly seems to be tied to it by some kind of rigid formula.

Trading on the stock market also does not result in "real investment." The only type of equity investment that results in real investment is a public offering of new shares. Generally the only investors that can purchase shares in a public offering are large pension funds, endowments, hedge funds or mutual funds. Ultimately the money in such funds may have come from "savers" via retirement plans, gifts or investing in securities, but the connection is indirect at best, and most of the time such funds are trading existing securities rather than purchasing shares in a new offering.

Banks are one type of "financial intermediary." They are distinguished purely by the fact that they have depositors whose money provides the collateral that enables the bank to lend and borrow. Banks these days may also be publicly held corporations with equity financing from the sale of shares, and they are no longer restricted from engaging in all the types of investing that other financial intermediaries such as pension funds, insurance companies, money market funds and brokerage houses engage in. In fact a bank may be one subsidiary of a company that also owns a brokerage house. A brokerage house in turn may have accounts with cash deposits which are essentially demand accounts. In 2009 Bank of America bought Merrill Lynch and now my statement for an account at Bank of America comes ostensibly from "Merrill, A Bank Of America Company."

Banks themselves maintain accounts at the Federal Reserve Bank. This facilitates clearing drafts on one bank that have been deposited in another, and it makes it easier for banks to borrow money. Often if one bank's reserves temporarily fall below the required amount, it can borrow the money to make up the shortfall via a short-term loan from another bank. The interest rate on overnight loans of this sort is known as the federal funds rate and is often used as the basis for setting other interest rates. Similarly the London Interbank Offered Rate (LIBOR) is the average rate charged by a number of London banks for loans to each other.

Banks can also borrow directly from the Federal Reserve via the "discount window." The Federal discount rate is the charged for these loans and it is set by the Federal Reserve. One method of controlling the supply of money is by adjusting the interest rate which the Federal Reserve charges banks. In theory the "price" of money will affect the "demand" and therefore the "supply." In the case of the Federal Reserve it seems to work better when they attempt to "tighten" money by raising the interest rates which they charge banks. Making it more costly to borrow funds reduces the incentive of banks to borrow money from the Fed to lend to its customers. Reducing the "price" of money does not always seem to have the desired effect and is often compared to pushing on a string. It may be easier for banks to borrow money, but that does not insure that they will in fact borrow money or that the borrowed money will be used in ways that increase the "supply" of money circulating in the economy.

Banks can of course also increase their cash reserves by selling securities they may hold. Another way in which the Federal Reserve attempts to affect the supply of money is by buying or selling treasury bonds held by banks through what are called "open market operations."

Banks are essentially businesses making a profit by borrowing money at one interest rate and lending it at a higher interest rate. While a deposit in a checking account may not seem like a loan to the depositor, the net effect for the bank is the same regardless of whether the bank pays interest on the balance in the account. A savings account resembles a loan more in that there is a commitment to paying interest in exchange for a commitment (of sorts) not to withdraw the money right away. It is essentially a loan that is being renewed every day. A certificate of deposit is clearly a loan since there is a specified term and interest rate when the certificate is "bought." In some cases a CD is like a bond in that it can be sold on a secondary market before its term expires.

Making a profit from lending in this way may seem like a fairly innocuous and even boring business plan. It is, however, a business model with plenty of room for abuse. The abuse may have catastrophic consequences as in the case of Penn Square Bank in Oklahoma and its role in the failure of Continental Illinois in 1984.

> Penn Square was notorious in its wishful thinking. Its executives were the classic freebooters – entrepreneurial bankers who hustled new loans for oil drillers based on the most generous assumptions about the prospects for finding oil and gas, about the future price of oil, about the borrowers' ability to repay. The federal examiners found a general recklessness and even fraud in the loan portfolio.
>
> But the hustlers from Penn Square could not have done this by themselves. Their modest-sized bank simply did not have the capacity. A bank's assets, its loans, were supposed to balance with its liabilities, its deposits. A shopping-center bank with less than $500 million in deposits could not carry

> $2 billion in loans on its books. So Penn Square simply sold the loans – "upstream," as bankers say – to the larger banks that wished to share in the bonanza.
>
> Continental Illinois, largest bank in the Midwest and seventh largest in the nation, picked up more than $1 billion of loan participations with Penn Square. Lesser amounts, but still in the hundreds of millions, were absorbed by Chase Manhattan and the others. They gave Penn Square the capacity to lend more and more and take greater and greater risks. ...
>
> Penn Square, in effect, acted as a business scout in the "oil patch" for Continental and the others. When Penn Square booked loans and reached its lending capacity, it simply offered a share of the action to the larger banks, collected the equivalent of a finder's fee, then turned around and went out to find more oil prospectors who needed money. This was very profitable for everyone, while it lasted, and Continental Illinois's stock climbed from $25 to $40 a share in less than two years. The largest and most admired banks in America were, it developed, as inattentive to the question of loan quality – the prudential rules of banking – as the hustlers in cowboy boots from a shopping center in Oklahoma.[14]

The failure of Continental Illinois was the largest bank failure in history at the time. Its operations required it to borrow $8 billion every day. Its rescue by the Fed, the Federal Deposit Insurance Corporation, the Treasury and other regulators gave rise to the phrase "too big to fail."

Interest

The power of compound interest over two hundred years is such as to stagger the imagination.[15]

Interest on loans may be so embedded in our culture as to seem transparently obvious, but, if one really stops to think about it, it becomes fairly complicated. Plenty of things are lent with no thought of charging a price for their use. Transactions of this sort may occur primarily between friends or relatives and are not regarded as business transactions, while the same transaction between strangers may seem acceptable only as a business transaction in which the borrower has to pay for the use of whatever is lent. This may be a completely arbitrary cultural distinction. To present it as a norm implies all kinds of things about human nature and "normal" relationships between "strangers." I freely share my things with friends and relatives perhaps because I feel confident they will be returned in more or less the same condition. I may also be willing to do this because I feel a bond of shared interests or goals. I wish my friend well and am willing to help him achieve his goals by sharing my things with him. A stranger on the other hand may be, by definition, one who is not trusted and/or one whose goals are not shared. He may even be a threat or a competitor for scare resources. The only reason to lend him something is if it benefits me.

Ambivalence towards interest on loans has a long history. The holder of a mortgage is quite often the villain in old movies and 19th century melodramas. The hapless maiden or the struggling rancher is the victim of a cruel banker who takes away his or her livelihood by foreclosing on the mortgage. I suspect that this image of the banker has its roots in the notion of "usury" as a sin. Prohibitions against charging interest on loans seem to be almost as old as the practice of charging interest. The definition of usury has vacillated between prohibitions on any interest and prohibitions on excessive interest. Ancient Israelites were prohibited from charging interest on loans to fellow Israelites but not on loans to foreigners. Traditional Islam prohibits charging interest on any loans, and banks in Islamic countries often still find other ways to structure their investments. During the

Middle Ages prevailing Christian culture wanted to label usury a sin, but as a practical matter loans seemed to be necessary to make the economy function. The task of making loans was foisted off onto the outsiders, and the ambivalence towards money lending became one of the things fueling anti-Semitism.

The idea that interest is "rent" on money comparable to rent on any other type of property which is lent to another to use makes sense only if money is conceived as a commodity or scarce resource which is "property" like anything else I own. But if "money" is really more like good will or social status, then the fact that a certain amount has been conferred upon you may not necessarily entitle you to profit from letting someone else "use" it. That someone can make money simply because he already has surplus cash on hand is surely a social convention rather than a law of nature. We have, for whatever reason, set things up so that the rich get richer.

If money is understood as purchasing power, it may still be mine to "lend" to someone else. Instead of my writing a check to purchase something, which I then lend to him, I simply write a check to him to transfer the purchasing power to him, and he writes the check to purchase the item. The transaction between us can be categorized as a loan, and the amount he has to return to me will depend on how long it takes him to return the amount I lent to him.

A loan may also be understood in terms of credit. It is a short step from an installment purchase plan to a loan. With an installment purchase I agree to pay a bit more because I am be allowed to take longer to pay for the item. The longer I delay the payment, the greater the difference between what I pay and the normal retail price. Adding a third party turns this transaction into a loan. Someone lends me the money to buy an item. I pay the normal retail price and then pay back the lender in installments with a premium depending on how long it takes me to pay back the original amount.

Another justification for charging interest on a loan is that it provides the only incentive I can have for parting with my money. My money is my property just like everything else I own, and I am entitled to a "return" if I "put it to work." I am being rewarded for letting someone else put the money back into circulation rather than simply hoarding it for future use. I am rewarded for foregoing consumption. From the social perspective what matters is that the money continues to circulate. Hoarded money is a drag on the economy since it is not being used in ways that keep people employed and increase the amount of goods to go around. If the loan enables a business to start or expand, then so much the better.

There is a difference between lending money and investing it in an enterprise. We tend to think of them as just two ways of putting my money to work with different levels of risk and reward. The return on a loan is generally less than the potential return on an equity investment, because the risk is less. A debtor is obligated to pay back a loan regardless of how well his own ventures fare. An equity investor is essentially a part owner of the company who runs the risk of losing all of his investment, but he also enjoys the potential for having the value of his share in the company increase dramatically if the venture is successful. Islamic finance sees this as a moral distinction, but for the rest of us any misgivings about loans are probably associated with "loan sharks" preying on individuals in need of money for necessities rather than institutions buying bonds.

There may be a lingering suspicion of those who have accumulated money and exploit the fact that they have money other people need, even though this suspicion runs counter to the American Dream of achieving financial "independence." Part of the reason for this may be the common notion that the economy is a zero-sum game, so that anyone who has accumulated money has done so at the "expense" of others. The individual who accumulates wealth, however, may not feel that he is doing so at the expense of others. There is another common notion that anyone who accumulates wealth is "creating" something.

Perhaps we should ask instead what justification there is for objecting to the charge of interest on a loan. The Old Testament or the Koran may contain condemnations of usury, but they do not explain the judgment except by reference to the will of God. One current interpretation of the Islamic prohibition is that loans are an inappropriate form of investment because they involve an obligation to repay the principal without any shared risk. This obviously applies only to business loans and seems irrelevant to personal loans for consumption, be it a large screen TV or an emergency medical procedure. Another more contemporary theory about usury is that there is a point at which higher interest rates become self-defeating because they make it impossible for the debtor ever to repay the debt.[16]

Ancient Greek philosophy shared the prejudice against interest bearing loans and at least Aristotle attempted to explain his judgment. Aristotle's analysis of money seems to have been somewhat inconsistent – at least when one attempts to pursue it to its logical conclusions. He condemned the practice of charging interest on loans and is often credited with saying that money should not breed money. At the same time he acknowledged a legitimate function for money as a means of exchange facilitating trade. Aristotle approached the idea of money from two different angles. His analysis of the origin of money from barter is essentially the same as that of classical economics, and to some extent he wants to view the nature of money in terms of its "origin." In most of his thought, however, the essential nature of things is revealed by the form they take in their most developed state, and he could see that the nature of money meant that it inevitably developed into an end sought for its own sake rather than remaining a means for achieving other ends. This is not the place to enter into the deep waters of the interpretation of Aristotle, but there are some striking things in his comments on money. One has to do with the impact of money (and the existence of markets) on craftsmanship. He deplores the way in which the artisan's focus will shift from making the best possible object in terms of its usefulness (and perhaps beauty) to the most profitable one to trade. Aristotle lived in a society in which markets were at best a marginal phenomenon and most production was for consumption by the household or the estate where it was done rather than for sale.

Aristotle's ideas about interest on loans can be seen as a concern about the perversion of money from its function as a means of exchange. When money or the accumulation of money becomes an end in itself rather than serving as a means to acquire goods that satisfy genuinely human needs, then the pursuit of money becomes an unending project. It is a desire that can never be fully satisfied. J. Paul Getty, when asked how much money he needed, is reputed to have said, "A little bit more." In some sense for Aristotle an "end" that has no end is a self-contradiction. Aristotle seems to have had his finger on an issue that has never been adequately resolved. There is still a very strong suspicion that the unending accumulation of money is somehow inhuman or at least neurotic in some way, no matter how much we may have given up trying to distinguish genuine from spurious needs.

It seems impossible to base a condemnation of interest-bearing loans on a moral judgment about an obsession with the accumulation of money. Obsession turns a reasonable activity into a compulsion, which like any other form of "excess" seems irrational or sick, but the problem is the obsession not the activity on which it focuses. The suspicions about money and commerce, which form a seemingly permanent thread in our culture, are surely deep-rooted and probably beyond the purview of economics. The only argument that is going to persuade an economist that interest-bearing loans are a bad idea will have to be one that shows how interest charges undermine the functioning of the economy. Such arguments have been made.

Amato and Fantacci argue that the ultimate cause of the recent financial crisis is the confused notion that money is a commodity and that the only way to eliminate future financial crises is to eliminate financial markets. They insist that a market economy can exist without interest-bearing loans. They are fully aware of the social, political and intellectual obstacles to implementing such a market, and they do not have a fully developed plan for how to achieve it, but they do seem to think steps can be taken towards it. What is needed above all is an understanding of the goal. In their introduction to *Saving the Market from Capitalism* they summarize in no uncertain terms their perspective:

> To begin with, we have to distinguish between markets for actual goods and services, which should be as free, integrated and extensive as possible, and financial markets, which shouldn't even exist. ...Market economy and capitalism are not synonymous. Actually, they are incompatible. Capitalism is a market economy with one market too many: the money and credit market.[17]

> [Even people who don't invest in stocks and bonds, and possibly protest against the excessive power of Wall Street, are still hardly likely to call into question the underlying principle of the financial markets – the dogma of liquidity. This consists in the apparently natural idea that cash (liquidity, in other words) is the safest form of saving and, consequently, one will part with it only for an investment that is equally liquid or that yields sufficient interest to compensate for the lack of liquidity. This, in short, is the

> general creed we all respect: money is the supreme good, and must generate interest when it is lent. ...
>
> But there is still more to it. Independently of the financial markets, the idea that money is wealth and that the mere holding of it merits a reward is the root of an endemic evil that is both social and human. Call it as you will. Until a couple of centuries ago, it was called usury. Then the classical economists called it rent, and criticized it harshly. Today it's called rate of interest. In any case it is income obtained without working or running entrepreneurial risks and is thus quite distinct from both the worker's wage and the entrepreneur's profit.
>
> Now it may seem trite to point it out, but in times like these we'd better try to be basic: if somewhere someone is making money without working, somewhere else someone is working without making money.[18]

The concept of interest is so ingrained that economics assumes money has a "yield" and that holding money long term has an "opportunity cost."

> What is the cost of holding money? Money is costly because it has a lower yield than do other safe assets. Currency has a nominal interest rate of exactly zero percent per year. Checking deposits sometimes have a small interest rate, but that rate is usually well below the rate on savings accounts or money market mutual funds. For example, over the period 2000–2007, currency had a yield of 0 percent per year, checking accounts had an average yield of around 0.2 percent per year, and short-term money funds had a yield of around 4.6 percent per year. If the weighted yield on money (currency and checking accounts) was 0.1 percent per year, then the cost of holding money was 4.5 (4.6 - 0.1) percent per year.[19]

Financial advisors are fond of pointing out that cash actually loses value over time due to inflation. Since the inflation rate for 2000 through 2006 ranged between 1.55% to 3.42%, perhaps it makes sense to say that cash had a negative yield in terms of "real" dollars.

Economics views money as a capital asset or at least an asset with the potential of becoming capital, so that what the worker has earned if he does not spend it on consumption is the potential to receive a return on capital. Keynes marveled at the way compound interest facilitated the accumulation of capital which made the modern era possible.

> The modern age opened, I think, with the accumulation of capital which began in the sixteenth century. I believe – for reasons with which I must not encumber the present argument – that this was initially due to the rise of prices, and the profits to which that led, which resulted from the treasure of gold and silver which Spain brought from the New World into the Old. From that time until today the power of accumulation by compound interest, which seems to have been sleeping for many generations, was re-born and renewed its strength. And the power of compound interest over two hundred years is such as to stagger the imagination. [20]

What Keynes means by "the power of accumulation by compound interest" is probably not the same thing borrowers wrestle with when they try to figure out how long it may take to repay a loan. He is talking about the growth made possible by reinvestment of at least a portion of the return on an investment, but the passage is too rich to pass up without some commentary. Keynes says nothing about how Spain was able to persuade the inhabitants of the New World to let them bring all that gold and silver back to the Old World. He is, however, a little blunter when he explains how England benefited from Spain's newfound wealth.

> Let me give in illustration of this a sum which I have worked out. The value of Great Britain's foreign investments to-day is estimated at about £4,000,000,000. This yields us an income at the rate of about 6½ per cent. Half of this we bring home and enjoy; the other half, namely, 3¼ per cent, we leave to accumulate abroad at compound interest. Something of this sort has now been going on for about 250 years.
>
> For I trace the beginnings of British foreign investment to the treasure which Drake stole from Spain in 1580. In that year he returned to England bringing with him the prodigious spoils of the Golden Hind. Queen Elizabeth was a considerable shareholder in the syndicate which had financed the expedition. Out of her share she paid off the whole of England's foreign debt, balanced her Budget, and found herself with about £40,000 in hand. This she invested in the Levant Company – which prospered. Out of the profits of the Levant Company, the East India Company

was founded; and the profits of this great enterprise were the foundation of England's subsequent foreign investment. Now it happens that £40,000 accumulating at 3½ per cent compound interest approximately corresponds to the actual volume of England's foreign investments at various dates, and would actually amount to-day to the total of £4,000,000,000 which I have already quoted as being what our foreign investments now are. Thus, every £1 which Drake brought home in 1580 has now become £100,000. Such is the power of compound interest![21]

Drake stole a treasure in order to start the ball rolling on the accumulation of capital in England. How or why the Levant Company or the East India Company proved to be so profitable is not explored, nor is it clear whether is was necessary for the investment to be "foreign." It seems as though it is just natural that an investment will "yield" 6½%. Does "accumulation" involve the creation of wealth or is it only a transfer producing a concentration of wealth in the hands of a few?

Explaining economic growth as a result of the power of compound interest only begs the question since compound interest is simply a mathematical representation of growth. The idea that we can leave half the profits from foreign investment abroad to accumulate at compound interest makes it sound like foreign investment is a savings account and does nothing to explain why it is profitable.

A savings account may be the only place where the idea of compound interest makes sense. Interest paid periodically on the balance in the account stays in the account to become part of the balance on which the next interest payment is calculated. It seems like automatic growth because the deposit is insured and the rate seems to be stable.

If one thinks of interest as "rent" on a commodity which is "lent" to someone for a period of time, compound interest may seem like a slick trick. When I rent a car or a piece of equipment at a daily rate, I expect the rental charge when I return the car or tool simply to be the daily rate times the number of days I had it. Why should different rules apply when I am borrowing money? In some cases the amount due to pay off a loan may be a similar calculation of the principal amount times the a periodic rate. It can also, however, involve compound interest where the principal grows with the accumulated unpaid interest. Money it seems is a very special type of commodity. Cars and tools depreciate as they age and are used. Money is supposed to grow perhaps like a fine wine that improves with age, unless of course inflation causes the money to depreciate.

Regardless of its origins or the metaphors we use to describe it, interest is firmly ensconced at the very foundations of mainstream economic theory. It is the price of money, which like any other commodity is subject to the laws of supply and demand in the market. Money is a peculiar type of commodity, however, and its "price" seems to have unique features. Money is not generally "bought" – unless you consider a currency exchange a purchase. Perhaps you "buy" euros with dollars. Normally money is "rented." At least that is the way interest on a loan is generally explained. I suppose you could say that I "bought" the money with which to purchase my house when I took out a mortgage. I am paying for the money over time rather than the house and the markup includes all the interest over the term of the mortgage. Money also seems to have different prices simultaneously. Perhaps this is like the difference between the wholesale and retail price of other goods, but the price of money also seems to depend on the status of the buyer in an odd way. The buyer who can least afford it is charged the highest price. Normally I expect an affluent consumer who buys something in a "high end" store to pay a bit more for it. Unlike rent on other things the rate for money seems to be higher for a longer term "rental." Normally if I rent a car or tool for a longer time, I expect the rate to be discounted slightly. With loans the interest rate for a long term can be higher than the interest rate on a short term.

Economic theory seems to have some trouble explaining exactly how supply and demand determine the "price" of money. Keynes offered his "liquidity-preference theory" of the rate of interest as an improvement on the classical theory about supply and demand for money. It has been interpreted and debated, but the standard economics text seems to step around the issue by defining interest rate as a special case of the return on investments. It starts by saying that the theory of capital and interest can explain how supply and demand for capital "determines returns such as real interest rates and profits." [22] It later uses an idealized case of a closed economy with perfect competition and without risk or inflation to illustrate the basic relationship between interest rates and return on capital.

40 - Rethinking Money & Finance

> In deciding whether to invest, a profit-maximizing firm will always compare its cost of borrowing funds with the rate of return on capital. If the rate of return is higher than the market interest rate at which the firm can borrow funds, it will undertake the investment. If the interest rate is higher than the rate of return on investment, the firm will not invest.
>
> Where will this process end? Eventually, firms will undertake all investments whose rates of return are higher than the market interest rate. Equilibrium is then reached when the amount of investment that firms are willing to undertake at a given interest rate just equals the savings which that interest rate calls forth.[23]

In this simplified model the money for investment is borrowed rather than being taken from previous profits as it was in Keynes example with the East India Company. Rather than showing how the supply and demand for capital determines the interest rate, it seems to show that the interest rate determines the demand for capital. Obviously there is a complex interaction between investment decisions and the market interest rate. The tendency towards equilibrium is driven both by the willingness of firms to invest and the willingness of people to save. The interest rate "calls forth" a certain amount of savings. Higher interest rates provide more savings but less willingness to invest; lower interest rates provide less savings but more willingness to invest.

For some reason supply and demand analysis likes this strikes me as suspect or even tautological. It adds a description that seems like an explanation of the facts but does not really get to the root causes. I am not at all sure that an individual's "willingness" to save is a function of the current interest rate rather than his income and his commitment to a certain life style and the expenses it entails. What incentivizes savings is uncertainty about the future or the need to accumulate sufficient funds for a retirement income. The idea that the supply and demand for capital determines the interest rate also seems to ignore the way in which the Federal Reserve sets some interest rates in its attempt to control inflation or achieve full employment.

The fundamental issue with the explanation of interest may be the assumption that investment is only possible with savings and that only interest can induce someone to let someone else use the money he or she has saved. Not all loans are investments in the "real" economy, and loans with interest are not the only way savings can be channeled to real investment. Credit can also be extended without any "savings." Ultimately the justification of interest boils down to the feeling that I should be rewarded for letting someone else use my money.

Interest is supposed to be compensation for foregoing consumption and taking a risk. If savings is not really necessary for investment in the real economy, then foregoing consumption is no longer a virtue to be rewarded. It is simply a choice to wait and use the money for consumption later. Letting someone else "use" it while I am waiting to spend it is an act of generosity which may be virtuous (depending perhaps on what the money is used for). It is also not clear to me how receiving interest compensates for having taken a risk. If I don't trust the person to return the money to me, the perhaps I am a fool for letting him use it or perhaps I am just choosing to make a charitable donation. Obviously there may be unforeseen circumstances which prevent the borrower from returning the money even though he or she had every intention of doing so, but does charging interest really "compensate" me for that risk. If the borrower defaults on the whole deal, the interest I was supposed to get does not help. If he manages to pay interest for a while and then defaults on the principal, is that bit of interest really any compensation?

The idea that interest on savings gives me an incentive as an autonomous economic agent to do something that is good for the overall real economy makes sense only if my savings are necessary for investment. If businesses use retained earnings or profits to invest in growth, then the consumer has already contributed to that growth. If banks or other firms can extend credit to enable a business without my savings, then my incentive to save is irrelevant. The real impact of interest is that it eventually redistributes money from those who needed more to those who had more than they required for current expenses. If the loan is repaid with interest, the lender has more money than he started with. Whether the borrower is significantly better off will depend on why he needed the money and how things went when he spent it. At the very least one hopes he has gotten himself out of a hole he was in.

If I have surplus cash on hand and want to put it to work, I can make an equity investment in an enterprise. Both the risk and the potential for return may be greater, but my money is being put to use in the "real" economy. With the current setup it is difficult for individuals with modest savings to find equity investments of this sort rather than just buying existing shares being traded on the stock market, but it is certainly possible for things to change in a way that would make it easier via collectives or partnerships for investing. Cloudfunding is an example of how this might work.

Suppose I could wave a magic wand and declare that money would no longer be a commodity with a price determined by supply and demand in a market. What if charging interest on loans was illegal? What difference would it make in my day-to-day use of money? I would still have a bank account and could certainly pay for purchases with a debit card. I could still conceivably have a credit card, although the issuer could no longer charge me some outrageous interest rate on unpaid balances. Credit cards would be more like the original Diners Club card where the balance always had to be paid at the end of the month. So maybe I lose a cash flow management tool. On the other hand, if I have a good relationship with my bank perhaps they could revert to doing things the way my bank in England did in 1965 when I had an overdraft while I was traveling. They sent me a polite letter calling my attention to the overdraft and suggesting I take care of it at my earliest convenience. In other words there is no reason a bank cannot extend credit to customers whom they trust. There also may be no incentive for them to do so, however, other than valuing the customer's business and hoping it will be a stable long-term relationship.

In most cases if you pay the balance on your card every month, you don't pay interest on it. The card is simply a convenience that facilitates purchases or a short term cash flow management tool. Perhaps the bank where you have a checking account could issue a credit card that would enable you to pay for items over time to a limited extent. Other banks or financial institutions who know little or nothing about you could not offer you credit cards in order to earn interest payments on your balances. Merchants who want to attract your business could offer charge accounts with some provision for paying off large purchases over time, but they would not be charging interest on the balance due. Perhaps like gas stations they would offer one price for cash and another for credit or installment purchases.

The first question the average person is likely to ask in response to talk about eliminating interest-bearing loans is "How am I going to make the big-ticket purchases that are so important to me like a car, a house or a college education?" A car purchase is often financed by a loan with the car serving as collateral. The loan is paid off over a period of years with the understanding that defaulting on the payments incurs the risk of having the car "repossessed." The interest on the loan is built into the monthly payments, and the interest rate may depend on who is making the loan and who is buying the car. From the point of view of the buyer this is really no different from paying a higher price for the car in monthly installments without any "interest." Sometimes car dealerships offer financing with a 0% annual rate for the loan. In other words they are willing to accept payment over time for the right price on the car (and whatever other fees they may hide in the fine print). If interest-bearing loans were illegal, this form of "financing" might be the norm.

The same thing is true on a larger scale with buying a house. Instead of paying rent to a landlord every month, I make mortgage payments to a lender which cover the interest on the loan as well as the principal and perhaps even taxes and insurance via an escrow account. My budget has to include monthly payments for my housing either way. The main difference between a car loan and a mortgage is that unlike a car whose value depreciates every year the value of a house may increase over time. The possibility of "refinancing" or selling at a profit lets homeowners view their house as an investment asset. It also encourages lenders to offer mortgages with abnormally low interest rates for the first few years and little or no down payment. If the crisis of 2007-2008 taught us anything, it is the danger posed by such mortgages.

It may be a strategic error to regard ones own home as an investment. It is not an asset that produces income unless one refinances it or otherwise borrows money against it. Home ownership has long be promoted as a means of stabilizing a community, and it does provide a family with more security than they might have in renting with the possibility of eviction always looming. People will always want to own their own homes, but how would people buy and sell houses without mortgages involving interest?

It is possible to imagine a real estate exchange that lets people buy and sell houses on credit without any interest being charged.

Such an agency would not be a for-profit business, but more like a public utility answerable to the community it serves rather than to investors. There could be transaction fees to cover the operating costs of the agency, but they might not even be tied to the price of the house, and they could be split between the buyer and the seller. It is even conceivable that the operating costs for the agency would be paid for by property taxes. The managers at such an agency would be faced with the same tasks as those faced by loan officers at a traditional bank. They would have to appraise the value of the house, evaluate the credit-worthiness of the buyers and perhaps set down payment requirements. They would do all this with an eye to the overall needs of the needs of the community.

If a home being sold was previously purchased with credit from such an agency, much of the sale price might go towards paying off the balance on that previous purchase. Perhaps some of the profit from the sale of the house would be used in a down payment on another house, so the impact of the transaction on the amount of money circulating in the economy would be minimized. The really interesting question to speculate about is what the impact of such an institution would be on real estate prices.

One consequence of the elimination of mortgage interest is that the homeowner's equity in his home would grow more rapidly than with a typical mortgage which uses compound interest combined with fixed monthly payments heavily weighted towards interest payments initially. It is probably anybody's guess as to how this might affect a particular homeowner's willingness to sell his house at a particular price.

Student loans for college education are a very different type of loan. There is no collateral involved unless you are inclined to view certain types of employment as indentured servitude. There are already a lot of proposals for eliminating or drastically reducing the burden student loans. If college education cannot be free, then perhaps interest-free student loans should be considered an investment in infrastructure to be paid back over time at a rate consistent with the individual's earnings.

The other big-ticket items that most people worry about are unexpected things like medical expenses or career setbacks. Again, the air is full of proposals for reforming health insurance so that people are not bankrupted by unexpected medical bills.

For other personal loans, making banks more like public utilities might enable them to extend credit to help customers and the community during hard times. If the bank is answerable to the community instead of to stock holders, then its officers can consider human needs rather than just profitability or shareholder value in deciding whether to extend credit to a particular customer.

Another perspective on interest in commercial loans is that it is the cost of "financing." If you are planning a construction project with a view to selling the finished building, chances are you will not use "your own money" but will "finance" the project; and the interest you pay on the borrowed money is a "cost" of the project which is recouped along with the other costs when the building is sold. If all of the suppliers of the materials were willing to extend credit until the sale of the finished building and all of the work was done by sub-contractors equally willing to extend credit, you could eliminate the "cost of the money." This type of financing might be achieved with a commercial credit clearing exchange formed by a network of contractors and suppliers.

Obviously banks which were non-profit entities, cooperatives or public utilities could extend credit to developers without charging interest. In this way the developer could pay all the workers and suppliers as the work was done and the bank would have the finished building as collateral for their loan. None of this requires "interest" even if there are "origination fees" involved in extending credit to the developers.

The big problem with eliminating interest, however, is not the impact it will have on the use of money by normal consumers, but the way in which it would pull the rug out from under monetary policy which attempts to fight inflation and eliminate unemployment. Current monetary policy uses interest rates to control the amount of money in circulation. This is because banks can make money by borrowing from the Federal Reserve at one rate and lending at a higher rate to its loan customers. Raising or lowering the interest rate charged to banks will raise or lower the "price of money" their customers and thereby affect the "demand" for loans and the money supply.

To the extent that credit "creates" money it can be used to control the supply of money in the economy and thereby prevent excessive inflation or deflation even without "interest." If banks were free to extend credit without having to borrow money at interest, and bank loans were interest free, there would obviously be a greater demand for bank loans than the bank could process. In addition to assessing the credit-worthiness of the applicants the bank would have to limit how much money it poured into the local economy based on statistics about the state of the economy including unemployment levels.

Making such a system work strikes me as difficult but not impossible. Loan officers at banks would have to go back to being serious students of local businesses and the economy rather than just rubber-stamping everything that comes across their desk in the secure knowledge that it is heading to a place where it will be someone else's problem. Even though money is no longer viewed as a limited resource or commodity, credit extended to one company will still have an impact on the credit that can be extended to other companies. Banks would have to be regulated. One bank's allotment of credit would have to be balanced with that of all the other banks serving the same community. If banks do not have enough customers asking for credit in a recession, the government would probably have to take up the slack with infrastructure projects in the region.

Needless to say the biggest obstacle to eliminating interest in this way would be the "financial sector" in which a lot of people make a lot of money by arranging various types of financing involving interest. Aside from this the real obstacle to eliminating interest in the ways I have described is probably the feeling that it is just a slight-of-hand trick that accomplishes nothing in terms of the real functioning of the economy. This is because "interest" is tied to "growth" and growth results in progress and increased prosperity for all. The root of interest is the "yield" that "capital" is supposed to have and the way in which "wealth" can grow.

Wealth and Growth

My immediate association with the idea of wealth is the term "wealthy" which describes people who, unlike me, have consistently earned more than they spent so that they have accumulated reserves of money. I probably fit into the category of the "in some sense wealthy" since my major asset is a house which is now worth 10 times what I paid for it 45 years ago. To speak of the "wealth of nations" strikes me as a metaphor which views a nation as a person with income, expenses and reserves. Obviously wealth means something different to an economist, especially when it is described as being "created" by economic activity.

In a zero-sum game like Monopoly the money that one player accumulates comes at the expense of the other players. Much of what is regarded as "wealth" today is the result of a redistribution of money. When a day trader makes a killing on a stock transaction, the money he acquires comes out of someone else's pocket. I am unable to see anything "creative" in this process. One might argue that the appreciation in value (i.e. market price) of the stock is an indirect result of the creation of value by the success of the underlying company, but I am not inclined to buy this without further probing into how the company achieved its success and whether that success is accurately reflected in the fluctuations in the market price of its stock. Stock prices that fluctuate enough to benefit a day trader surely do not reflect hourly changes in the success of the underlying company. They reflect differing expectations of traders with regard to the future of the company or simply with regard to trends in the price of its stock.

Consulting Wikipedia I find that Adam Smith saw wealth creation as "the combination of materials, labour, land and technology in such a way as to capture a profit (excess above the cost of production)." I'm afraid I balk at this concept because it hinges on "profit," which, of course, depends on market pricing. Did Wham-O really "create wealth" when it capitalized on the aerodynamic qualities of the cake pan by marketing the Frisbee?

There is a mystery gear somewhere in the wealth creation machine if persuading people to pay more for a Frisbee than it costs to make and market results in the "creation of wealth." At first glance it seems to result simply in the redistribution of money so that more of it is in the hands of Wham-O. It does cause money to circulate in a way that involves wages, and circulation is as vital to an economy as it is to the human body, but the only accumulation is the profit skimmed off this flowing stream. The owners of Wham-O became wealthier only when the demand for Frisbees became enormous and economies of scale kicked in. A warehouse full of Frisbees has value only so long as the craze persists. The owners of Wham-O were, of course, "job creators" since they had to hire more employees as their marketing efforts produced greater and greater demand for Frisbees. Creating jobs sounds more philanthropic than creating (personal) wealth, but I am still a long way from understanding the relationship between greater employment and greater wealth or between the rate at which money circulates in an economy and some measure of the health or wealth of the economy.

Surely the notion of wealth creation has its roots in agriculture where human labor cooperates with nature to produce goods (food). It is much easier to view an abundance of food as wealth, even if most of the "creation" is handled by nature. This seems especially true when the seeds for next year's crop can be gleaned from this year's crop. Cultivation technique may increase the "yield" of a plot of land, so there is some validity to the idea that humans create wealth through their labor.

A craftsman who makes a piece of furniture out of raw materials has obviously created something. Whether the piece of furniture has value beyond its usefulness in the craftsman own home is a bit more complicated, and the craftsman can only be said to have "created wealth" if there is a market where the furniture can be sold for more than it cost to make. Part of its "cost" of course is the craftsman's labor and expertise and if the style of his furniture is regarded as outmoded, he may not have created any "wealth."

One definition of wealth is the abundance of valuable resources or valuable material possessions. An individual's wealth is generally measured as his net worth. It includes assets as well as cash. I assume a nation's wealth includes untapped natural resources, such as oil, minerals or timber. Timber can be viewed as an agricultural product since it is theoretically possible to manage forests in a sustainable way so that they continue to produce a certain amount of usable timber for centuries. With oil and minerals it seems as though there is a fixed amount of the resource available. New technology may make it more easily accessible, but if a nation's wealth consisted purely of its natural resources the "creation" of wealth would appear to be mostly a zero sum game.

At the risk of getting ahead of myself, I'll go ahead and voice the suspicion that Adam Smith was able to conceive of the "wealth of nations" because he lived in a nation that was beginning to exploit natural resources beyond its own borders (or to extend its borders to include the resources). Wealth seems to be a relative term. One person is wealthy because he has more resources at his disposal than others or than he used to. Perhaps in paradise we can all be wealthy, but I still need to understand better how "wealth" can be created.

It is obvious that an individual can accumulate resources by being successful in business. It might seem by extension that a nation can accumulate wealth only if it is trading with other nations. There is a concise piece in Forbes in which a disciple of Ayn Rand argues that only individuals create wealth. He is objecting to the use of a pie metaphor by in discussing the distribution of wealth

> Wealth grows. True. But the pie metaphor carries with it another implication.... It treats wealth as owned by society. We happen to find ourselves in possession of a pie. How did it get here? That's never made too clear, but it's here, and now we have to decide how to divide it up fairly.
>
> In accepting the pie metaphor, we concede a moral point that should not be conceded. Wealth does not arise from an amorphous social process; "society" owns no pie.
>
> Wealth is created by, and morally belongs to the individual creator. As Rand observes, since "man has to sustain his life by his own effort, the man who has no right to the product of his effort has no means to sustain his life. The man who produces while others dispose of his product, is a slave."
>
> Let's break that down a little. Suppose Robinson Crusoe is tired of trying to scoop up fish with his hands and figures out how to turn a tree branch into a spear, increasing his daily catch tenfold. Can Friday, who never thought to make a spear, properly complain that Crusoe has received an "unfair distribution" of fish?
>
> Whatever the complications and intricacies involved, the basic issue is the same whether we're talking about a

remote island or a complex division of labor economy like America's: a man uses his mind and his existing property (i.e., previously created wealth) to bring new wealth into existence. He doesn't gobble down an already-baked pie – he produces.[24]

He goes on to describe how Richard Branson built his empire by starting with a bunch of record albums in the trunk of his car. In an aside he reconciles the reliance on wage labor to produce wealth with Rand's notion that a man whose product is disposed by others is a slave by emphasizing that the laborers were paid according to their productivity. The problem with all this is that a "market" is precisely the kind of "amorphous social process" that he wants to eliminate from the creation of wealth. Producing something does not create wealth unless that something has "value" in a "market." If his Robinson Crusoe caught more fish than he and Friday could eat before they spoiled, he was wasting his time. If he made a deal where Friday would clean the hut in exchange for enough fish to relieve him of the task of fishing for survival, he has set up a social network involving a division of labor made possible by technology. If he decided to lord it over Friday by consuming a larger share of the fish, he has created a social hierarchy based on his own fishing innovations, but if Friday was as smart as I suspect he was, he would have learned how to fish with a spear and let Crusoe clean his own mess. None of this really has anything to do with the "creation of wealth."

The point of the analogy is obviously that technology makes possible a surplus of goods. The analogy seems to be compromised by the fact that dead fish are not a stable asset that hold value in the long term. Suppose Friday knew how to smoke fish or discovered a salt lick on the island which could be used to preserve the fish. He could perhaps leverage this knowledge in a partnership deal with Crusoe that enabled them to create wealth in the form of enough smoked or salted fish to see them through lean times or free them to devote their time to other pursuits. If, however, we are attempting to specify the wealth of the society on that island, do salted fish count for more than the seemingly endless supply of fresh fish swimming in the water around them. And if a ship of starving pirates showed up in the lagoon, the value of the preserved fish might skyrocket. We could go on ringing changes on this analogy, but the upshot of it all may be that simple analogies are of limited use in understanding the complexities of economics.

Surely the key to wealth as a social phenomenon is the ability of human labor to produce more than is required for survival. There are intriguing descriptions of surviving hunter-gatherer cultures which convey the impression that their members have much more leisure time and seem much more content than most members of "advanced" cultures, and I gather that the emergence of the drive to produce ever increasing surpluses is still a bit of a mystery for anthropology. Nonetheless it obviously happened, and we appear to be stuck with it.

The simplest version of how the market sets prices seems to assume that the producer can know what kind of sales volume to expect at every price level. He adjusts his level of output to insure that sales will provide the greatest profit. If he can't make a profit selling widgets, he just closes up shop and moves on to something else no matter how many customers are clamoring for affordable widgets. It is up to someone else to figure out the cost-savings method that will enable him to profit from the huge demand for widgets. The entire premise of this model is that economic transactions only take place when there is a profit to be made, even though the model is often derived from a model of primitive barter. If one starts with a simple model for direct barter between individuals with differing resources or differing preferences for consumption, it is possible for there to be a mutually beneficial exchange without any profit in the sense of accumulated wealth. Each party satisfies his own consumer desires and neither ends up with a surplus.

Similarly a model based on division of labor has room for mutually beneficial exchanges without profit to either party. I do what I'm good at and you do what you are good at and together we produce just enough to go around.

If you start with an industrious farmer who is capable of producing more than he needs for his own subsistence, he may have no incentive to do so unless a market exists for his surplus produce. If there are a lot of hungry people in his community, he might enjoy the status of being their benefactor or simply give them food out of generosity. If there are goods available other than farm produce, then he may sell his surplus food in order to buy tools or toys. If there is a fully developed market, he may just sell his surplus and save the money for future projects. In other words the profit motive explains nothing without the prior or simultaneous existence of fairly developed markets.

There is another arena in which the profit motive may play a role: trading between communities with different resources. A merchant may be able to buy things from one community and sell them for a profit in another simply because the demand is higher there. Trading in this sense seems to have a long venerable history. In fact in some primitive cultures trading was only permitted with outsiders. Within the community exchange was governed by different customs more akin to gift giving.

Most economic theory probably assumes that the accumulation of wealth is only possible where there is private property. Mises even says that money has no function without private property and the division of labor. Explanations of the origin of (and justification for) private property are as varied and slippery as the explanations of money. We shall have to dig into them eventually, but for now it seems to me that the crucial thing is how you define wealth. A "primitive" society in which everything is communally "owned" may still be capable of production surplus. It may manifest itself mainly in rituals, sacrifices, temples or wars, but I would still be inclined to call it wealth.

The question then becomes, if a community or society is capable of generating a surplus of goods, what are the options available to it for determining what to do with the surplus and how is an option chosen. Perhaps there is still also the question of what the motivation for creating the surplus is in the first place. Surely there is some circularity in the relationship between the motivation and the choice of what to do with the surplus. Individuals are motivated by the customs of the society in which they live. To some extent a culture can be defined by how it disposes of its surplus productivity, and anthropology is full of eye-opening alternatives. Ours has settled into a mixed bag combining a "public sector" and a "private sector" and allowing a relatively small number of individuals to control vast amounts of wealth.

"Wealth creation" is primarily associated with the accumulation of wealth by individuals. Economic growth of the society as a whole is normally discussed in terms of gross domestic product (GDP). Wikipedia explains that GDP is "a monetary measure of the value of all final goods and services produced in a period of time (quarterly or yearly)." The explanation of how it is calculated, what it includes and what it ignores, however, is enough to make my head swim, and I am sure the brief article is mere scratch on the surface of a very complex attempt to measure the output of an economy. I am willing to let the experts determine how to measure GDP so long as the method chosen does not affect policy recommendations based on how growth is good or bad for the overall health of society.

Clearly just from the simple definition of GDP, the output of an economy can be increased by 1) putting more people to work, 2) having people work longer and harder or 3) achieving greater efficiency through technology and innovation. To take a nice loaded example, the invention of the cotton gin made feasible much larger cotton crops. It combined with a five-fold increase in the labor force (imported slaves who could be forced to work as long and as hard as their health permitted) to yield an increase in cotton production in the South from 750,000 bales in 1830 to 2,850,000 bales in 1850. In terms of GDP the economy was booming and this might be described as explosive growth.

Some would argue that this is a good example of why economic growth is not always good for society no matter how much the plantation owners may have benefited in the short run. The Southern economy became completely dependent on cotton exports and most of its "capital" was tied up in slaves. Dependence on Southern cotton did not persuade England and France to actively side with the South in the Civil War and defeat involved not only wiping out capital tied up in slaves but also destruction of much of the infrastructure required for rebuilding the economy. But I digress…

Increase in output does not necessarily produce a corresponding increase in the monetary value of the output. Excess production of a good can cause a drop in the price commanded by the good. Farm produce is notoriously susceptible to over-production, and governments have resorted to extreme measures to protect farmers from bankruptcy. GDP measures the value of the output. That value may decline simply because of a decline in the demand for the product. Growth in GDP may also come at the expense of damage to the environment that is not adequately factored into calculations of cost. A farmer who depletes his soil by maximizing his output for several years running is undermining his own long-term economic viability.

A manufacturing plant that pollutes the air and water may not be undermining its own viability, but it may be undermining the longer-term viability of the whole society.

One way an economy can grow while avoiding overproduction of any given good is to increase the diversity of goods produced. This may happen spontaneously because of creative people or it may be engineered by stimulating demands with advertising. There seems to be no end to the things people can desire once they have enough to survive. Technology and desire feed off each other in a way that seems inevitable, but for the economist an increase in GDP attributable to the Pet Rock, Hula Hoop, or Frisbee is just as real as the increase due to the personal computer or cell phone.

To the extent that economic growth is a goal of policy it would seem to be justified either by the fact that it satisfies more (and more diverse) individual desires or by the fact that it promotes fuller employment (which in turn permits more individuals to satisfy their desires). Satisfying seemingly frivolous desires of some may produce jobs for those whose most basic needs are going unsatisfied. Reducing unemployment is obviously the best justification for continued growth. There is also the possibility of raising the average standard of living even if full employment is never achieved. This benefit is often characterized as the way in which "a rising tide lifts all boats," but it may not be noticed by the people drowning because they have not been able to get into a boat.

In the end I fear that the benefits of economic growth may well depend on how growth is measured, what is included or excluded in the calculation of the GDP. I shall probably have to return to this before I can draw any conclusions, but my instinct tells me that there may be better ways to measure the success or health of an economy. Bhutan has conceived of an intriguing alternative in their idea of Gross National Happiness.

If there is real economic growth, the amount of money circulating or the "velocity" with which it circulates should be increasing or perhaps money is becoming more valuable as prices across the board fall. In the current system, the creation of money is accomplished primarily by credit. A given level of money in circulation is maintained by rolling over loans or extending new credit as old loans are paid off. Theoretically the amount of money circulating is determined by supply and demand, but the ability of a central bank to set interest rates for certain types of loans means it can be managed to some extent. It is assumed that all of this is driven by the profit motives of autonomous economic agents.

The relationship between profit-seeking and growth may be more complex than the simple models seem to suggest. Profits may just reflect a redistribution of wealth. Suppose I start a business producing widgets and am willing to sell them at cost for a while in order to introduce them. After a year I decide to raise the price in order to make profit. Sales continue to grow and economies of scale offset my increased production costs. I am "producing" something and the economic transactions in the production and sale of the product show up in the GDP. Unless the buyers are using bank loans in order to buy the widgets, there would be no increase in the amount of money circulating. Perhaps sales of some other less desirable product fall as widget sales rise, so that money flowing through consumers wallets is ending up in my pocket rather than someone else's.

Or to take a simpler example: I decide to start a consulting business. My net income shows up in the GDP, and maybe the company that hired me shows slightly less profit. Has the country's wealth grown?

Real economic growth is clearly driven by technology and innovation. Some of this may be the result of profit seeking, but I suspect most major technological advances were the result of the desires on the part of engineers and scientists to understand things and develop techniques or machines for their own sake. Profit seekers will quickly latch on to new technology, but the impetus to find a better way to do something may not be the same as the impetus to make more money. Much of the core technology underlying the digital age was developed by governments in their efforts to provide defense or to explore space. Obviously a lot of creative work done by all types of artists or even craftsmen is not the result of profit-seeking. It may not find its way into the calculation of the GDP, but it is surely a product worth considering in evaluating the health of an economy or society.

The person who argues that we as a community or society cannot afford to do things that need urgently to be done is ultimately saying we are choosing to use our wealth for other things. This is, of course, precisely the pie-chart interpretation that the Ayn Rand follower rejects – that any collective "we" has any say over how "we" allocate use "our" wealth. He might just suggest that we should consume less and vote to raise taxes so the government can spend more doing the things we tell it to do. Perhaps the more relevant question is whether pumping money into the economy can stimulate growth. The conventional wisdom seems to be the "printing money" just causes inflation, but an argument could be made that having the government initiate infrastructure projects paid for by "printing money" would give consumers more money to spend thereby increasing revenues and profits for businesses and encouraging them to expand or develop new products.

There are two things in the Samuelson/Nordhaus explanation of growth which struck me as odd. First in discussing the need for investment in capital and "capital deepening, which is the process by which the quantity of capital per worker increases over time,"[25] they conclude

> ...the wage rate paid to workers will tend to rise as capital deepening takes place. Why? Each worker has more capital to work with and his or her marginal product therefore rises. As a result, the competitive wage rate rises along with the marginal product of labor.[26]

This just sounds like wishful thinking to me, especially when I consider one of their examples of capital deepening: "a road builder uses a backhoe instead of a worker with a pick and shovel."[27] I can see that a backhoe operator requires different training or skills than a worker with a pick and shovel and therefore might command a higher wage, but the number of workers required to build the road has been dramatically reduced and the competition for the job of backhoe operator will surely tend to hold down the wage rate, especially as more workers learn how to operate the machine. To say that each worker has more capital to work with seems to imply that the worker owns the backhoe and his wages must include rent on the equipment. It is unclear to me why the wage rate must rise with the marginal product of each worker rather than the road building company's profits. It is presumably the desire to increase profits with greater productivity that motivated the company to invest in a backhoe. This is not to suggest that investment in capital is not a major component in growth. It is more a suggestion of why the rising tide may not lift all boats.

The other point in their explanation of growth where I balk is the way in which personal savings is related to accumulating capital:

> Accumulating capital, as we have seen, requires a sacrifice of current consumption over many years. Countries that grow rapidly tend to invest heavily in new capital goods; in the most rapidly growing countries, 10 to 20 percent of output may go into net capital formation. The United States shows a stark contrast with high-saving countries. The U.S. net national saving rate, after averaging around 7 percent during the first four decades after World War II, began to decline and actually fell to near-zero in 2008. The low saving rate was the result of low personal saving and large government fiscal deficits. The low saving was seen primarily in the large external (trade) deficit. Economists worry that the low saving rate will retard investment and economic growth in the decades to come and that the large foreign indebtedness may require major adverse changes in exchange rates and real wages.[28]

First of all a profitable company may have retained earnings which it eventually uses to invest in capital goods without having any dependence on personal savings. In fact maximized consumption would seem to increase the possibility of this.

More importantly the underlying assumption of a connection between personal savings and capital investment may be applicable to the current system but seems to me to be based on mistaken ideas about the nature of money.

Finance

My son grew up at a time when everyone interested in making "serious money" wanted to be an investment banker. I had no idea what investment bankers did (other than make obscene amounts of money). When I went to college, few of my classmates discussed their life plans in terms of making money. Those who did I regarded as something of an anomaly. This is not to say that many of them did not go on to make large amounts of money. One of my classmates co-founded the Quantum Fund with George Soros and "retired" in 1980 when I was just beginning to struggle with the financial realities of adult life. When I knew him he was studying history and apparently knew little about the stock market. When another classmate announced some time after he graduated from Columbia Law School that he was going to work for Bernie Cornfeld, I was a bit surprised. Bernie Cornfeld created something called Investors Overseas Services which sold mutual funds and recruited customers and employees with the slogan "Do you sincerely want to be rich?" I had always assumed my friend was as idealistic as I was and headed for a career of public service. I concluded he was disillusioned by the Vietnam war and the conduct of the Nixon administration. That is to say I still regarded going for the money as a cynical choice.

Once I bought my house, I no longer had any money invested in the stock market and largely lost interest in it. When I inherited some stock from my father I put it into an account for my son and basically let it sit there. For years I played tennis with a guy who was a financial advisor and managed portfolios for individuals. He had an MBA from USC and had worked at a bank for years before becoming an independent financial advisor. He seemed to know what he was talking about, but I eventually discovered he was a con artist who liked gambling with other people's money. A client won a judgment against him for mishandling a portfolio, but the financial advisor just declared bankruptcy, walked away from the judgment and did the same thing to another client a few years later. By the time of the 2007-2008 financial crisis I had developed a very jaundiced view of the stock market. I had also "retired" because the company where I was working ran aground, and I was trying to figure out how to maximize my retirement income.

The logic implied by the existence of the stock market seems unassailable. Companies need financing to start or expand their operations. People want to invest their surplus funds in a way that promises a better return than a savings account or government bond even if there is an element of risk involved. A market for buying and selling shares in companies needs to exist, and the more people can have access to it the better. The problem is the way a stock market seems to evolve into the world's largest casino. Perhaps I wouldn't mind having people gamble on stock prices if the price fluctuations did not seem to have such an impact on the economy as a whole.

The more I read about the causes and proposed cures of the 2007-2008 crisis, the more convinced I became that there is something fundamentally wrong with the way in which our society "finances" its activity. To say that something makes no sense to me may, of course, just be a reflection of the limitations of my intellect and expertise, but I cannot accept the notion that a modern society will inevitably be plagued by increasingly catastrophic business cycles plus massive unemployment and poverty combined with extreme wealth in the hands of a minute percentage of the population. To say simply that it has always been so and ever will be is not a convincing argument. Surely there is a better way.

No one will argue with the idea that investing is necessary for the development of the economy or even just for maintenance of infrastructure and the adaptation to changing circumstances. Technology will continually create opportunities for new (and perhaps better) products and services. The question is where the money should come from.

Companies finance their investment with loans or sales of shares. Public financing for government investment in infrastructure or research comes from taxes or loans (bonds). In theory each of these sources of financing imply that the money is already "out there" somewhere in terms of accumulated cash and needs to be "channeled" into investments. As we have seen, however, loans from banks essentially create new money for the duration of the loan. Many argue that government expenditures can do the same thing. If the Treasury just issued checks to pay for infrastructure or research projects, the checks would be deposited and become part of the money supply in circulation. The problem that people have with this idea is that letting the government "just print money" gives rise to concerns about inflation because one of the factors associated with inflation is the amount of money in circulation.

In the current system when the government "prints money," what it is doing is "monetizing debt" using the unique relationship between the U.S. Treasury and the Federal Reserve. The Treasury issues bonds, notes and bills which are essentially standardized loan contracts designed to be "securities" which can be traded in a market. Originally they were printed in a way to make them difficult to counterfeit, and, if the loans paid periodic interest, they would include coupons which were cut off and turned in to a bank for redemption when the payment was due. I am old enough to remember that my mother had a safe deposit box at the bank where she kept bonds and would clip off the coupons. Bonds that pay all the interest in a lump sum at the maturity date are called "zero coupon" bonds. As a kid I used to buy 25¢ savings stamps at school to put into a book until I had $18.75 worth and I could trade it in for a savings bond which would be worth $25 in 10 years. Savings bonds were not marketable, but other zero coupon bonds are, and the market price, which will obviously vary with the maturity date of the bond, is allowed to float. On maturity the bond will be worth its face value, but when bought and sold on the market prior to its due date, its price will determine the effective rate of return that the buyer will receive on the investment. This fluctuating rate of return on U.S. Treasury securities, especially on short term bills and notes, has a ripple effect on other interest rates in the financial market.

When the Treasury issues securities, it can transfer (i.e. sell) some of them to the Federal Reserve and its account at the Federal Reserve is credited with the purchase price. This is comparable to the way normal banks credit the account of a borrower with a loan agreement. The government is borrowing money from the Federal Reserve. The "cash" credited to the Treasury's account is "created out of thin air." The purchase of the securities by the Federal Reserve may actually take place on the open market via other financial institutions but the net result so far as the Treasury is concerned is the same.

The Federal Reserve, although it operates as a profit making enterprise like other banks, is required to turn all of its net profits over to the government. If it holds a Treasury bill or note until its maturity, it simply returns any interest it has earned to the

Treasury. The Treasury can choose to "pay back" the Federal Reserve for the principal amount (i.e. the face value of the bond or note or bill) by having its account debited or it can "roll it over" by issuing another security to cover the amount and "selling" it to the Federal Reserve. The net effect is that the Treasury can borrow money indefinitely from the Fed "for free."

Even though I have read several explanations of this process of "monetizing debt," I think I am not alone in feeling there is something weird about the government creating money by lending money to itself. It seems at first like a bit of sleight of hand or at least an unnecessarily circuitous route for "financing" government operations or investment. Why not just have the government create money by issuing checks to pay for things without pretending that it is borrowing the money from the Federal Reserve? Is this just a vestigial artifact from the evolution of money and finance? Regardless of how it came about, the monetization of debt in this way is an indication of how central interest is to finance and the economy.

When the Federal Reserve was created in 1913, the stated goal was "to furnish an elastic currency, to afford means of rediscounting commercial paper, to establish a more effective supervision of banking in the United States, and for other purposes." In 1933 this was amended to include promoting "effectively the goals of maximum employment, stable prices, and moderate long-term interest rates." Elasticity of money refers to the ability to have the supply of currency or credit expand and contract in response to the needs of business. The rediscounting of commercial paper refers to the ability of banks to use their loans to customers as collateral for borrowing money from the Federal Reserve. Obviously the Federal Reserve is intended to be more than a way of facilitating transfers between banks. It is tasked with keeping the economy running smoothly, and it has attempted to do this primarily by controlling the amount of money in circulation or by influencing interest rates. It also deals with issues related to foreign exchange rates which can have an impact on our own economy.

So part of what the Federal Reserve is about is making sure that credit is available for investment in private enterprise as well as for financing government. The best way it has found for encouraging investment is through the influence it can have on interest rates. This seems in keeping with the way economics regards interest as the "price" of money in the interaction of supply and demand.

Theoretically if the economy is slow or in a recession, lowering the interest rate will encourage businesses to invest. Conversely if inflation is the problem, "tightening" money by raising interest rates will make businesses less able to expand and will slow things down. It doesn't always work this way. In the 70s there were periods of high inflation even though interest rates were extremely high. Also low interest rates alone may not entice business to invest in ways that increase output. Business investment decisions are influenced by a host of other things, and inflation may be caused by things like the manipulation of international oil prices by OPEC that occurred in the 70s. Nonetheless influencing interest rates seems to be the best tool available to the Federal Reserve for keeping the economy on track.

The Federal Reserve cannot just mandate interest rates for the entire financial market. It can only set the interest rate at which it lends money to banks and influence the price of Treasury bonds by buying or selling large amounts so that the supply available to investors will cause their prices to rise or fall. Normally the rate which banks have to pay the Federal Reserve will determine the rate at which they are willing to lend money to their customers. The effective interest rate on short term Treasury bills should also have an effect on the rates other bonds competing for investor's dollars will have to pay. In theory it should even affect the expectations for the return on other types of investment. Again reality does not always conform to the theory because there may be other factors determining investment decisions. In recent decades many businesses have sought short term profits by strategies other than investing in long term plans for growth or sustainability.

In a simplistic model of business finance investment comes from the sale of shares, and bank credit is just used for cash flow management if revenue tends to vary during different seasons. Money for expansion is supposed to come from profits generated by the business. In reality large corporations seem to have relied increasingly on loans even to the point of borrowing money in order to buy back their own stock.

Debt financing comes in different forms. Corporate bonds normally have a fixed interest rate. The price of a bond in the secondary market will vary with changes in the prevailing interest rate, but this does not affect the amount that the issuer will have to pay in periodic interest or on the bond's maturity. In order to get lower interest costs, the company may issue convertible bonds which can be converted to shares of stock under certain conditions. Companies that are struggling and have a lesser credit rating may resort to another type of debt financing known as "leveraged loans." The terms of these loans are custom tailored and may involve a variable rate of interest based on something like the London Inter-bank Offering Rate (LIBOR). They may also have priority over other corporate debt in a bankruptcy. Like more conventional "junk" bonds, leveraged loans are often used for mergers and acquisitions where proceeds from the loan are used to buy up sufficient shares of stock to take control of a company.

Whether there is anything detrimental about the reliance on debt financing is debatable. Hyman Minsky concluded that the use of debt in corporate finance was a major factor in making capitalism inherently unstable. He distinguished between three different kinds of debt financing: hedge finance, speculative finance and Ponzi finance.

Hedge finance is betting that revenues will grow sufficiently to pay off the loan. During periods of prosperity Minsky observed that entrepreneurs are inclined to become more adventurous and take on greater risks. So long as revenues can be counted on to cover the interest payments, they may take on debts with the expectation that when the loan comes due it can be refinanced. Minsky calls this speculative finance rather than hedge finance. The current revenue is not sufficient to pay down the principal on the loan, but it can carry the loan by covering the interest payments. In more extreme situations where revenue in the shorter term is insufficient even to cover the interest payments, businesses may engage in what Minsky calls "Ponzi" finance, where new investment is used to pay accrued interest as well as rolling over the principal. The use of speculative and Ponzi financing for business eventually leads to pressure to increase prices so that there is sufficient revenue to service the debt. Minsky sees this pressure as a major cause of inflation.

Any business can have slow periods or seasonal fluctuations in revenue, and short term bank credit is clearly the best way to help smooth things out. Needing to continually refinance debt, however, makes a company more vulnerable and perhaps more inclined to pursue short term profits rather than long term stability. The extreme case of this is the leveraged buyout where the buyer is so burdened with debt that they may be forced to liquidate much if not all of the company and thousands of people are thrown out of work.

With equity financing there is a limit to the number of shares a company can sell without losing control or diluting the value of existing shares too much. Debt financing makes it easier (and perhaps more tempting) to keep raising the ante to the point of risking bankruptcy. Traditional bank loans are reasonably straightforward, and prudent loan officers may be able to prevent excessive speculative borrowing. Most large corporate loans now, however, are likely to be complex transactions with institutions like hedge funds, pension funds and insurance companies rather than old fashioned banks. They are driven partially by the desires of traders or dealers to earn bonuses and of fund managers to maximize their short term returns. Even banks have found ways to pass loans along to other investors and may be much less concerned about the long term viability of the borrower.

The term "financialization" has been coined to describe a fundamental change in the economy over the last 50 years. It has been variously defined, but in its broadest sense it "refers to the increasing importance of finance, financial markets, and financial institutions to the workings of the economy." Working from this definition, Gerald F. Davis and Suntae Kim of the Ross School of Business at the University of Michigan provide a helpful overview not only of the increasing importance of finance but of the causes and consequences of financialization in a paper entitled "Financialization of the Economy."[29] They emphasize that "the fundamental feature of financialization is a shift from financial institutions to financial markets." The key to this shift is the ability to "securitize" loans.

> One of the most critical yet under-appreciated enablers of financialization is securitization. Securitization is the process of taking assets with cash flows, such as mortgages held by banks, and turning them into tradable securities (bonds). A single mortgage is illiquid and its payment is often unpredictable: the homeowner might lose his or her job due to a medical emergency, or win the lottery and pay off the mortgage early, or the neighborhood might be leveled by a tornado. But when bundled with hundreds of

other mortgages in other parts of the country, the payoff becomes more predictable due to the law of large numbers, and suitable for being divided up into bonds, with different tranches having different risk profiles. Mortgage-backed bonds are the most familiar form of securitization, but the same basic process can be done with almost any kind of cash flow, including auto loans, college loans, credit card debt, business receivables, insurance and lottery payoffs, veterans' pensions, property liens, and more…

Securitization may seem obscure or peripheral, but it represents a fundamental shift in how finance is done. A loan represents a relationship between a bank (or other institution) and a borrower. A traditional 30-year mortgage or business loan reflected a lasting mutual commitment, and both banker and borrower had reasons to maintain that relationship for mutual benefit… From the bank's perspective, a loan is an asset. Selling that asset through securitization fundamentally changes the relationship. From the borrower's perspective, the bank looks more like an underwriter rather than an ongoing partner. Securitization thus shifts debt from a concrete relationship with an entity (a bank) to an abstract connection to the financial markets. This became clear during the mortgage meltdown, when far-flung buyers of asset-backed securities that were plummeting in value sought to locate the borrowers on the other end, relying on the haphazard "paperwork" documenting their "ownership."

Commercial banks, traditionally the most powerful financial institutions, look very different when their loans are merely temporarily illiquid assets intended to be re-sold on the market. Commercial banks traditionally took in deposits (or issued bonds) and used the proceeds to fund loans to borrowers. Their marble-pillared facades conveyed a sense of permanence and security. But if the loan will be quickly re-sold, then the bank was little more than a one-time intermediary. There is little functional difference between underwriting a bond issue (which investment banks did) and issuing a loan that will be quickly re-sold and securitized (which is what commercial banks came to do). In this sense, the wall between commercial banking and investment banking erected by the Glass-Steagall Act had become largely moot. With widespread securitization, the largest American commercial banks were transformed into universal banks with substantial investment banking operations. Meanwhile, whether they knew it or not, borrowers had become "issuers" on financial markets.[30]

I don't know if it makes much difference to me as a homeowner who actually owns my mortgage so long as they do not foreclose on me. I hardly had a personal relationship with the loan officer at Home Savings of America in 1977 when I took out my first mortgage, nor did I even speak directly with anyone at Countrywide when they held my mortgage after I refinanced in 2004. Perhaps I should have, since everyone was affected by the financial crisis largely precipitated by sub-prime mortgages with Countrywide leading the pack. I also question the idea than an individual mortgage is too risky to "sell." When I refinanced a mortgage in 2014, I originally sought to do it with Wells Fargo where I had had multiple checking accounts over the past 20 years. I got a better quote from a mortgage broker and decided to deal with him. After the refinance was completed I was told that it was being transferred to Wells Fargo Mortgage. I have no idea if this transfer was part of some convoluted bond deal, but it seems to be the reverse of the normal process of securitization by banks.

The issue with securitization of loans is the effect it has on financial institutions and the risks it creates for catastrophic financial crises. First of all the bank making the loan may be more likely to focus on pocketing the origination fees rather than validating the soundness of the loan. The risk the borrower will default is just passed along to some other investors who know even less about the borrower than the bank did. Prior to the 2007-2008 crises banks had been under some pressure from government agencies to make more loans available to lower class or minority borrowers. The introduction of variable rate mortgages had made it possible for them to offer loans to borrowers who might not otherwise have been approved. The ability to pass the risk along to others encouraged them to focus more on their own profits and obviously tempted them to cheat on the loan approval process in one way or another. With no one policing the securitization process, bad mortgages got packaged along with sound mortgages and all were regarded as sound investments. It was virtually impossible for an investors buying a mortgage backed security to know who the home owners were. All the investors knew was that they were getting a better return on a bond that had passed muster with a rating agency than they might be able to get elsewhere.

The connection between securitization and the risks of a major financial crisis are complicated. Securitization is just one aspect of financialization, and it is the combined effects of all these tendencies which give rise to the risk of massive failures. Davis and Kim ultimately see financialization as a broad "qualitative change in the nature of power relations" in society. They say that historically financial markets have an inherent tendency "to limit the concentration of power in the hands of particular actors by endorsing coordination through impersonal rules and the aggregation of economically 'rational' actions." The connections they make between securitization and other consequences of financialization such as corporate focus on share holder value and growing inequality in wealth are not clear to me, however. It may be because what they see as "the shift from relationship-based businesses (such as commercial banking) to markets" involves an idea of "markets" that I cannot grasp. I can see that securitization results in a dispersal of accountability or responsibility. It encourages an atomization of finance where decisions seem to result from individuals pursuing gain rather than any kind of coordinated effort to guide investment in the "real" economy.

To understand how a "credit crunch" or "liquidity trap" can threaten an entire economy and how a bank can be "too big to fail," it is necessary to have a better understanding of what the "products" are in financial markets. Financial markets theoretically exist for two reasons: to provide liquidity for investments and to facilitate risk management.

Risk Management and Liquidity

Of the maxims of orthodox finance none, surely, is more anti-social than the fetish of liquidity...[31]

Investors naturally look for ways to maximize their returns while minimizing their risks. Bernie Madoff's consistent returns seemed like a sure thing for smart money if you could get in the door – until, of course, they were actually revealed to be too good to be true. A tremendous amount of ingenuity has been devoted to devising schemes to reduce or even eliminate risk in investments. It is probably safe to say that all of them depend on some contingency which is either overlooked or dismissed as negligible.

Risk management in investing is often compared to insurance. I am willing to pay an annual premium for fire insurance on my house because the premium is so low in comparison to the cost of rebuilding my house after a fire. It can be low because the insurance company insures so many houses, and the odds are that only a small percentage of them will ever catch on fire. So far as I know it is not possible to take out insurance against loss on an investment portfolio at least not with an insurance agency, but credit default swaps, which played a major role in the 2007-2008 financial crisis, are in effect a form of insurance. They are just dressed up as "investment vehicles" so that they avoid regulations which apply to insurance contracts. They are justified as a way of spreading the risk around.

Another comparison used in investment risk management is hedging a bet in gambling. In certain circumstances a gambler who is betting on a long shot can place a second bet which will limit his losses or even guarantee a profit if his long shot does not come through.[32] Hedging an investment was originally a strategy of holding both "long" and "short" positions in a stock. Investopedia offers a helpful explanation of what "long" and "short" positions mean:

> If an investor has long positions, it means that the investor has bought and owns those shares of stocks. By contrast, if the investor has short positions, it means that the investor owes those stocks to someone, but does not actually own them yet.

For instance, an investor who owns 100 shares of Tesla (TSLA) stock in his portfolio is said to be long 100 shares. This investor has paid in full the cost of owning the shares...

Continuing the example, an investor who has sold 100 shares of TSLA without yet owning those shares is said to be short 100 shares. The short investor owes 100 shares at settlement and must fulfill the obligation by purchasing the shares in the market to deliver.

The magic of selling something you do not own is provided by a broker who is willing to lend you shares to sell at the current price and allow you a certain amount of time to buy shares to return to the broker. If the price of the stock goes down you buy the shares for less than you sold the borrowed shares for and get to pocket the difference. In other words the broker simply requires that you "return" the number of shares borrowed regardless of the stock's price. If the price of the stock goes up you lose on the deal, but if you had both a long and a short position in the stock you can use the shares you own to return to the broker and the whole deal is a wash so far as you are concerned. Combining a long and short position on a given stock effectively protects you from losing money and may enable you to make a little, but it may also prevent you from getting the full benefit of an appreciation in the stock value.

Needless to say "hedge" funds do a great deal more than just hold long and short positions on certain stocks. They deal in all sorts of "derivatives."

A derivative is a financial security with a value that is reliant upon or derived from, an underlying asset or group of assets—a benchmark. The derivative itself is a contract between two or more parties, and the derivative derives its price from fluctuations in the underlying asset.

Perhaps the most basic type of derivative is the option. An option is essentially a futures contract. A futures contract is most easily understood with agricultural produce. A farmer who has planted his crop knows what his costs are and may be interested in protecting himself against some unforeseen drop in price for his crop by entering into a contract to sell his crop for an established price well before harvest time. He is willing to forego the possibility of greater gains if prices for his produce go up more than expected in order to know what his income will be. This seems to be a beneficial arrangement for the wholesaler as well, since it enables him to know well in advance what his costs will be. It may enable some people to speculate on commodity prices, but on the whole it seems like a reasonable arrangement.

If an investor owns stock and wants to protect himself against a significant decline in its value he can enter into a contract to sell shares at a set price for a period of time. The contract can be such that he has the option to sell or not, but he pays for that option.

Conversely if an investor thinks the value of a stock is likely to go up significantly in the near term, he can purchase an option to buy at the certain price some time in the future. If its value increases beyond the set purchase price, he can buy it and then sell it on the market and make a profit. Similar contracts are possible to hedge against fluctuations in interest rates and foreign exchange rates. Sometimes the terms of the contract can become ridiculously complex.

Today's "hedge fund" is an investment fund set up as a partnership so that it is not subject to the same kinds of regulations as publicly traded mutual funds. Hedge funds use every conceivable type of derivative to maximize their returns. To a naïve moralistic outsider like me derivatives just seem to offer exotic forms of gambling, but defenders of the faith will argue that derivatives allow individual investors to manage risk, and even make the financial markets more efficient and less volatile. I'm not sure that the two views are contradictory. It has become common in discussing investment strategies to describe investments as bets.

An individual investor has a limited number of "risk management" strategies available to him. He can sell short or purchase options, but many of the esoteric "investment vehicles" are available only to large investors like pension funds, endowments or hedge funds.

The main consideration in an individual's risk management strategy may be the liquidity of his investments. When the market seems to be going to hell, he can always cash out and wait for things to settle down – if his investments are sufficiently liquid. Liquidity requires an active market for the "securities." If you lend your brother-in-law money to start a restaurant and the restaurant flops, you are not likely to be able to sell your share of the ownership in the restaurant. If you invest it in blue chip stocks, you can probably always sell the shares even if the economy starts to tank. The stock market can, of course, be subject to something comparable to a run on a bank. If everyone starts to fear the economy is tanking and pulls out of the stock market, share prices will go into free fall and you will get a "recession." For most of my life it has been a mystery to me why stock prices have such an impact on the overall economy and unemployment.

Keynes used the phrase "fetish of liquidity" to emphasize the fact that ultimately from a macro-economic point of view there can be no liquidity. To some extent the needs of the individual investor contradict the needs of the economy as a whole. Economic health requires long-term investments, not just trading of financial "instruments" with an eye towards short-term profit and liquidity.

> Of the maxims of orthodox finance none, surely, is more anti-social than the fetish of liquidity, the doctrine that it is a positive virtue on the part of investment institutions to concentrate their resources upon the holding of "liquid" securities. It forgets that there is no such thing as liquidity of investment for the community as a whole. The social object of skilled investment should be to defeat the dark forces of time and ignorance which envelop our future. The actual, private object of the most skilled investment today is "to beat the gun", as the Americans so well express it, to outwit the crowd, and to pass the bad, or depreciating, half-crown to the other fellow.[33]

Pundits and politicians in the U.S. have commented on how a focus on the short term harms the economy and contributes to the great disparity of wealth, but have gone so far as to advocate closing the stock market.[34] Even Keynes, who saw that financial markets encourage a pursuit of short term gains and liquidity, thought that regulation and taxes could suffice to restrain investors and encourage long term investing.

While in theory the function of the stock market is to allow businesses to raise capital for initial operations or expansion, in fact the main function is to provide liquidity for investors. The idea is that individual investors would not be willing to invest in long-term ventures if they could not liquidate their investment at any time. Theoretically the price of the shares should be a function of the health of the company, but share prices are really more a reflection of assessments of the company by investors rather than managers of the company, and eventually they tend to reflect what some investors think other investors will think about the future price of the shares. Most of the shares sold in the stock market are sold by one investor to another rather than by the underlying company, so the company itself receives no direct benefit from the sale. Nonetheless the value of a publicly traded company is often seen as a function of its stock price rather than its actual assets and long-term prospects.

If the company finances some of its operations with credit, its ability to secure credit may be hampered by a decline in its value as reflected in its stock price. The more difficulty the company has in securing credit, the more investors will devalue its stock. It is easy to see how apprehensive investors can send a company into a downward spiral even if there was no real reason for concern initially. So it becomes imperative for management to focus on short-term strategies that sustain or boost the price of the stock. This tendency is amplified by compensation packages involving stock options which obviously give management personal incentives to focus on the stock price.

Another way in which the stock market affects businesses is via consumer confidence. If consumers have investments in the stock market, the value of their assets will directly impact their willingness to spend or incur debt. Financial "news" also encourages the consumer to view the stock market as an indication of what the future holds even if one has no personal stake in stocks. If the stock market is taking a beating, we know to batten down the hatches and prepare for hard times. Maybe we should wait to buy that new washing machine, and another feedback loop kicks in as washing machine sales fall and workers get laid off.

In the end, though, it seems to be the availability of credit that enables businesses to flourish rather than the stock market, and credit seems mysteriously tied to the liquidity of financial markets. If there is no ready market for one type of financial "vehicle," the market for another will tighten and there will be a chain reaction until credit dries up. The reason for the huge bailouts in 2007-2008 was apparently the absolute necessity of preventing credit from drying up completely to the point where banks and their customers could no longer continue operations.

The point of all those "financial vehicles," though, was to spread the risk around to those who could handle it. What they seemed to have done instead was to spread the risk around to the point where it threatened everything and everyone. A mortgage lender laid off risk by "securitizing" the mortgages. A bunch of them were combined into a "product" and sold to another financial institution. They in turn split up several mortgage packages and recombined pieces of them into new "products" which they sold (with the help of rating agencies) as AAA bonds. These highly rated bonds were used as collateral to borrow funds for other investments. Nobody knew or cared whether the homeowner was going to be able to continue making payments when his adjustable rate tripled. The homeowner assumed he would just be able to re-finance the loan since the value of the property would have increased so much. Then AIG found a new income stream by insuring some of these bonds. Some people made a lot of money. The rest of us took a huge blow to the solar plexus when it all blew up. I'm not doing justice to either the complexity or the absurdity of all this, but it does seem to me that it has to do with credit and "risk management." At some level it is based on the idea that you can eliminate risk by sloughing it off onto the next fellow.

Would the elimination of financial markets solve this problem? Certainly it would eliminate all the speculation and convoluted financial "products." The question is whether it would dry up credit to the point where businesses could not operate. In the old fashioned model, small businesses were financed by loans from bankers who knew how to weigh the prospects of the business and evaluate the risk of lending them money. The bank accepted the risk in exchange for the potential for earning a return on its investment. In the best of all worlds it was viewed as a cooperative venture in which the bank might help the business through hard times in order to see the long term return. Businesses would also extend credit to each other in order to manage cash flow and insure long-term relationships. If a business were on the verge of bankruptcy, perhaps its creditors might work with it to keep it afloat until things improved. Maybe an occasional debt would be forgiven completely if it would benefit the community at large in some way.

What would be the incentive for anyone to extend credit to anyone else? It is easier to imagine how this works on a local scale. The rhetorical distinction between "Wall Street" and "Main Street" reflects this sense. Somehow the financial markets seem divorced from the realities of local business. Multinational corporations might not be possible without financial markets, but the dry cleaner or restaurant on the corner certainly should be, even if the equipment they currently use is manufactured by a conglomerate incorporated in Liechtenstein. Just how much would come unraveled if we pulled the plug on Wall Street? Do we need Jimmy Stewart as George Bailey to make things work on Main Street?

The prevailing idea about investment is that it comes from savings. People whose income exceeds their expenses accumulate money which they lend, directly or indirectly, to people who want to start a business but do not have sufficient funds to do so. But as we have seen investment need not be tied to individual savings. Extending credit to someone by agreeing to accept deferred payment does not require any accumulated money. It simply requires trust and a willingness to accept risk. Banks which are clearing houses for commercial transactions are in a unique position to extend this kind of credit to new or expanding businesses. The question is what it means for a bank to assume risk. What happens if their trust is misplaced or their assessment of the risk is mistaken? With the financial markets available today, the bank may be able to "securitize" the loan and pass the risk along to others. Any loss would then be a small part of numerous investment portfolios that could presumably absorb it without dire consequences. Or the bank could use the loan on its books as collateral to borrow funds at a lower rate and at the very least defer the impact of the loss in the event of a default. Without these financial markets the bank would be stuck with the bad loan and would have to absorb the loss if the borrower defaulted. But if the bank "printed the money" for the loan in the first place, what are the real repercussions of that loss? In trying to imagine a banking system in a market economy without financial markets, I feel as though I am missing some parts. A bank in such a system is clearly not a "business" in the normal sense. Perhaps it is a cooperative, like a credit union, or maybe it is a public utility, but how do you regulate a bank's ability to "print money."

There is a non-profit group in the UK called Positive Money which has a set of proposals for the reform of the banking system designed to restore investment in the real economy or as they say, "to democratise money and banking so that it works for society and not against it." Part of what they advocate is a clear separation between two functions of banking. In a sense it is a restoration of the distinction between savings accounts and checking accounts, although they refer to them as "investment accounts" and "transaction accounts." The investment accounts would be time deposits not subject to immediate availability, and they would not be guaranteed against loss. Money from pooled investment accounts could be invested in or lent to businesses, but they could not extend credit in a way that amounted to creating money. In their scheme only the government could "create" money, but they would do so based on an analysis of the need for money for further investment in the real economy. They would distribute the money in a variety of ways including expenditures for infrastructure projects, direct payment to citizens as a kind of negative taxation and possibly loans to banks for the sole purpose of investing in businesses. Their proposals can be found at http://positivemoney.org.

Positive money envisions the investment in businesses as loans, and the risk of default would be shared by the depositors and the bank:

> If some borrowers failed to repay their loans, then the loss would be split between the bank and the holders of the Investment Accounts, according to the terms and conditions of the specific account. This sharing of risk would ensure that both the bank and the investor's incentives were aligned correctly. Any investor opening an Investment Account would be made fully aware of the risks at the time of the investment, and those who did not wish to take a certain level of risk would be able to opt for alternative accounts that offered lower risks and consequently lower returns. Risk and reward would therefore be aligned, and much of the moral hazard associated with the current banking system would be removed.
>
> If a commercial bank suffered such a large number of defaults (borrowers who were unable to repay their loans) that it became insolvent and failed, the bank would be closed, the remaining assets liquidated and the creditors paid off. Investment Account holders would have depositor preference (i.e. they would have priority in the queue of creditors waiting to be repaid) over bondholders and shareholders. Amongst all Investment Account holders, those who opted for the lowest risk accounts would be repaid before those who opted for the higher risk accounts.[35]

One of the important items in their proposals is that loans made by banks using funds from investment accounts could not be "securitized" to get them off their books. There is, however, no proposal for eliminating financial markets, much less interest-bearing loans. In fact customers putting money in investment accounts can choose to have their funds invested in financial markets. The real goal of the proposal is to insure that sufficient money is always available for loans to businesses that contribute to the GDP. The focus is on money creation via credit accounts, and the solution involves shifting the ability to create money from banks to the government. Bank loans would not create money, but would simply channel existing money into investments. It is recognized that currently only a small percentage of bank loans go to businesses that contribute to the GDP, and there seems to be no indication that the proposals would result in more bank loans to the "real" economy. If the government (or the independent body established for the purpose of monitoring the need for adjustments in the amount of money in circulation) decides to create more money, one of its options is to channel that money into the real economy via venture capital groups, loans to banks or even direct investment in business.

> Problem: Because most of our money is created as a result of bank lending, the lending preferences of banks determine where new money starts its life in the economy. In practice, this has resulted in the bulk of money going into property markets and to the financial sector. According to Bank of England figures, between 1997-2007, of the additional money created by bank lending, 31% went towards mortgage lending, 20% towards commercial property, 32% to the financial sector (including mergers and acquisitions, trading and financial markets). Just 8% went to businesses outside the financial sector, whilst a further 8% financed credit cards and personal loans. Yet it is only ultimately the last two - lending to businesses and consumer credit – that have a real impact on GDP and economic growth. In short, we have a system where very little of the money created by banks is used in a way that leads to economic growth or value creation. Instead, the majority of the money created has the effect of inflating property prices and therefore pushing up the cost of living.
>
> Sovereign money as a solution: In a sovereign money system, new money is created by the central bank and then

spent into the real economy through government spending. Depending on how the money is spent, this will have a much higher impact on GDP and economic activity than the money created by banks. This is primarily because a) it will all be spent directly on activities that contribute to GDP, whereas most bank lending is not, and b) it does not come with the cost of servicing additional private debt, which could act as a brake on spending. This means that the real economy is better supported in a sovereign money system.[36]

There is considerable debate about the implications or feasibility of the Positive Money proposals, and there may be some inconsistencies in the proposals. Some discussions seem to imply that banks would still be making decisions about how to invest in businesses, even if they were investing money lent by the central bank with restrictions on how it could be invested. (Money created by the government and lent to banks could not be invested in the Finance, Insurance, or Real Estate sectors.) Other discussions seem to say that the government could invest in businesses either directly or via something like venture capital groups. Ultimately the question is whether the amount of money available for investment in the real economy and the ability of banks to create money through the extension of credit are the root problems. So far as I can tell there is nothing about the proposed reforms that would alter or limit the way in which speculation in financial markets affect the overall economy. While the proposals specifically say that newly created money lent to banks could not be used for mortgage loans and that the amount of existing money is (always?) sufficient for mortgage financing, I see nothing that would prevent a mortgage lender (which is not a bank) from securitizing its loans and passing them along to the financial markets.

As we have seen, however, liquidity is a double-edged sword. It may encourage "investment" but it also encourages "trading" and "speculation." Financial markets theoretically designed to spread the risk and keep the wheels of industry turning end up making it possible for George Soros to make a billion dollars in 1992 by "shorting" the pound sterling and forcing the British government to alter its monetary policy. While an expert might be able to point out that Soros was simply seeing an opportunity created by a mistaken monetary policy and insist that regulations and enlightened government policy can prevent financial crises, it may also be that there is something fundamentally wrong with the way investment in business is generated.

Clearly the first mistake is assuming investment requires "saving" or the accumulation of excess funds by individuals. Granting credit either in the form of accepting delayed payment for goods and services or in the form of bank loans does not require savings. It is a bookkeeping entry based on trust. The idea that investment can only come from savings is derived from the idea of money as a scarce resource, i.e. a commodity.

The flip side of this question is what should be done with savings if they are not required for investment. "Hoarding" money is generally viewed as counterproductive, but this may also be based on the assumption that money is a scarce resource. Hoarding is bad because it means there is less money in circulation, which in turn presumably means the economy is being less productive. If monetary policy compensates for the money siphoned off in savings, perhaps the real concern should be that hoarded money may be dumped into the economy causing an excess amount of money in circulation which in turn results in "inflation." The real point here is that even if money is not a "scarce resource," the amount of money circulating needs to be tied somehow to the productivity of the economy. Perhaps it would suffice to require large savings withdrawals to be signaled well enough in advance to permit monetary policy to adjust credit levels.

If we discard the notion that saved money should "grow," i.e. that the simple possession of money entitles the holder to more money, along with the dream of living without working or as we say living on "unearned income," then individuals can accumulate retained earnings for large future purchases or as a buffer against emergencies, but they are not encouraged to speculate with that money. There is no issue of "liquidity" for the individual saver since he is not personally investing his savings in risky ventures. His only concerns are taxation and inflation. He can still of course choose to risk his savings by starting his own business alone or in partnership with others. Only in this sense will individual savings lead to investment in business, and as any "entrepreneur" knows this will not be a "liquid" investment.

Have we punctured the American Dream? It depends on which dream you having. If you dream of upward mobility based on hard work, frugality and bright ideas, it seems to me to be intact. If, however, you dream of making it big by gaming the system so that you can then enjoy status and material comfort without having to work, then you may need to wake up.

Would the elimination of financial markets substantially change the way investment decisions are made? We are of course only talking about investments in the "real" economy – businesses, research, infrastructure, etc. Speculation in stocks, bonds, commodities, derivatives and other "financial products" would no longer exist. The talent involved in conceiving, evaluating and selling such products would have to be employed elsewhere in what one might hope would be more productive endeavors. It is conceivable that private equity funds would still be able to finance risky innovative enterprises, but most of the investment decisions would probably be in the hands of banks and public entities which are subject to control by federal or local government. The mention that the government would be involved in making business investment decisions will probably trigger pyrotechnic displays of paranoia about "statism" and "socialism," but it is not clear that the role of government would really have to be any bigger than it already is. Bank loan officers would probably have to be a new breed combining the best of the old-fashioned conservative loan officer with the aggressive innovation of today's investment bankers or venture capitalists.

What would happen to the idea of a "publicly held" company where shares are owned by millions of individuals? Suppose a start-up wants to solicit financing via crowdfunding? Is there any way to prevent a secondary market for selling shares in the new company from giving rise to a new stock market? There is probably room for creative thinking here. Perhaps crowdfunding could be regulated in a way that would prohibit short term ownership of shares and only permit sales of shares back to the company based on some standardized accounting of the value of the company. The same restrictions might apply to partnerships in general to insure that ownership of part interest in a venture does not become a marketable asset. The guiding principle would always be that investment in the economy is a long-term (or longer-term) commitment. Whether being a partner in a venture could be "collateral" that could convince a bank to advance credit to the individual for unusual expenses might be left to the discretion of the bank.

If investment primarily takes the form of credit advanced to ventures by a public utility bank, who bears the risk? Can such a bank go bankrupt? If the bank makes a series of bad investments in businesses which fail, who else is harmed besides the owners and employees and perhaps customers of the failed businesses? This is a question of whose money it is that is financing the businesses. Presumably the banks depositors (if it is in fact a bank that has depositors) are insulated from the failed investments by federal deposit insurance if not some other mechanism that separates their money from the money invested. If we think of the bank as some kind of local development agency, we can hope that its managers who made the bad choices are subject to oversight and even replacement by some body answerable to the public at large. The money that was created when the credit was advanced to the businesses would still be at large circulating somewhere in the economy (unless there was some corruption involved and it is being hoarded by a crook until the dust settles). The "loan" would turn out to be a "grant." The fact that these loans were forgiven or written off would presumably create potential inflationary pressures which would limit the ability of any bank to pour more money into the economy via investments. Taxes of some sort could be used to compensate for excess money so the risk ultimately is borne by the public at large or by the portions of the public subject to the increased taxation. If the point of investment in the "real" economy is to foster businesses which benefit society as a whole, then it seems appropriate that society as a whole should shoulder the risks. This would certainly incentivize the public to keep a close watch on the managers at whatever institution is making the investment decisions. It might make it difficult to publicly fund "frivolous" ventures, but presumably the more adventurous individuals who have accumulated some reserve purchasing power would be happy to gamble on these ventures. Austerity might mean cutting back on luxury items rather than skimping on education or infrastructure maintenance.

Any venture involves the risk of failure or limited success. In the current system a business that consistently breaks even is not really considered a success, since it is a venture whose goal is to produce a profit. Muhammad Yunus is a great advocate for "social businesses" whose goal is to solve problems not to generate profits,[37] but they are still meant to be self-sustaining businesses.

In other words they can fail if they do not generate enough revenue to be self-sustaining in the long run. The desire to avoid risk in economic ventures is a bit like the desire to avoid death in life. It is an understandable desire but ultimately an unrealistic goal. The best way to manage risks is to share them with our fellow citizens, not to sell them to them.

If one has accumulated reserves of purchasing power, are there other avenues for investing it, if it cannot be used for interest-bearing loans? Perhaps the only investment vehicle available would be either direct investment in small businesses or investment via a cooperative venture capital operation. I am guessing such investments would require a commitment of several years, and perhaps there would be alternatives like CDs where the commitment might be 3, 5, 7, 10, 15 or 20 years with the longer commitments offering greater profit participation in some way. Perhaps the return on the investment would only be paid at the end of the term rather than doled out as "dividends" along the way. In any case the return on my investment would be a function of the success of the venture it was funding, and there would be a risk involved. Any attempt to use surplus cash to generate even more money will involve risk since it will be a direct investment in the "real" economy.

If I cannot lend my cash reserves and expect interest on the loan, can I use my cash to buy assets which I can rent to others for more than the rate at which the assets lose value or will there still be a market in "assets" (other than financial instruments) which have the potential for appreciation? The most obvious asset in this category is real estate, but people also rent vehicles, tools, furniture and apparently now even clothing and jewelry. Of these perhaps only real estate can be expected to hold its value indefinitely or even appreciate. Other things may become "collectibles" with age, and I have to wonder if there is any way to stamp out speculation in collectibles. The same may be true of commodities, especially ones that can be stored indefinitely without deteriorating. How do you distinguish between a middle man who is simply enabling goods to be distributed efficiently and a speculator who is attempting the corner the market?

Ownership of real estate, be it buildings or arable land, seems to me to present special problems for any alternative economic system. It was after all the privileges enjoyed by the landed aristocracy that provoked much of the interest in revolution and "socialism" or "communism." Owning "real" property seems to be one of the best ways to enjoy an income based on the labor of others, so if each of us dreams of being able to live without working, we are unlikely to vote for a society in which this is impossible or illegal..

We may be getting closer to the issue of whether money should be a "store of value." Conventional economic theory about individual savings and investment is based on the assumption that society needs savings invested in order to remain healthy and grow. All the talk about money growing over time if it is "put to work" is really just a way of saying investment requires savings. As we have seen, businesses can be "financed" via credit that does not require the contribution of any individual's reserve purchasing power. So we don't have to "incentivize" individuals to "invest."

Similarly there is no natural law that says an individual's savings "should" grow. In fact I suspect that I am not alone in finding it morally repugnant that someone can make more money simply because he already has more money than he requires for his current expenditures. We think he is being rewarded for his virtuous frugality because we think his money is required for investments which keep the society healthy. It is repugnant to me because it seems to involve a redistribution of purchasing power for no good reason. I have yet to see how this aspect of the economy is not a zero sum game. If my money grows, either someone else's money is shrinking, or else there is more money in circulation resulting in the risk of inflationary pressure making everyone's money less valuable. When people talk about "wealth creation" or "wealth management," they are not really talking about wealth in the sense of newly created resources or products which will contribute to the overall health or growth of the economy. They are talking about an individual siphoning off a larger share of the money circulating in the economy and making sure he can keep it for his own benefit. In a Ponzi scheme it looks as though everyone involved is benefiting – until the chickens come home to roost.

Once we understand the true nature of money, the idea that one gets a medal as a "job creator" for "investing" his or her money begins to crumble – unless we also award job-creator medals to everyone who pays taxes. The difference between paying taxes and investing is that an investment is supposed to result in the accumulation of wealth by an individual. Even a business that fails creates jobs for a while, so perhaps we should applaud those who lose money in their investments as well as those who get a return.

"Store of value" does not necessarily imply that the value appreciates. It simply implies that purchasing power can be used in the future as well as the immediate present. The only justification for allowing reserves of purchasing power to grow is to counteract inflation that will cause them to diminish over time. This strikes me as a bandaid for the injuries of inflation which does more harm than good. If one of the causes of inflation is excessive money in circulation, surely the cure is not to be found in giving more money to wealthy individuals.

The idea that money is not functioning properly unless it is circulating leads some to advocate negative interest on idle money. It can also result in rather convoluted suggestions that "savings" should be in the form of stores of commodities. Both these suggestions seem to me to miss the point about the nature of money. I see no reason why it should not be possible to hold reserves of purchasing power for future use. How individuals can accumulate such reserves is a separate issue, and I confess that I am intrigued by the idea that in a truly democratic society individuals should not be "investors." This is not to say that investment decisions have to be "centralized" in some federal bureau. There are a host of other ways to implement investment in the "real economy."

Investment, Capital and Property

Investment is what enables productivity to grow. The simple model for a "free enterprise" economy involves the "entrepreneur" who has accumulated enough money to launch his own business or who has hustled up investors who are willing to let him use their money in exchange for a piece of the action. The implication is that the decision to start or expand a business is made by an individual or a small group of investors. They risk their own money in the belief that the product or service they are going to offer will eventually generate enough income for them to recoup their investment and make a profit. The main argument one hears in favor of this type of capitalism rather than some form of socialism is that individual entrepreneurs are more efficient at sussing out what type of business is likely to thrive at any given time or place. Would an economic development sub-committee looking for ways to build up magazine publishing and all the businesses that support it in Chicago have come up with the idea for Playboy?

Suppose investment decisions were made by some form of governmental bureaucracy rather than individuals with savings. Let's assume that in 1953 regional and local branches of the bureaucracy were relatively autonomous and the group in Chicago happened to include some fairly open-minded and adventurous types. There is an open door process in which they accept applications for funding for projects since they are smart enough to know the limits of their own imaginations. In walks a young college graduate with a few years of magazine work under his belt who wants $8,000 to start a new magazine about which he is clearly passionate. Perhaps he is a bit more nervous pitching the idea than he would be to relatives and friends of friends, but it is not inconceivable that some members of the committee might be taken with his enthusiasm and willing to gamble a small part of their annual budget on this idea. What would the difference be in terms of how it played out?

Perhaps the more relevant questions are what would be the guidelines used by the committee to evaluate proposals and what would be the motivation of the people presenting projects for funding. There are actually meetings like this taking place every day at film and television production companies or studios.

Somebody comes in with an idea, maybe even a completed script, and no one on either side of the table has a clue as to whether it could be a successful film or TV program. It is conceivable that the person pitching the idea only wants to make money and be famous, but the chances are good that he is moved by something else as well. The people on the other side of the table know that they are gambling, if not with their own money then with their careers and their ability to send their kids to private school. No one pretends to be able to predict the box office potential of the project, and the decision they make is probably justified with talk about "the story" and the presenter's "passion for the project" which is infectious. If the buyers really are hard boiled bean counters, then imagine instead what happened when the Russian Ministry of Culture agreed to put up 35% of the financing for *Leviathan*, a film they subsequently criticized for its negative depiction of ordinary Russians but nonetheless selected as Russia's official submission for the Oscar for foreign language film. Or try to figure out how Tarkovsky could have made any of the films he made in Russia. I can't.

My point is simply that worthwhile investment decisions can be made by some group other than "entrepreneurs" looking for a profit, but for most of us in the U.S. "investment" implies the use of individual savings and private property.

It is probably impossible to know the ultimate origins of the notion of private property. Perhaps the caveman who crafted a tool or weapon regarded it as his in some way, but how would we know? The point at which the idea of private property changed the course of history is surely the moment when people agreed that land could be "owned." Private property is often explained with a myth about the ownership of land, most famously formulated by John Locke.[38] It is the cultivation of land that entitles an individual to "own" the land. This has a special resonance with an American reader because of the image of the "settler" which is fundamental to our idea of the history of the United States. The settler finds a plot of land in the wilderness where he builds a home, clears the fields, and cultivates crops. We think it is appropriate that he be granted "title" to the land for his efforts. In fact the government went a step further in its efforts to settle certain parts of the country and made it possible for "homesteaders" to own a plot of land simply by staking out a claim and filing the necessary paperwork. These days "settlers" in the West Bank might be regarded with a little less enthusiasm.

Strict Libertarians do not think it was appropriate for Columbus to claim Spanish ownership of an entire island or continent simply because he set foot on its shores. It is the mixture of human labor with the natural resources that entitles one to claim ownership of land. It is not clear to me though why the settler is entitled to ownership of the land itself rather than just the produce he cultivates. If I chop down a tree to sell for firewood, does that make me the owner of the space previously occupied by the tree? Admittedly clearing land so that it can be cultivated to produce crops which had not grown there naturally seems like a different thing, and building a house on a plot of land seems to wed the product of ones labor with the land in a way that might be difficult to separate. There are, of course, leasehold arrangements where the ownership of a dwelling is not tied to the ownership of the land on which it stands, and in assessing the value of property we distinguish "improvements" from "land." Mineral rights are another interesting aspect of property. Does the fact that I planted vegetables on my plot of land really mean I am entitled to royalties on all the oil that can be pumped out of the ground when it is discovered beneath my farm?

Any conundrums resulting from a labor theory of property are probably the result of the fact that Locke was not introducing the idea of private property, but attempting to put it on a new footing. To some extent he was probably rebelling against the prevailing ideas about land ownership in a feudal society. My impression is that land ownership derived from a social hierarchy (rather than vice versa) and that originally entitlements with regard to land were established by social status if not force.

Many Americans think that the only alternative to an economy based on private property is communism, which is conceived as a totalitarian dictatorship in which the individual is subjugated to the state. Libertarianism seems to be based on a dichotomy between individualism and "statism" with a dangerous slippery slope inclined towards statism. It may well be that individualism as celebrated in American culture can not be separated from private property, but there may also be a wider spectrum of definitions of private property than we acknowledge, and the slippery slope may tilt both ways.

Is it possible to imagine an advanced economy without private property? For many people the idea of private property probably starts with a paycheck. This is my hard-earned money, and I am entitled to use it however I want. "Buying" something seems to imply "ownership," although it is possible to use things we do not "own." I can live in a house I don't own, and much of what I buy I "consume" one way or another rather than hold as an "asset." Property, when it does not refer specifically to land and buildings, is generally something that has relatively lasting value. Keep in mind that economic value is a function of the desires of the rest of the people with whom I live. The hoarder may see value in the piles of stuff in his living room, but the rest of us know it is garbage.

After the Russian revolution there was a brief period where the leadership tried to implement an economy in which everyone received an equal monthly stipend regardless of what he or she did. The goal of this policy can be interpreted in various ways, but one way to look at it is that by divorcing income from work every individual in the society was being regarded as equally valuable. The output of the economy belonged to everyone, and profits did not accrue to individuals or businesses. We all know how well this worked out, but the impulse behind it is intriguing.

Note that the Russians did not attempt to eliminate money from their economy (although Cambodia did briefly in 1975 under the Khmer Rouge). So long as there is money, there is some form of property. The Russians could choose to spend their stipend on potatoes or vodka or whatever else was produced, but individuals were theoretically not able to accumulate wealth through "investing." Most Americans would simply scoff at the idea that such an economy could work at all, saying that no one would choose to work if they did not have to.

As much as free market economists may argue that private property is the best way to maximize efficiency in the allocation of resources, the appeal of private property to the individual seems to me to be largely three things: a desire for "independence," a desire to acquire status and power in society and a desire to provide similar status and power or independence to ones children. For much of European history marriage among the upper classes was essentially a merger of two enterprises and inheritance laws were designed to preserve the estates created by consolidation in marriage. The desire to accumulate wealth is based to some extent on a competitive sense of economics as a zero-sum game, and it seems only natural that someone would strive to acquire as much wealth and live as "well" as possible. It also seems natural to us that one would want to give ones children a head start in the game.

Financial independence is to some extent an illusory goal since the value of ones assets depends on a market. One cannot be literally financially independent from a society in which one lives. Obviously plenty of people achieve financial independence in the sense that they have enough income-generating assets that they can safely assume that they will never have to work again – unless there is some sort of apocalyptic catastrophe. Some folks thought they were well on their way to financial independence in 1929.

Private property is fundamental in the Libertarian understanding of society and economics. Murray Rothbard calls "the precious concept" of property "the base and groundwork of the entire social order," and attempts to explicate the logic of private property in his book, *For A New Liberty: The Libertarian Manifesto*. It is basically an interpretation of Locke's labor theory of property. He begins by saying, "The libertarian creed rests upon one central axiom: that no man or group of men may aggress against the person or property of anyone else." The idea of property is assumed as something obvious or self-evident, although he does attempt to ground it in a "natural law" analysis of man's essential nature. He explains private property by an interpretation of Locke's labor theory of property so that eventually he can say

> The central core of the libertarian creed, then, is to establish the absolute right to private property of every man: first, in his own body, and second, in the previously unused natural resources which he first transforms by his labor. These two axioms, the right of self-ownership and the right to "homestead," establish the complete set of principles of the libertarian system. The entire libertarian doctrine then becomes the spinning out and the application of all the implications of this central doctrine.[39]

One conundrum in this labor theory of property is that I absolutely own the product of my own labor – except when I don't, as in when I am a hired hand. Libertarians squirm out of this by classifying "my labor" as something which I can sell on the market. I am only a slave if I am coerced into working for less than the market value of my labor. Is it coercion if I only seem to have a choice between starving and working for $8 an hour? Marxism, of course, jumped on this and made a capital case out of the fact that a worker does not own the product of his own labor. It turns the tables on classical economists by saying that someone who does not own the product of his labor is alienated from his own nature.

The labor theory of property seems to me to be a rationale for one of many possible social conventions regarding the distribution of control over resources and produce. It is a nice and fairly persuasive metaphor, but in reality very little property these days is acquired directly through the transformation of unused natural resources into a product which has market value. Most property is purchased or inherited. Whether the ownership is legitimate then becomes a matter of the provenance of the property. What if I stole it or purchased something from someone who acquired it illegitimately? Suppose the estate I buy in England was originally part of an area seized by Viking hoards who slaughtered all the previous inhabitants. Or my inheritance comes ultimately from an olive oil importing business whose revenues were enhanced by racketeering.

Libertarian economics is all derived from an idea of the human individual. It starts with the individual and conceives of society in terms of interactions between individuals. On the surface this seems to make complete sense, but part of me balks for some reason. For free-market economic theory individual human desire is the opaque given which drives everything. Any consideration of how social forces generate and shape desire is considered irrelevant to economics.

The libertarian idea of the individual also results in the conclusion that society is not an entity in any meaningful sense.

> The individualist holds that only individuals exist, think, feel, choose, and act; and that "society" is not a living entity but simply a label for a set of interacting individuals. Treating society as a thing that chooses and acts, then, serves to obscure the real forces at work.[40]

When Margaret Thatcher said "There is no such thing as society" she also said, "There are individual men and women and there are families and no government can do anything except through people and people look to themselves first."[41] The strict libertarian would maintain that, like society, even the family is a "fictive entity:"

> Society is a collective concept and nothing else; it is a convenience for designating a number of people. So, too, is family or crowd or gang, or any other name we give to an agglomeration of persons. ...When the individuals disappear so does the whole. The whole has no separate existence. Using the collective noun with a singular verb leads us into a trap of the imagination; we are prone to personalize the collectivity and to think of it as having a body and a psyche of its own.[42]

The point of this, of course, is to resist any assignment of responsibility to society for individual behavior. Rothbard attempts to reveal the absurdity of holding society responsible by defining society as "everyone but yourself." What the argument misses, however, is the fact that every entity except for some subatomic particle is composed of interacting "individual" elements and disappears when the elements disappear. It may well make more sense to view society as a self-perpetuating system comparable to an organism. How individuals should be held accountable for their behavior is a separate issue.

Mainstream economics avoids the conundrums of a libertarian labor theory of property by framing the whole discussion in terms of "capital."

> The two great input partners in the productive process are labor and capital. We know what labor is, because we are all workers who rent our time for wages. The other partner is capital—a produced and durable input which is itself an output of the economy. Capital consists of a vast and specialized array of machines, buildings, computers, software, and so on.[43]

What is missing from this partnership of course is the element of natural resources which are not an output of the economy. The definition of capital seems to expand to include the natural world or at least those parts of it owned by individuals or corporations.

> In a market economy, capital typically is privately owned, and the income from capital goes to individuals. Every patch of land has a deed, or title of ownership; almost every machine and building belongs to an individual or corporation. Property rights bestow on their owners the ability to use, exchange, paint, dig, drill, or exploit their

> capital goods. These capital goods also have market values, and people can buy and sell the capital goods for whatever price the goods will fetch. The ability of individuals to own and profit from capital is what gives capitalism its name.[44]

The settlement of the American west provides a nice example of how every patch of land can have a deed or title of ownership.[45] The land was considered "public domain" owned by the government and then given or sold to homesteaders, railroads, or speculators. How the government dealt with the previous inhabitants of the land has been well documented.

The textbook discussion of property rights acknowledges that property rights are not absolute.

> Interestingly enough, the most valuable economic resource, labor, cannot be turned into a commodity that is bought and sold as private property. Since the abolition of slavery, it has been illegal to treat human earning power like other capital assets. You are not free to sell yourself; you must rent yourself at a wage.[46]

Two things emerge from this: property rights are subject to regulation rather than being absolute natural rights, and human labor is not a commodity, no matter how much literature there is regarding "human capital."

How to regulate property rights is surely a matter of social consensus which may evolve with a society. In other words the nature and extent of "property rights" are the result of political decisions.

Human labor may no longer be a commodity, but there is a "labor market" and education is classified as an investment in "human capital."

> The term "human capital" refers to the stock of useful and valuable skills and knowledge accumulated by people in the process of their education and training.[47]

This enables education to be viewed as an investment and "economic studies of incomes and education show that human capital is a good investment on average."[48] In other words the high cost of a college education is justified because it is an investment which yields a return as higher earnings later in life. Whether this is actually true is debatable.[49]

The real question is who controls the capital and who decides what (or whom) to invest in. Capitalism is an economic system in which individuals (or corporations) can own and profit from capital. When the textbook says that "almost every machine and building belongs to an individual or corporation," it is gliding over the possibility that capital can be publicly owned and still used in ways that do not produce profits for individuals or corporations but nonetheless provide benefits for the whole economy. There has obviously been a trend towards "privatization" which seems to want to replace "can own" with "should own" based on the assumption that private companies are always more "efficient" that public "bureaucracies."

There is a similar elision in the textbook description of capital investment:

> If people are willing to save—to abstain from present consumption and wait for future consumption— society can devote resources to new capital goods.[50]
>
> Economic activity involves forgoing current consumption to increase our capital. Every time we invest—building a new factory or road, increasing the years or quality of education, or increasing the stock of useful technical knowledge—we are enhancing the future productivity of our economy and increasing future consumption.[51]

This makes it sound like individual decisions to forego consumption and save make possible the increase in capital required for growth. Building interstate highways or intercontinental ballistic missiles may involve forgoing consumption in some indirect way, but it is not the aggregate individual decisions to set aside some cash that makes such investment happen. Whether it depends on taxation affecting everyone is a question to be addressed later.

Let's try to view investment through a different mythical window. Suppose we start with a small community with access to a certain amount of resources, both natural and human. They have a town meeting to decide how to allocate those resources among various projects proposed by anyone and everyone. It is safe to assume that different citizens have different priorities. Some think a hospital is more urgently needed than a beauty parlor; others think the primary focus should be on farms supplying sufficient food for everyone. The format for the town meeting is direct democracy in which each citizen has an equal voice or vote. Probably each would have a number of votes. Presumably I could not just vote to have my neighbors do all the unpleasant tasks while I tended the apple orchard or sculpted the statue for the town square. Perhaps the first round of voting determines the top priorities and a subsequent round of bargaining determines who does what. Maybe in order to persuade someone to collect the garbage he would be rewarded with extra votes to give him more influence over the allocation of other resources. If I'm going to be in charge of waste management, I at least want to have a nice park available to me in my off hours, maybe even one with a swimming pool.

The immediate obvious objection to this story is that "communism" of this sort can only work with a small and relatively primitive community. The point, however, is that the votes each person has are what becomes "money" in an economy where the "market" replaces the town meeting. The difference is how we decide who gets more "votes" in a market economy. Obviously we don't provide extra "compensation" for those who perform onerous tasks; in fact the market generally finds a way to pay such workers less than those with cushy jobs. Clearly the citizens with the most money exercise the greatest influence over the allocation of resources and the direction of "projects." They also are probably the ones leading the campaigns to prevent any town hall meetings from interfering with their ability to do so. As Calvin Coolidge said:

> After all, the chief business of the American people is business. They are profoundly concerned with producing, buying, selling, investing and prospering in the world. I am strongly of the opinion that the great majority of people will always find these the moving impulses of our life.[52]

If you throw a man into a lake, he is going to try to swim to shore, but if you ask him to participate in the design of a dam to make a lake, he may well also be interested in insuring that people have fishing boats and life preservers. The idea that most people are motivated by "producing, buying, selling, investing and prospering in the world" makes complete sense from the point of view of the individual who finds himself having to "sink or swim," i.e. having to "earn a living" in the midst of an economy driven by market forces over which he has little or no influence.

The difference between trying to swim and designing a lake is like the difference in perspective I encountered when a friend lost patience with my attempts to understand money:

> I'm sure you believe you have reached a great level of understanding about money—if one measures that by the

> sheer volume of words on paper. Try telling your grocer how much you've learned. Try putting that new wisdom to use in investing. Be thankful you were able to buy a house in Brentwood when you did. I have learned a few things about money in the last 40 years and I have the assets to prove it. Can you say the same?[53]

I may or may not be swimming as well as my friend, but I refuse to accept the implication that it is a waste of time to examine the assumptions on which our economic system is based.

What happened to the "self-evident" idea that all men have an unalienable right to "life?" Is it sufficient that one have a pulse or do we all have a "right" to sufficient food, clothing and shelter to be able to plan what we are going to do tomorrow? What we really believe is that the right to life is not God-given, but "earned" by making oneself useful to others. If you cannot find a way to be useful, then you are not entitled to use any of the resources "owned" by others. The difference between a child and an adult is that a child deserves to be taken care of while an adult can be left to fend for himself even if it means sleeping in an underpass and begging.

How do we decide what to invest in? With the current system a billionaire who thinks colonizing Mars is a great idea can pour money and resources into a long-range program for doing so even though most people might think the resources would be better devoted to solving problems on earth. On the other hand the decision to send astronauts to the moon was made by the federal government. A group of millionaires can develop a stylish electric car to the point where they can sell stock in their company, but the roads and bridges on which to drive such a car are built by the government. A "market" economy is supposed to be driven by "consumer preferences," but in 2019, government expenditure amounted to 35% of the gross domestic product.[54]

A lot of politicians insist that "big government" is not only bad for the economy but a threat to individual liberty. How big is too big, and why exactly is government spending bad for the economy?

Most people assume that the government is an entity like a household or a business where expenses must be covered by income. If a business consistently spends more than it earns, it will "go out of business" and cease to exist. If an individual lives beyond his means for too long he will be forced into bankruptcy.

He may not cease to exist, but he may well end up homeless and unemployed. A government's primary source of income is generally thought to be taxation, and if its expenditures exceed its tax revenues, it must borrow to make up the difference. Deficit spending and escalating government debt is generally considered a major problem, and it is assumed that allowing a government to default on its debt wreaks havoc on the global as well as the national economy.

Deficit Spending

Does the fact that the government is in a unique position of being able to "create money" mean that the analogy to a household or business does not apply? For many people financing government expenditures by "printing money" seems suspect, if not fraudulent. The government, of course, does not create new money by literally printing dollar bills. Only about 10% of the money in circulation consists of coins and dollar bills. The rest is just entries in bank account ledgers and the like. The most common explanation of how the government creates money is that the Federal Reserve lends money to banks at an interest rate that makes it profitable for the banks to extend more credit to its customers. (Does it have to "borrow" the money it lends to the banks?) It is the bank loans that actually put more money into circulation. The most appropriate description of how money is created and which institution actually creates it is the subject of some debate among economists and one of the things that separates "modern money theory" from some "Post-Keynesian" theory.

Malcolm Mitchell, one of the proponents along with Warren Mosler of "Modern Monetary Theory," is emphatic about the implications of the government's ability to create money.

> Because our Monetarily Sovereign nation has the unlimited power to create its sovereign currency, the dollar, it never needs to ask anyone for dollars. It doesn't need to tax or borrow, and it never can be forced into bankruptcy. It can pay any dollar-denominated invoice of any size at any time.
>
> In fact, the federal government creates money by paying its bills. The U.S. has created many trillions of dollars, simply by pressing computer keys, and will continue to do so. It does not "owe" anyone for creating these dollars.
>
> The U.S. government cannot live beyond its means; it has no means to live beyond.
>
> By contrast, if the debts of France, Germany et al, exceed their ability to obtain euros they, as monetarily non-sovereign nations, could be forced into bankruptcy. They did not create the euro, nor do they have the unlimited ability to pay bills.

Deficit Spending - 97

> Everything you believe about your personal finances — debts, deficits, spending, affordability, saving and budgeting — are inappropriate to U.S. federal finances. For this reason, your personal intuition about U.S. financing likely is wrong.
>
> Because the U.S. cannot be forced into bankruptcy, none of this nation's agencies can be forced into bankruptcy. The U.S Supreme Court, the Department of Defense, Congress, Social Security, Medicare and any of the other 1,300 federal agencies cannot go bankrupt unless the federal government wishes it.
>
> (All the talk about Social Security or Medicare going bankrupt is misguided. Even if FICA were eliminated, Social Security and Medicare would not need to go bankrupt, unless Congress wished it. They could pay benefits, forever.)
>
> The unlimited ability to create money is an uncontested fact for Monetarily Sovereign nations, although at any given time economic growth, inflation, deflation, recession, depression and social factors may influence a nation's decision to create money.[55]

The caveat contained in this last sentence may be a point that many critics of the theory overlook. At the very least it indicates that things may be more complex than simply creating money to pay for everything. Most critics insist that unlimited creation of money will produce hyperinflation and point to the hyperinflation created when the German government tried after World War I to solve its economic problems by literally printing money. Another summary of modern monetary theory by Cullen O. Roche takes pains to emphasize that the theory does not entail a license for government to spend recklessly.

> So what's the bogey here? What's the catch? Because surely you must be asking yourself why this sounds like a free lunch. We can just spend to our hearts content, right? Absolutely not. The bogey here is inflation which is constantly moving up and down with the amount of money in the system based on my tax rate, spending, borrowing, etc. Thus, government cannot just spend and spend and spend or the extra dollars in the system will chase too few goods and drive up prices. It's important to understand that government cannot just spend recklessly. This is important so I'll say it again. This does not give the government the ability to spend and spend and spend. If they spend in excess of productivity and tax

too little they can create mal-investment and inflation. Likewise, if the government taxes too much and spends too little they create a government surplus and private sector deficit (by accounting identity). This can result in deflation and/or excess private sector debt levels as the private sector literally suffers a dollar shortage.

Some people claim that Modern Monetary Theorists say deficits don't matter. That is a vast misrepresentation of MMT. No Modern Monetary Theorist would ever say such a thing. Deficits most certainly do matter. Maintaining the correct level of deficit spending is, in many ways, a balancing act performed by the government. It is best to think of the government's maintenance of the deficit like a thermostat for the economy. When the economy is running cold the deficit can afford to be higher. When it is hot the deficit should be lower.[56]

Keynesian economists have long argued that deficit spending is a way to pull the economy out of a slump. The public works program under the New Deal was similar to the proposal of Modern Monetary Theory that the government should be the employer of last resort guaranteeing that every person seeking employment has a job. Some commentators insist that there is nothing new about "modern monetary theory" since all of its basic tenets are contained in Keynesian or "Post-Keynesian" theory. The main difference may be the way Modern Monetary Theory interprets the means by which the government creates money to finance its expenditures.

Reading debates about monetary theory can make my brain feel like a soccer ball. Sometimes I can see that people are talking past one another without seeming to get the point of what the other has said, but often they seem to be using completely different conceptual frameworks to talk about the complex procedures by which the Federal Reserve attempts to regulate the economy. Modern Monetary Theory, of course, says that is precisely the point, because traditional frameworks for understanding the economy and formulating monetary policy became obsolete when we went off the gold standard. The same is true in an even more radical way, of course, for the ideas of Amato and Fantacci:

> We need a phenomenology of finance precisely because its underlying features tend not to manifest themselves. Those involved in the general economic discourse – staunch supporters or stubborn opponents, posthumous or

springtime prophets – tend in fact not to see what turns finance into something it really should not be. Above all, they are so caught up in the present-day dogma that they cannot even see it as such.[57]

Amato and Fantacci also agree that going off the last vestiges of the gold standard had a profound effect on the nature of money, which was not fully recognized at the time:

> In fact Nixon's decision, however unwittingly, had disruptive effects on the very nature of money. Three distinctions that had hitherto remained – albeit with increasing vagueness – at the basis of the international monetary and financial system were abruptly and definitively wiped out: the distinction between money and credit; the distinction between national and international currency; and the distinction between money and commodities.[58]

Modern Monetary Theory strikes me mainly as an attempt to step back and see the big picture, to see the U.S. economy as a whole and to take a fresh look at how the fiscal and monetary policies of the government function as part of a system. Some of its advocates may overstate their case or get carried away by their own rhetoric. They seem at times to conflate logical priority with historical origins, and there may be some validity to the criticism that the theory is based on generalizations which oversimplify how the system works, but the issue of whether something fundamental changed when we went off the gold standard seems valid. Needless to say I am sympathetic to the idea that we need to understand money before we can develop policies to fix what is wrong with the economy.

The idea that it is a mistake to even think about government spending in terms of a need to balance the budget is perhaps the most striking contribution of Modern Monetary Theory. This may not be new – the concept of "Functional Finance" advanced by Lerner in 1943[59] was intended to shift the focus of fiscal policy from a goal of balancing the budget to that of insuring maximum productivity without inflation – but it clearly seems alien to the rhetoric of almost every member of Congress. Even liberals view deficit spending as a corrective measure which is only required during recessions and appear to believe the ultimate goal is a balanced budget and "manageable" national debt. The idea that government budgeting and financing is essentially the same as household budgeting and financing seems firmly engrained in all our political debate. (One notable exception: Stephanie Kelton, one of the most visible advocates of Modern Monetary Theory was an economic advisor for the Bernie Sanders' campaign. She was also the Chief Economist for the Democratic Minority Staff of the Senate Budget Committee.)

Deficit spending does not seem to involve the creation of money if it involves the sale of bonds. It seems appropriate to use the metaphor of "printing money" if the government is just issuing checks to pay for spending on defense or infrastructure or welfare, but is it "printing money" if it borrows money to cover government expenditures? In this case expenditures are covered by borrowed money which presumably already exists. In fact the most striking thing to me about the "creation" of money is that it seems to be achieved by "loans." I can see that banks extending credit to customers are in effect creating money out of thin air. A bookkeeping entry "creates" money which is dispersed through the economy as the borrower "spends" it. When the loan is eventually repaid, the newly created money evaporates, even though some kind of wealth (marketable products?) that it has been used to create may remain. The federal government can similarly "create" money by extending credit or making loans or even conferring grants. The mechanisms by which it can do so are complicated by the fact that both the Treasury and the Federal Reserve Bank are involved.

Rather than try to sort out the differences between open market operations, the federal funds market, the discount window, repurchase agreements, and the term auction facility, I am content to recognize that all of these methods seem to involve loans or bonds in some way. The question I have is whether any of them (or some other method at the government's disposal) involves simply entering a number in a ledger in the way that Modern Monetary Theory seems to imply when it describes the combined actions of the Federal Reserve and the Treasury as one governmental entity "creating" money. If the Treasury "issues" a bond, note or bill which the Federal Reserve buys, the Federal Reserve credits the Treasury's account in the same way a bank credits a customer's account in a loan. If you regard the Federal Reserve as part of the government, then the government is selling the bond to itself. The difference between this transaction and literally printing new money to deposit in the account is that the bond, note or bill is a loan that theoretically must be repaid and involves interest (which may be 0%). The question is why money creation has to be in the form of a loan, especially if the interest on the loan is 0%.

The concept of a loan seems to imply that the money already exists and is being "lent" rather than "created." The concept of "credit" seems a bit looser. Extending credit means you are willing to wait to receive payment and the transaction itself does not require a transfer of pre-existing money. When a bank extends credit, though, it is in effect creating money, because the customer can write checks against the amount to pay for goods and services. Nonetheless a bank credit line results in a loan which must be repaid. When the loan is repaid, the money that was created by the loan goes away. Maybe this is the point.

If "printing money" is conceived as a kind of loan, the money created potentially has a term or a limited life. If the loan is not "rolled over," the amount of money circulating will be reduced. Money is not a "resource" of which there is a fixed or limited supply. In 1923 the German government may have literally printed trillions of marks worth of banknotes, but that is not what happens now when the U.S. government "prints money." Money creation is a record of a transaction and not the creation of something "permanent." It is an adjustment to the purchasing power in the economy for which we have yet to find a better name than "a loan." Like the extension of credit by a bank, it is essentially an expression of trust – trust that the purchasing power will be put to good use and the amount eventually repaid if necessary.

Obviously not all the money in circulation was created by loans or credit. Surely some of it (perhaps the 10% that is actual printed money) stays around permanently. What would happen if all the loans on everyone's books were paid off? Would there be a catastrophic amount of "money" drained out of the economy?

There is one school of monetary theory which emphasizes the idea that interest-bearing loans involved in the creation of money can never be paid completely so that the loans must be perpetually renewed. The reason the interest could never be completely paid is explained by a simple formula involving the amount of money created by the loans, P, and the interest charged on those loans, I. Obviously P is less that $P + I$, so in terms of the big picture it is never possible simultaneously to pay off all the principal and interest. (The money required for the interest does not "exist" unless it was created in some other way.) One conclusion that can be drawn from this is that interest on loans is a pernicious thing. Another may be that simple algebraic formulas may not be the most reliable way to understand the actual functioning of the economy or the creation of money.

What is the real net effect of a loan which must be perpetually renewed. (There is actually such a thing as a "perpetual bond," aka "perp," which is a bond with no maturity date. It may be callable, but it has some kind of restriction on how soon it can be called or redeemed. Financially it is generally regarded as a kind of equity rather than a loan.) If the national debt is a loan which must be perpetually renewed, then "servicing the debt" is really just an income redistribution program or a government subsidy to holders of Treasury bonds.

It is very hard to break free from the assumption that the government must have "income" to cover its "expenses." Explanations of modern monetary theory tend to repeat over and over again the mantra that monetarily sovereign nations or their government programs can never go bankrupt as though hammering on the reader's head will finally break the ice. Let's assume for a moment that the government is in fact creating money and pumping it into the economy in some way guided by an understanding of the effect it will have on productivity, employment and prices. Let's assume also that all the decisions about where the money goes are based on democratic expressions of political will – whether the money goes to local school districts or for interstellar weapons. How do you describe this economically or even sociologically?

Are there metaphors which are appropriate for characterizing this from a big-picture perspective? One that occurs to me is the irrigation of arid land. Money flows into institutions or businesses and is channeled via wages and contracts to individuals or other businesses, all of which can now flourish because they have the means to survive and support one another. This is a very different image from the extreme libertarian view that all government action destroys wealth.[60] The question, of course, is why the land is arid. Is there something about economic activity or society that requires a collective expression of political will to get things started or keep them going? Is there a point at which the system becomes self-sustaining and no longer requires the constant infusion of new money? Classical economic thought which starts with autonomous self-interested individuals bartering with each other assumes no "political will" is necessary. It almost seems to believe that such a collective expression of political will is impossible and any attempt to achieve it will inevitably result in a tyrannical dictatorship. It also views money as a commodity or a limited resource. ("The problem with socialism is that you eventually run out of other people's money."[61])

Another metaphor for the role of money in society is that of the circulation of blood in the body. Money functions by circulating. The government may be the lungs and heart which maintain the "purchasing power" of money and keep it circulating. Most of the circulation is, of course, accomplished via the myriad transactions constituting markets. In this metaphor the "creation" of money is less prominent than its circulation, and the conduits through which it flows seem vast in comparison to the pump. Perhaps inflation and recession are caused by a failure of the "heart and lungs" of the government to function properly. If the purchasing power of money is too weak (not enough oxygen?) we suffocate. If the pressure is too high, vessels burst.

There is one interpretation of Keynesian theory in which deficit spending is called "pump priming" with the implication that once the pump is primed the system can carry on without additional priming. For the classical economist the pump is simply the aggregate of all the decisions of individuals (or perhaps the "invisible hand"). Classical economics shies away from organic metaphors ("There is no such thing as society."), although it may invoke evolutionary biology when it ventures into accounts of social institutions and custom.

Once money is circulating is there any reason the rate of circulation will inevitably decline? Here again one must beware of thinking in inappropriate metaphors. Is the economy like some giant machine with a flywheel that will eventually slow down if it is not driven by some external source of power? In other words, what causes recessions? Do we understand the interdependence of employment, consumption and investment well enough to know where to push to keep the wheel turning? I sometimes have the impression that we are flailing around blindly and maybe even sticking our fingers in gears rather than turning the crank.

The main argument against deficit spending is that it is irresponsible, that it forces future generations to pay for our consumption by running up a debt that must eventually be paid. It is also said that the interest on the debt may become unsustainable as it becomes a larger and larger portion of the budget. Credit cards may be alright as a means of managing cash flow until things improve, but they are not a viable source of income in the long run. However if the creation of money does not involve incurring debt, what becomes of the notion of the notion that we are foisting off the cost of our current consumption onto future generations? Money is created so that the supply of money can grow along with the economy. The critical issue becomes the exact relationship between healthy economic growth and the supply of money.

One of the ways Modern Monetary Theory and some strains of Keynesian theory attempt to alter our thinking about deficit spending is to use accounting concepts and algebraic definitions to describe the role of government spending in the national economy. If you define the gross domestic product as the sum of consumption, investment, government spending and net exports (or exports minus imports), then government spending becomes one variable in an equation. For any given level of GDP it varies depending on levels of consumption, investment and net exports. In the same way Gross National Income is defined as the sum of consumption, savings and taxes. Once you begin to analyze the overall economy at this level of abstraction, it is possible to view deficit spending (or government surplus) as one element in an accounting process reflecting the state of the economy at a given time and not necessarily as an accumulating debt that must eventually be paid. It is not the federal budget that needs to be balanced; it is just the overall economy, and that balance is achieved either by altering the total GDP or simply by definition.

Summarized in this way the theory seems like sophistry or sleight of hand, but this is largely because the initial abstract framework is a vast simplification of a very complex system and that to move from descriptive to prescriptive the theory must incorporate many more variables including attempts to generalize the "economic behavior" of individuals.

Almost all economists use mathematical models to describe the way the economy works. Often my eyes start to glaze over when I encounter pages filled with equations, even if they are simple algebraic equations rather than the complex mathematical expressions that must ultimately be used to connect data that may or may not be causally related. One of the problems I have with mathematical models is that it seems easy to lose sight of the distinction between a relationship which is true by definition and one which is capable of being the basis for predictions or estimations of outcomes of policy decisions. A definition like

GDP = C + I + G + (X- M)

is fundamentally different from an equation in physics like

$e = mc^2$.

Einstein's theory about the relationship between mass and energy enabled scientists to create a bomb. Defining gross domestic product as the sum of consumption, investment, government spending and net exports does not enable anyone to do anything without additional theories about how human behavior will affect any of the variables in the equation. Textbooks may attempt to keep this distinction clear. The definition of gross domestic product is an attempt to provide an accounting framework within which we can analyze each of the components. What has to be added is some indication of the factors which affect, for example, the levels of consumer spending and how changes in consumption actually affect the other variables. The problem I have is that the first pass at fleshing all this out may involve a factor which is a constant representing something like the "marginal propensity to consume." The assumption seems to be that it is useful to represent all the factors involved in all of the decisions by consumers as an average constant for some initial analysis and then go back later and figure out what really influences consumers' choices. Perhaps at some point before it all gets too complicated some number can be used "temporarily" as a value for the marginal propensity to consume in order to evaluate the impact of some policy about government spending. If a model contains too many of these kinds of coefficients, I can't help but question its validity, even if every one agrees at the end of the meeting that now we have to figure out what the marginal propensity to consume really is. The real question I suppose is whether something like a marginal propensity to consume is in fact an independent variable or whether it is inextricably linked with all the other variables in the model.

For the layman perhaps the real value of this branch of economic theory is the questions it raises about the creation of money and the real goals of fiscal policy. Responsible fiscal policy surely should focus on providing necessary services and insuring that the economy is "prospering" rather than on balancing the federal budget, but most politicians insist that the economy cannot prosper in the long run if the government is constantly running a deficit. Everyone seems to fear that the "national debt" will become unsustainable.

What is needed is the ability to think about "government spending" without classifying it in terms of a deficit or surplus. The "national debt" is normally viewed as the accumulated deficits from an "unbalanced federal budget," but if government spending is "financed" by the creation of money, the "national debt" is simply a record of the net amount of money the government has injected into the American economy over the years. If the money injected was created with interest-bearing loans, the expense of servicing the debt just becomes part of the investment. There is a problem only if the growth of the economy has not kept pace with the supply of money. The main symptom of this failure to keep pace may be inflation.

It is with the issue of inflation that Modern Monetary Theory and Keynesian theory both end up wrestling the same demon. The metaphor of "printing money" often conjures up images of hyperinflation where prices rise so rapidly that people feel compelled to do their grocery shopping at lunch time rather than after work. The main example that seems to haunt us is that of Germany after the First World War when Germany mass printed marks in order to buy foreign currency to pay reparations. The value of the mark fell from 90 marks to the dollar in 1921 to over 4 trillion to the dollar in 1923. While the causes of this hyperinflation may be clear to historians and economists, it remains the most surreal example of what happens when the government literally prints too much money.

Inflation and Recession

"Inflation" and "recession" are two economic terms bandied about by politicians and pundits perhaps even more than "growth" and "job creation." We all know that inflation means everything is getting more expensive and recession means times are hard all over. Both are problems, and we want to vote for the magician who can make them disappear. I probably first realized "what inflation means to me" when my adjustable rate mortgage rate soared into double digits a few years after I purchased my house. Recession is what I wanted to blame when I got laid off from a job where I had just single-handedly completed the first phase of the company's transition from hardware-based to software-based image processing.

Inflation on the surface seems like a simple concept. Wikipedia tells me

> In economics, inflation is a sustained increase in the general price level of goods and services in an economy over a period of time. When the price level rises, each unit of currency buys fewer goods and services. Consequently, inflation reflects a reduction in the purchasing power per unit of money – a loss of real value in the medium of exchange and unit of account within the economy. A chief measure of price inflation is the inflation rate, the annualized percentage change in a general price index, usually the consumer price index, over time.

It's easy to see inflation in the long term. My son's kindergarten tuition was more than my tuition at Yale. A new car today cost 20 times more than it did when I first bought a car. It is harder to see clearly in the short term when technology makes some things less expensive while prices for other things reach exorbitant levels. The trick in measuring inflation is selecting the "basket" of goods whose prices are tracked for the consumer price index.

Recession is a bit more difficult to define than inflation. One of the most common definitions involves "negative growth." Investopedia offers the following:

> A recession is a significant decline in activity across the economy, lasting longer than a few months. It is visible in industrial production, employment, real income and wholesale-retail trade. The technical indicator of a recession

> is two consecutive quarters of negative economic growth as measured by a country's gross domestic product (GDP); although the National Bureau of Economic Research (NBER) does not necessarily need to see this occur to call a recession.

The most striking thing about this definition is that some group decides whether to "call" a recession when other factors beside GDP seem to be declining. Ultimately it is a decline in "economic activity" which constitutes a recession.

The cure for a decline in economic activity is surely to increase economic activity, and the government is in a unique position to do this by investing directly in the economy. Infrastructure projects will increase economic activity by employing more people. Their income will presumably result in more retail sales. In the longer term, government funded research will eventually result in new products and services adding to the economic activity. Once economic thinking is liberated from what Stephanie Kelton calls "the deficit myth",[62] we should no longer fear recession. We need only figure out how to avoid accelerating inflation rates.

The textbook response to this is to imply that deficit spending by the government inevitably leads to "a particularly damaging form of demand-pull inflation."

> The large deficits and the rapid money growth increase aggregate demand, which in turn increases the price level. Thus, when the German government financed its spending in 1922–1923 by printing billions and billions of paper marks, which came into the marketplace in search of bread and fuel, it was no wonder that the German price level rose a billionfold. This was demand-pull inflation with a vengeance. This scene was replayed in the early 1990s when the Russian government financed its budget deficit by printing monetary rubles. The result was an inflation rate that averaged 25 percent per month, or 1355 percent per year.[63]

The hyperinflation in Germany in 1922 and Russia in 1992 were both precipitated by extraordinary historical events - the crippling reparations payments imposed on Germany after WW I and the turmoil resulting from the dissolution of the Soviet Union in 1991. Whether deficit spending by the government under more normal circumstances can ever lead to hyper-inflation is not clear.

Regardless of what causes it or how it is measured, inflation is a real phenomenon. The most common explanation of inflation is the monetary theory focusing on the correlation between inflation and the amount of money in circulation or the availability of credit. Milton Friedman famously said that inflation "is always and everywhere a monetary phenomenon in the sense that it is and can be produced only by a more rapid increase in the quantity of money than in output."[64]

In the simplest model when there is a dramatic increase in the amount of money in circulation without a corresponding increase in the amount of goods and services available for purchase, prices will rise. The idea is that they will be "bid up" when people have more money at their disposal. The first question that occurs to me is why consumers will "bid prices up" rather than save or invest. Obviously a shortage of a particular product may induce sellers to jack up prices to profit from the "excess" demand, but I do not see why the converse applies. With the onset of the COVID-19 pandemic, prices of some items did go up temporarily when there was a shortage due to increased demand, but this increased demand was not caused by an increase in the supply of money. Perhaps it all depends on who has the "extra" money, but surely the more pertinent question is why there is no increase in production to meet the increase in demand.

The Samuelson-Nordhaus textbook saves the discussion of inflation for the penultimate chapter, and it does not really offer a coherent account of the causes of inflation. It takes inflation as a given historically and focuses mainly on its impact on the economy or "costs" along with policies that have attempted to prevent it or cure it. The closest it comes to explaining the causes of inflation is to point out that while inflation prior to the industrial revolution might be explained by the supply of money, recent history shows that "shocks to the economy" are what make inflation deviate from its expected rate.

> The economy is constantly subject to changes in aggregate demand, sharp oil- and commodity-price changes, poor harvests, movements in the foreign exchange rate, productivity changes, and countless other economic events that push inflation away from its expected rate.[65]

Perhaps what this reveals is that the economy is not a closed system of producers and consumers. It is dependent on natural resources which may be subject to depletion or at least extreme fluctuations, and it is dependent on economic decisions of foreign suppliers of energy or raw materials. It is even dependent on the weather. Perhaps the ultimate cause of long-term inflation is the increasing dependence on non-renewable natural resources. If more and more products and services require energy that comes from limited resources (and may be controlled by foreign governments or multinational corporations immune to competition), then it seems likely that the price charged for the energy will keep rising. What is not explained by these "shocks to the economy," however, is why prices continue to rise rather than stabilizing after the shock has been absorbed. This is almost universally attributed to a vicious circle between wages and prices.

Economists distinguish between "cost-push" inflation and "demand-pull" inflation. Cost-push inflation is rising prices associated with rising costs of production. This is easy to understand, especially if it is the cost of raw materials which rises. OPEC decides to cut oil supplies in retaliation for U.S. involvement in the Yom Kippur war, and we get not only lines at the gas pump but also double digit inflation which persists for years. Since the entire economy depends largely on energy generated from oil and gas, an increase in energy costs is bound to result in an increase in prices across the board.

What is not immediately obvious is why inflation continues or accelerates rather than just having a one time bump-up in prices. The standard answer to this is that price increases result in demands for higher wages, which in turn require further price increases. The problem I have with this explanation is that it seems to imply a one-to-one relationship between labor costs and pricing. Labor costs are only one factor determining prices, even if "wages" include all the costs of sub-contracted services associated with marketing and distribution as well as the salaries of managers who are not normally included in the category of "labor." If a 1% increase in labor costs does not require a 1% increase in prices to yield the same profit, then there should be a dampening of the feedback effect rather than accelerating inflation. Perhaps the whole system has too many feedback loops to be simplified to this degree, and, as economists are fond of pointing out, expectations of further inflation can actually amplify the inflation as contracts are written to compensate for it.

Demand-pull inflation is rising prices associated with growth in demand which exceeds supply or production capacity. The more I thought about it, the more difficulty I had grasping the economic concept of "demand." The measure of demand seems to be simply the total amount of goods and services purchased, but surely in some sense demand for more or better goods and services is infinite. Most grownups accept that "you can't always get what you want."

Trying to understand "demand" takes us back to the very foundations of mainstream economic theory. After describing the fluctuations in gasoline prices during the last half of the 20th century, Samuelson and Nordhaus introduce the theory that explains how a market economy sets prices:

> What lay behind these dramatic shifts? Economics has a very powerful tool for explaining such changes in the economic environment. It is called the theory of supply and demand. This theory shows how consumer preferences determine consumer demand for commodities, while business costs are the foundation of the supply of commodities. The increases in the price of gasoline occurred either because the demand for gasoline had increased or because the supply of oil had decreased. The same is true for every market, from Internet stocks to diamonds to land: changes in supply and demand drive changes in output and prices. If you understand how supply and demand work, you have gone a long way toward understanding a market economy.[66]

The diverse range of individual desires, needs, wants, preferences, or taste are the foundation of economic theory. They are taken as an opaque given even though we all know they are culturally conditioned or even manufactured by advertising. Economics abstains from judging or evaluating individual desires and tries to describe how they drive the system that determines what gets produced and who gets it.

To quantify "demand" in a way to make it useful in economics, a graph is imagined which plots the quantity of a single good purchased at a range of different possible prices. It makes more sense to me to think of this as a "sales" curve rather than a "demand" curve. We all know that lowering the price of something may increase the number of sales. A 50% off close-out sale may well clear the inventory. Apparently data has been collected on enough different commodities to enable economists to confidently formulate the "law of downward-sloping demand."

> When the price of a commodity is raised (and other things are held constant), buyers tend to buy less of the commodity. Similarly, when the price is lowered, other things being constant, quantity demanded increases.[67]

This just seems like obvious common sense, but what may not be obvious is what the "other things" are that are being "held constant." It is these other things which will make the bedrock foundation of mainstream economics seem more like quicksand.

The textbook takes care to distinguish "demand" from "quantity demanded."

> A change in the quantity buyers want to purchase, prompted by any reason other than a change in price (e.g., increase in income, change in tastes), is a change in demand. In graphical terms, it is a shift of the demand curve. If, in contrast, the decision to buy more or less is prompted by a change in the good's price, then it is a change in quantity demanded. In graphical terms, a change in quantity demanded is a movement along an unchanging demand curve.[68]

The relationship between "demand" and price is a great deal more complex than the two-variable "demand curve." Apparently one of the other things being held constant in plotting a demand curve is consumer preferences (aka demand). If data indicate that sales have changed when prices changed, there is no way to know whether this represents a shift in the imagined demand curve or a movement along it. Consumers may have had more or less money to spend or their desire for the product may have changed.

One might wonder how it is possible to plot the demand curve for a particular product at a particular time. It is instructive to read a review of the top 10 techniques for the empirical estimation of demand.[69] It describes and critiques the various methods a business manager might use to estimate a demand curve for his product, including forms of market research as well as the use of mathematical techniques like regression analysis. None of the methods seems to be completely reliable.

Nonetheless, this demand curve is generalized by imagining a curve which represents "aggregate" demand as the total of all the individual demand curves for products on the market at a given time in the economy.

> Aggregate demand. Total planned or desired spending in the economy during a given period. It is determined by the

aggregate price level and influenced by domestic investment, net exports, government spending, the consumption function, and the money supply.[70]

Given the complexity of the factors affecting the demand curve for a single product at a given point in time, one may well wonder how it can be useful to speculate about "aggregate demand" in the long or short run. Of course if aggregate demand is the same thing as "planned or desired spending" in a given period, it can be derived from the figure for the Gross Domestic Product. The corresponding "aggregate price level" can presumably be derived from the consumer price index. The question is whether this really enables us to draw any conclusions about how price determines demand or vice versa. Moreover since a demand curve represents a relationship between prices and sales at a given moment in time, there is no way to know what the curve will be in the future.

A corresponding "supply curve" is similarly defined:

> The supply schedule (or supply curve) for a commodity shows the relationship between its market price and the amount of that commodity that producers are willing to produce and sell, other things held constant.[71]

The supply curve is depicted as an upward sloping curve shaped and ultimately limited by the law of diminishing returns. One of the things being held constant in this case is capital investment which increases efficiency and lowers unit production costs. This obviously enables a producer to offer increased supply at the same price and represents a shift in supply as opposed to a change in the amount supplied:

> When changes in factors other than a good's own price affect the quantity supplied, we call these changes shifts in supply. Supply increases (or decreases) when the amount supplied increases (or decreases) at each market price.[72]

So the relationship between price and "supply" is also not a simple two-variable function, but the curve is still used as the model for an "aggregate" supply curve for the whole economy.

> Aggregate supply (AS) curve. The curve showing the relationship between the output firms would willingly supply and the aggregate price level, other things equal. The AS curve tends to be vertical at potential output in the very long run but may be upward-sloping in the short run.[73]

The shape of the short run aggregate supply curve is apparently difficult to explain:
> Economists generally agree that the AS curve slopes up in the short run — which is to say that both output and prices respond to demand shifts. It has proved very difficult to develop a complete theory to explain this relationship, and controversies about aggregate supply are among the most heated in all of economics.[74]

In the long run the only way to increase output is by capital investment, which should result in a shift of the curve. If capital investment is one of the factors held constant, then there can be no further increase in supply beyond the equilibrium point no matter how much the price goes up.
> Aggregate supply differs depending upon the period. In the short run, inflexible elements in wages and prices lead firms to respond to higher demand by raising both production and prices. In the longer run, as costs respond fully, all of the response to increased demand takes the form of higher prices. Whereas the short-run AS curve is upward-sloping, the long-run AS curve is vertical because, given sufficient time, all prices and costs adjust fully.[75]

Samuelson and Nordhaus acknowledge that they are putting forth one of several controversial theories about the relationship between aggregate supply and demand, but it seems that this is the theory underlying their explanations of inflation. At some point increased demand results in higher prices with no corresponding increase in supply. If the economy is truly operating its maximum potential, the producer can do nothing to increase the supply and workers will continue to demand higher wages to keep pace with the increased cost of living. Producers will raise prices again to cover increased costs and inflation will be off and running.

Criticism of the theory of supply and demand takes various forms. The points of attack that resonate the most with me are the idea that the theory is tautological in some fundamental way or at least immune from empirical confirmation and the emphasis on the fact that prices rise not just due to some pressure from an amorphous "demand" or "market forces" but because some producer makes a decision to increase the price of his product.

Clearly for any business to be viable there has to be a "demand" for its product. The business may create the demand along with the product, but investing in a business is worthwhile only if enough people want to buy the product. Market research or some sixth sense may enable a businessman to find a price point as close as possible to what the market will bear. He probably hopes that the product will catch on in a way that will enable him to sell more and make a fatter profit. He will invest in advertising or additional manufacturing capability if he thinks it can increase his profit either by lowering his costs or increasing his sales. The main thing driving all this is a profit motive, not some consumer "demand."

The theory of supply and demand involves the idea that an economic system inevitably seeks a kind of equilibrium the way water seeks its own level. This seems to lead to thinking in terms of "market forces" which are somehow comparable to physical forces. Consumer demand pushes up prices. Prices pull up supply or push down demand. Supply and demand naturally find a balance at a "market clearing" price:

> A market equilibrium comes at the price at which quantity demanded equals quantity supplied. At that equilibrium, there is no tendency for the price to rise or fall. The equilibrium price is also called the market-clearing price. This denotes that all supply and demand orders are filled, the books are "cleared" of orders, and demanders and suppliers are satisfied.[76]

The "demanders" that are satisfied are, of course, only those who decide to buy the product at the equilibrium price. The rest of us can only dream of buying it when our income increases or the price goes down. How satisfied the "suppliers" are may depend on their profit margins. They may be willing to operate at a loss for a year or two because they believe that their product will catch on in the long run. The whole idea of this kind of equilibrium in an economy strikes me as a fantasy based on imagined phenomena and unrealistic assumptions about human behavior. Giving it a mathematical expression may make it appear more "scientific," but it still rests on the foundations which make it impossible to project into the future or test empirically. Adding "behavioral" complications appears to be an effort to correct some shortcoming in the theory, but it does not improve the foundations.

This might all be academic speculation of no consequence if it were not for the fact that it drives government policy. Inflation and the cost of living are hot political issues, and they depend on the prices of things. In order to keep things from getting more expensive, we have to have some idea of the factors that determine prices.

In the past the U.S. has made attempts to stabilize prices by direct legislation. My father was in fact a regional director for the Office of Price Administration from 1942 to 1946 and the Office of Price Stabilization from 1951 to 1953, although needless to say I had no idea what he was doing. These days I have the impression that most people agree that "price fixing" is not a good idea regardless of whether it is done by a government agency or cartel. We do, however, feel that consumers need to be protected against "price gouging." We may also support government subsidies to industries whose products are deemed essential but for which the market price is not sufficient to yield a profit. Lower prices may seem good to the consumer, but they can spell disaster for some producers. This is especially true for farmers. In the 19th century falling prices for crops created the fervor behind the Progressive political movement, and government subsidies have been used to stabilize prices of farm produce. These have even included paying farmers not to grow a crop at all, or purchasing "excess" and literally throwing it away. It is hard to believe there is not something fundamentally wrong if we ever have to do this.

One way consumer demand may contribute to inflation is through credit card debt. If consumers use credit to purchase things with no intention of paying off the debt in the near term, they are effectively increasing the amount of money in circulation. How much of this type of consumer debt it would take to drive up prices is difficult to say. Revolving consumer debt in the U.S. (credit cards, home equity lines of credit, store charge accounts, gas cards, etc.) exceeded one trillion dollars during the financial crisis and again from 2017 to 2019. This, of course, includes the use of charge accounts simply as a convenience or for short term cash flow management. Apparently Americans paid $121 billion in credit card interest and fees in 2019 and an estimated 42% of those who use credit cards do not pay the full balance at the end of the month.[77] So this may be a way in which consumer "demand" increases the money supply directly and pushes "supply" towards its limit. These consumers are already paying more than the "list price" for whatever they are buying since the average interest rate on credit cards is 16.61%, but whether consumer card purchases induce suppliers to increase there prices is probably hard to determine. The suppliers may not have been operating at full capacity so that they are more than happy to increase their supply at the same price to satisfy the consumers who want or need their products enough to go into debt to purchase it.

Consumer debt of this sort only started to be significant in the late 1960's, so it can hardly be a sufficient explanation for the persistence of inflation over the last 200 years. The real explanation must lie somewhere in the factors involved in growth in an industrial economy.

Another obvious example of demand driving up prices may be the real estate market, or at least the upper end of the real estate market. Buying or selling a house is an economic transaction in which buyers or sellers compete with each other and price is established by bidding. In Los Angeles there seems to be a huge demand for "affordable" housing. Developers have no interest in jumping in to meet the demand for affordable housing, because they can make so much more money with unaffordable housing.

Real estate, however, may be a unique and unrepresentative sector of the economy. Clearly the real estate bubble leading to the financial crisis was a distortion of the "market economy" because housing became a speculative investment. The real estate market in many cities is also infected with all kinds of social hierarchies, prejudices and preferences. ("Location, location, location!") There is a limited supply of land near the coast in Southern California so no amount of increased production can increase its supply to meet a growing demand. Does this mean that the Consumer Price Index will inevitably rise? Housing costs are included in the CPI via a rental index which reflects the rent equivalent for someone who owns his own home. So an increase in house prices requiring larger mortgages will push up the CPI to some extent even if a booming real estate market is not accompanied by rising prices of other goods and services. More importantly a booming real estate market means that homeowners are sitting on more "wealth" and can more easily borrow money. This opens the door to increasing consumer credit that can lead to "excess" demand which might cause inflation.

The real question is whether inflation is inevitable with growth and technological progress. Is the car I buy today really comparable to the car I bought 50 years ago in terms of what I got for my money, not to mention the used 1953 Chevrolet I bought in 1960.? The Consumer Price Index has no way of breaking down the components in a contemporary car to compare them with the price of the closest approximation of those components in a car 50 years ago.

> One of the more difficult problems faced in compiling a price index is the accurate measurement and treatment of quality change due to changing product specifications and consumption patterns. The concept of the CPI requires a measurement through time of the cost of purchasing an unchanging, constant-quality set of goods and services. In reality, products disappear, products are replaced with new versions, and new products emerge.[78]

Obviously it makes no sense to compare the cost of using a cell phone with the cost of a telephone installed in a house 50 years ago. It may not even make sense to compare the cost of an iPhone with a Nokia mobile phone from 1990. What people are primarily concerned about are price increases in the relatively short term. An annual inflation rate in double digits wreaks havoc with a household budget and makes investing feel like running in place. They may, of course, be concerned about what inflation in the longer run will do to their retirement income. Social Security benefits are tied to the Consumer Price Index, but returns on personal retirement investment accounts are not.

If you think about the growth of a new business, it is possible to imagine how price increases result from a conflict over the distribution of wealth. Suppose a manufacturing business starts with a certain number of employees and a business plan that leads to a profit. The business might expand by investing its profits so that it can sell more products with perhaps more employees being paid the same wage. Eventually the business may become profitable enough that the owners start taking the profit as bonuses or dividends rather than re-investing all of it in the business. The workers see the owners getting rich and want a piece of the action. They unionize and demand higher wages. The company may have to raise the price of its products if they want to maintain the same level of profits they have started to enjoy. The obvious way to break the vicious circle of increased prices and increased wages is employee ownership of the business.

One must be careful about using stories like this as a basis for economic theory. In fact one of the principal criticisms of mainstream economics is that it attempts to explain "macro" economic by analyzing "micro" economic behavior. In other words it starts with individual autonomous economic agents and generalizes to come up with concepts like 'aggregate" supply and demand to explain something like inflation.

It may well be that inflation can only be understood by examining all the specific circumstances associated with any particular instance of inflation rather than attempting to explain it with models derived from the imagined behavior of autonomous economic agents often assumed to have total knowledge and purely "rational" behavior.

Some economists cite other types of inflation that are caused by speculation and currency exchange rate fluctuations. Speculative inflation is mainly a matter of trading in commodity markets. If a speculator buys up enough of a commodity, they can cause an artificial shortage and drive up prices. Rising commodity prices then become a kind of cost-push inflation in other markets.

Exchange rate inflation is associated with currency crises where a nation's currency loses value relative to other currencies and its imports become more expensive. Depending on how dependent the economy is on its imports, this can also lead to cost-push inflation or simply higher prices in consumer goods.

There is, of course, one market in which rapidly rising prices are a cause for celebration rather than concern: the stock market. People who look for some correlation between stock prices and inflation seem mainly interested in the effect of inflation on stock prices rather than vice versa. Currently the consensus seems to be that stock prices rise when fears of inflation subside, but historically it appears to be difficult to ferret out a clear correlation between inflation and the stock prices.[79] It may be fears of recession have more of an impact on the stock market than concerns about inflation.

Average investors just think of the stock market as the place where their money is supposed to grow so that they can survive when they retire. One of the reasons they may feel compelled to invest is because inflation will eat away at the real value of savings.

Total stock market prices indicate the "capitalization" of all publicly traded companies, but that total does not figure into the calculation of gross domestic product or total "economic activity." The stock market is like a shadow play projected behind the arena of "real" economic activity. Economic activity can affect stock market prices, but probably more often stock market prices affect economic activity. Stock prices affect how people think or feel about their finances, which will in turn influence their decisions as consumers. Sometimes it seems as though controlling the economy boils down to controlling how people think and feel, and I'm not at all sure this is a job for mathematicians and congressional committees, not to mention a chairman of the Federal Reserve given to making oracular pronouncements about the future.

There is one aspect of discussions of inflation in mainstream economics which is particularly crucial in government policy: the relationship between inflation and unemployment and the concept of the "non-accelerating inflation rate of unemployment (NAIRU)." It began life as the "natural rate of unemployment," and its current form is an attempt to improve on its theoretical underpinnings or at least paper over the implication that there is anything "natural" about unemployment.

> The nonaccelerating inflation rate of unemployment (or NAIRU) is that unemployment rate consistent with a constant inflation rate. At the NAIRU, upward and downward forces on price and wage inflation are in balance, so there is no tendency for inflation to change. The NAIRU is the lowest unemployment rate that can be sustained without upward pressure on inflation.[80]

This attempt to analyze the relationship between inflation and unemployment has it roots in a paper by A.W. Phillips in 1958 entitled "The Relation Between Unemployment and the Rate of Change of Money Wage Rates in the United Kingdom, 1861-1957." Applying the theory of supply and demand to the labor market, Phillips analyzed data from almost a century of statistics on unemployment and wage rates in the U.K. to confirm an hypothesis "that the rate of change of money wage rates can be explained by the level of unemployment and the rate of change of unemployment, except in or immediately after those years in which there is a sufficiently rapid rise in import prices to offset the tendency for increasing productivity to reduce the cost of living."[81] He used mathematical techniques to derive a function which yielded a curve which fit the data as well as possible. His curve dealt with the rate of change of money wage rates, but other economists translated it into the "Phillips Curve" depicting a relationship between inflation and unemployment. Analyzing data for the U.S., Samuelson and Solow generated a curve which implied two things:

> 1. In order to have wages increase at no more than the 2½ per cent per annum characteristic of our productivity growth, the American economy would seem on the basis of twentieth-century and postwar experience to have to undergo something like 5 to 6 per cent of the civilian labor force's being unemployed. That much unemployment would appear to be the cost of price stability in the years immediately ahead.
>
> 2. In order to achieve the nonperfectionist's goal of high enough output to give us no more than 3 per cent unemployment, the price index might have to rise by as much as 4 to 5 per cent per year. That much price rise would seem to be the necessary cost of high employment and production in the years immediately ahead.[82]

The implications of this curve led to the concept of a "Natural Rate of Unemployment" and to idea that there was an inevitable trade-off between inflation and unemployment. Further analysis indicated that there was not a single "natural" rate, but that for any given state of the economy a reduction in unemployment below a certain level would nonetheless result in some degree of inflation. The level of unemployment for a stable inflation rate is the NAIRU. The assumption seems to be that it is not possible to have stable prices without high unemployment or full employment without high inflation. The best compromise that can be hoped for is a relatively low and non-accelerating inflation rate with relatively low unemployment.

Samuelson and Nordhaus describe the Phillips Curve as "the major macroeconomics tool used to understand inflation."[83]

> An important piece of inflation arithmetic underlies this curve. Say that labor productivity (output per worker) rises at a steady rate of 1 percent each year. Further, assume that firms set prices on the basis of average labor costs, so prices always change just as much as average labor costs per unit of output. If wages are rising at 4 percent, and productivity is rising at 1 percent, then average labor costs will rise at 3 percent. Consequently, prices will also rise at 3 percent.[84]

Several things strike me about the Phillips Curve. First even though Phillips assumed that increasing productivity tends to lower the cost of living, his data never showed a decrease in the cost of living. He assumed this was because wages were always increasing and looked for a correlation between wages and unemployment. The textbook example does not elaborate on the assumptions involved in its "inflation arithmetic." If productivity is rising at a steady rate, either workers are always getting more proficient or capital expenditures are improving the equipment they use. Presumably some price increase would be required to compensate for the amortized capital expense. Assuming prices are set based simply on average labor costs seems to bias the calculation in a way that encourages one to place all the blame for inflation on wage demands rather than looking at the reason wages are rising at 4 percent.

Even though the data for the U.S. analyzed by Samuelson and Solow seemed to correspond to what Phillips had found in the U.K., subsequent data from the 70s was completely at odds with the theory. As every mutual fund prospectus is legally required to say, "Past performance is no guarantee of future results."

Once it was realized that there was nothing "natural" about unemployment or the rate of change in unemployment, no one jumped to the conclusion that it might be possible somehow to achieve zero unemployment. The reason there is no place in mainstream economic theory for actual full employment seems to just be that both inflation and unemployment have always been a "fact of life" in industrialized market economies. There is also an assumption about the effect of widespread anticipation of continued inflation.

> Why, you might ask, does inflation have such strong momentum? The answer is that most prices and wages are set with an eye to future economic conditions. When prices and wages are rising rapidly and are expected to continue doing so, businesses and workers tend to build the rapid rate of inflation into their price and wage decisions. High or low inflation expectations tend to be self-fulfilling prophecies.[85]

Employment and Work

We may regard life, liberty and the pursuit of happiness as God-given rights, but everyone knows you must "earn a living" in order to exercise these rights. Unless you are a hermit with extraordinary survival skills, you've got to play along to get along. Your value to society, your status and your "purchasing power" are determined by how others view the contribution you can make towards the satisfaction of their desires.

Classical economics seems to treat labor in the same way it treats goods. Labor has a price in the market which is determined by supply and demand. As an alien visiting the land of economics I balk at the idea that human beings or their "labor" are in any way commodities to be purchased via a market. This smells wrong for me from the get go.

The social world I knew as a kid seemed relatively stable. My parents were not scarred from the Depression, and most of the grownups I encountered had steady if not permanent jobs. I knew that my father's career had some frustrations, but my main experience was of his having a steady job and a secure place in the community. I had relatively little exposure to the underbelly of the world in which I lived. Even the household servants seemed to me to have relatively stable lives despite the high turnover in cooks due to my mother's treatment of them. We had a "yardman" who had had a colorful career and was a pillar of his own community even though his status in the community at large was fairly low on the totem pole. In retrospect obviously I was completely oblivious to the realities of lower class existence in Birmingham in the '40s and '50s, not to mention the true nature of the racism involved. I bought into the idea that I could expect a place in a community that supported me in the manner to which I was accustomed. If I had gone to law school and returned to Birmingham, I probably would have enjoyed a stable career and comfortable life no matter how much I might have been at odds with the conservative establishment. But for a variety of reasons my siblings and I all wanted to get the hell out of Birmingham. We each navigated the open waters of the professional world in our own ways and with varying degrees of success, but it was a fairly rude shock to me when I discovered what "involuntary unemployment" meant. I know at least one college classmate who worked for the same employer his entire career, but the initial choices I made threw me into a white water of free lance work for which I was ill equipped, and my later attempts to find and hold "normal" jobs were undermined by my own personality as well as the impact of problems with the economy at large. As a result I all too often found myself in a conversation with someone where I was convinced I needed his money a lot more than he needed my services.

Even though I have sometimes hated my job, I like to work. I need to feel that I am being productive and useful. To some extent I thrive on solving problems or making things work. I prefer the end product to be something I respect and feel has genuine social value, but given a task I am capable of throwing myself into it with what I have, I think justifiably, called an inhuman amount of perseverance. I tend to assume that everyone likes to feel productive and a part of something that matters. I prefer to work "with" someone rather than "for" them, and I assume others feel the same. I do not assume that the Average Joe is a slacker who needs to be "incentivized" by competition or threats, and I don't really think that work should be simply a means to earn money so that one can indulge other desires. When it is, I feel as though something valuable has been sacrificed by the society.

I have learned, however, that it is one thing to be able to do a job and quite another to be able to get it. It used to be that employment ads were summarized as "Help wanted," but now the message is more likely to be "Prove you are good enough to be a part of our dynamic team." A lot of literature about finding employment based on "doing what you love" strikes me unrealistic to the point of being delusional. I've digested too many sour grapes to be passionate about being part of a team creating the next new thing. Clearly my mind is agitated by a bunch of conflicting attitudes and emotions about work.

My only job as a kid was pulling weeds in the side yard, and I was paid according to the number of weeds I pulled. It didn't last very long because I probably sensed that it was make-work conceived by my mother as a way of acquainting me with the idea of gainful employment. It didn't really matter if there were weeds in the side yard, and I suspect that as soon as I had earned enough to buy some comic books I lost interest. Maybe this was before I began receiving a regular allowance which continued until I graduated from college. I never recall feeling constrained because I could not afford to buy or do something. I could generally afford to send off for a magic trick or buy comic books or a kit for a model. I think I eventually used my allowance to buy birthday or Christmas presents for others in the family. In a sense my "job" was to be a good student. I got a bonus for good grades on my report card, but I don't really recall how rigid my allowance was. I occasionally helped with some household chores like emptying wastebaskets, but I never felt my allowance was tied to the performance of tasks.

When I was a senior in high school, my mother made it clear to me that I was expected to get a job for the summer after I graduated rather than just goof off in the way I normally did. I managed to turn this into an opportunity to escape on a grand adventure by somehow persuading my parents to let me go out west and work in the wheat harvest. I took the bus to Kansas armed with literature from various state employment agencies and had the extraordinary good luck to hook up with a small crew that followed the harvest from Oklahoma to Wyoming. I drove a combine and grew a beard. At the end of the season I used my earnings to buy an old car with the idea of visiting a friend working at Yellowstone and then driving to California to see my brother who was in graduate school at Berkeley. I damaged the car beyond my ability to pay for the repairs and sold it for junk in Jackson Hole. I took a bus to California, arriving with not quite enough money left to pay the bus fare back to Birmingham. I considered the summer a great success.

During my first two years in college my father found me a summer job in the payroll office of an aircraft plant in Birmingham. At the end of the first summer, I blew my earnings on a trip to Nassau with a friend. The second summer I got fed up and quit early so that I could spend two weeks completely on my own at a cabin we had on a lake. While I met some colorful characters in the payroll office, neither of these two summers accomplished the moral edification or character building that I suspect it was intended to.

By this point I had dropped my plans to major in political science as preparation for making a difference in the real world and had switched to philosophy as a means of understanding what life was all about. If anyone asked me what I intended "to do" with philosophy, I enjoyed saying I intended to live with it. College was opening up a vast new realm of ideas, and I began to identify work with "the life of the mind." To the extent that I had any practical ambitions, I assumed I would be an academic since that was a way to stay in school all my life.

I weaseled out of working after my junior year by signing up to study French in Grenoble with a program called Classrooms Abroad. I assume my parents funded this as well as the two weeks of traveling on my own in Europe at the end of the program because they viewed it as a legitimate part of my education. My mother had done something similar while she was in college. They also approved of my plan to study at Cambridge after graduation.

The summer between Yale and Cambridge I had a job as a teaching assistant at a Liberal Studies program for bright, motivated high school students. I assisted a mildly eccentric philosophy professor in a course where he assigned reading in Freud, Nietzsche and Kierkegaard. To the extent that the job was an experiment to see how I might fare as a teacher or professor, it was completely demoralizing. I found it almost impossible to explain things I was still struggling to understand. I liked the students and enjoyed the summer, but I came away afraid that I could never have the confidence to teach well.

While I was studying literature at Cambridge, anxieties about how well I could teach combined with a desire to do something more "creative" than analyzing and commenting on other people's creative work. I decided that instead of being an academic, I would try to be a filmmaker. I had fallen in love with art films while I as in college, and a career writing and directing films seemed to me to be the best possible form of work. It would combine the opportunity to give tangible form to the amorphous feelings inside me with work involving collaboration rather than the isolation of ivory tower research and writing. Plus it had the lure of glamour and status.

After beating my head against the wall in Hollywood for about 25 years, I finally abandoned all my creative ambitions and focused on finding a "normal" job which would enable me to pay my bills. Eventually I ended up as a kind of engineer doing computer systems work and programming for visual effects for movies. I often found the work frustrating and aggravating – partially I think because I never abandoned my feeling that "work" was supposed to be "self-realization" in some way.

I know that it is unrealistic to think that work is supposed to be soul-satisfying. Labor is part of the curse of being expelled from the Garden of Eden. This applies to gainful employment as well as childbirth. One has to separate poetry from work. T.S. Elliott was a banker; Wallace Stevens was an insurance executive. As Dorothy Parker said you need to earn enough money to keep body and soul apart. And yet... Much of the blather in popular culture about following your bliss or pursuing your dream is an expression of this same yearning. People want to identify with the activities that consume most of their waking hours.

At one point in my "career" I got a job as editor and business manager of a magazine. I told myself it was going to be a nice steady 9:00 to 5:00 job, but I threw myself into it working long hours trying to improve the magazine because I wanted it to be something I could identify with. I got myself fired, because I was not attentive enough to the goals of the group that owned the magazine.

When I was trying to be a filmmaker I wanted to think of films as art rather than entertainment. The difference to my mind was that entertainment starts with the audience and art starts with the material. If I had a script or an idea, I never had the confidence to get beyond the idea that I was asking someone to fund my desire to express myself rather than offering him or her a chance to make money with something the audience was clamoring for. Some people are lucky in the way their desires for self-expression coincide with the interests of a large audience. Hugh Hefner made hundreds of millions of dollars because his own desires complemented the desires of a large segment of the population. He was not cynically pandering to the interests of readers. He was trying to make himself into what he wanted to be in the eyes of the world, and the world bought lots of tickets to the show.

Traditionally it has been primarily aristocrats and artists who have been able to devote themselves to activities that they love, although the cliché of the "starving artist" indicates that the work of artists is not always valued by society at large. Normal working stiffs have to do necessary jobs to earn a living. I doubt that anyone ever followed his bliss down into a coal mine. There is, of course, a wide spectrum between artistic self-expression and slave labor, and the traditional craftsman is supposed to be someone who can take pride in the skill with which he produces useful and often beautiful necessities. A lot of our political ideology is rooted in the myth of the yeoman farmer, whose sense of self is presumably nourished by his independence and his relationship to "the land." The idea that work should be "meaningful" has a strong hold on our imagination. Even now when a host of economic and social factors have undermined job security, social media seems to be promoting the idea that every person's work can be a journey of self-creation and fulfillment. Perhaps I'm just an old curmudgeon, but I don't buy it. It is going to take a great deal more than thinking in terms of "branding" to create a society in which everyone can lead a healthy, productive life thanks to a satisfying job.

Technology and automation, which were supposed to eliminate much of the drudgery in work, seem to me to have created as many mind-numbingly repetitive tasks as they have eliminated. Part of the problem may be the way digital technology and financial markets conspired to recast the American Dream as hitting it big in your 20s with a tech venture that goes public rather than working 40 years in an automobile plant so that you can own a home and send your kids to college – upward mobility as a rocket launch rather than a mountain climb.

Perhaps the American Dream has always been conflicted about hard work. The worm in its heart is the fantasy of hitting the jackpot and achieving financial independence (i.e. voluntary unemployment). Before tech startups there had always been the Next Big Thing, some invention or marketing gimmick which would become a cash cow, or the dream of discovering gold or oil. I don't know when it started, but I recall in the 70s and 80s there was a deluge of opportunities to buy books or attend seminars to learn the secret of achieving financial independence – perhaps by marketing books and seminars about achieving financial independence. The stock market also morphed into a giant open-air casino in which the little guy could hit it big, though of course this was just a rerun of the run-up to the Crash in the 20s. We respect hard-working Americans, but it seems we would really prefer not to have to work.

I can't resist another aside about our attitude towards work. It seems to me that for some the real point of work is to attain a certain status in society. This status may involve having power over others or it may just require conspicuous consumption designed to elevate one in the eyes of the beholder. Perhaps people have always been motivated by a desire for fame, but it does seem as though the aspiration to be a celebrity is a much more common motivator these days, and it has nothing to do with the desire to be productive or contribute in some meaningful way to improvement of life on earth. An acquaintance in my youth, who went on to become a very successful and highly regarded writer and director, once referred to his salad days as "being a nobody." People are driven by other things that a need to feel productive.

Economics tends to present inequality or social hierarchy as an outcome of the system caused by differences in abilities, circumstances and luck. It may be that social hierarchy is more fundamental than economics, and what we know as economics is the perpetuation of that hierarchy even if there is a bit of musical chairs involved.

Surely one of the primary goals of economic policy should be full employment. Why isn't there an inalienable right to earn a living? Why is it OK if even 5% of the people who want to work cannot find jobs? Does that mean it is OK for 5% of the workforce and the families dependent on them to go without food, clothing and shelter? Article 23 of the Universal Declaration of Human Rights adopted by the UN General Assembly begins:

> (1) Everyone has the right to work, to free choice of employment, to just and favourable conditions of work and to protection against unemployment.[86]

Some unemployment may be inevitable with technological progress as older industries get displaced by newer ones, but surely providing new training to people who lose jobs due to "progress" should be a top priority on a par with any other investment. If the current economic system cannot produce full employment, then we need to keep looking for a better system. Is there really not enough work to go around, or is there just no access to the money to pay the wages involved in full employment? Even a superficial survey of the infrastructure in any community in the U.S. will surely reveal there is plenty of work to be done; so wouldn't it be nice if Ann Pettifor is right, and there is always "enough money" for socially necessary projects?

Muhammad Yunus, the father of microcredit, is convinced that the best way to fight unemployment is to enable more people to become small business owners. His microcredit and mentoring programs have demonstrated that small loans to individuals who could never qualify for normal financing can make a very large difference, not only in the lives of the individuals but in overall economy of their communities. While he initially focused on marginalized women in rural Bangladesh, he has demonstrated that the model can be adapted to urban communities in the U.S. or Europe as well. He has achieved impressive results, but I cannot buy the idea that a flood of small businesses could ever solve unemployment in an economy as large as that of the United States. If a plant lays off 500 workers in order to relocate to Asia, it seems unlikely that reverting to a cottage industry economy with 500 "entrepreneurs" offering homemade products or individual services can compensate for the loss of the plant payroll. In the current system small businesses have a hard time competing with large corporate franchises or on-line retailers, and it may be that fighting unemployment in a community will require insulating the local economy from the global economy in some way. The question of unemployment becomes the question of what it takes to make any given community economically viable and obviously there is no one-size-fits-all solution.

Birmingham, where I grew up, was known as "The Magic City" because it sprang up and grew so quickly during the last decades of the 19th century. It happened because the area had all three natural resources required for making steel: iron ore, coal and limestone. There was also an abundance of cheap labor and a political establishment that kept it that way – even to the point of "leasing" convicts to work the mines and steel mills. While there is still a steel industry in Birmingham, over the last 60 years progress and competition has resulted in the closing of most of the mines and mills, and now Birmingham is known mostly for its medical center and interesting restaurants rather than being "The Pittsburgh of the South." For a hundred years, however, the iron and steel industry was the backbone of the economy in the area. It required or attracted a host of other business and enabled the city to flourish.

Many cities are like this. Something about its location on a river or the presence of natural resources will provide the economic basis for the diverse businesses that permit a city to be self-sustaining and grow. My father grew up in a mill town, where the river was conducive to generating power for a cotton mill that could draw on the cotton fields in central Alabama. Again the mill and the town flourished for about a hundred years before competition made the mill no longer viable, and the city had to hustle up other industries to support the its economy. Local economies of this sort seem to depend on a larger external market to sustain them, and it is hard to imagine anything other than a relatively primitive agricultural community that could be truly self-sustaining. Now it seems there is a trend in which even the local businesses are replaced by outlets for large national or international corporations. It seems to be increasingly hard for a "mom and pop" retailer to compete with the likes of Walmart or Costco, not to mention Amazon.com. It might seem that corporate outlets would support the same level of employment, but they are also siphoning money off from the local economy so that there is less circulating to support local business. In any given community employment levels seem to be at the mercy of the ups and downs of the national or global economy. Insulating a local economy against global winds may be possible to some extent, but it is hard to imagine how any local economy can be self-sustaining these days without the help of a larger market.

One obvious remedy for at least some unemployment is publicly funded infrastructure projects including repair and maintenance ones that can use relatively unskilled labor. Even though the public works programs of the New Deal surely made a difference in the recovery from the Depression, many skeptics will say that it was really the Second World War that ended the Depression in the U.S. Voters today seem to view the idea of the government funded public works as a ticket to pork-barrel make-work projects plagued by bureaucratic waste and inefficiency – "bridges to nowhere."

Also job training programs could be provided for anyone who cannot find work. I have the impression that "on-the-job training" used to be much more common than it is now. Businesses and professions offering the potential for higher-paying careers seem to prefer non-paid "internships" as a way of screening new hires. Businesses at the other end of the spectrum seem to be struggling too much to hire untrained raw talent rather than someone who has already been trained or gained experience. The task of training workers has been "out-sourced" in a way to "technical schools" since public education seems to have abandoned any goals of "manual training" as somehow unworthy of the students. Struggling taxpayers do not want to turn over more of their hard-earned money to pay to train more workers, so the job falls to for-profit schools, some of which may offer valuable training while others are clearly focused on profiting from student loan programs.

Classical economic theory in its purest form seems to regard all unemployment as voluntary. This seemingly perverse assumption apparently derives from the belief that a free market economy naturally tends towards an equilibrium which produces full employment in the sense that anyone who is not working is choosing not to because his "rationally" evaluated leisure time is worth more to him than the wage he could earn. I hope that I am oversimplifying this theory as much as I hope that no serious economist still believes that all unemployment is "voluntary."

Clearly connecting every available worker with an appropriate job is a monumental task in large complex economy especially when it is subjected to external influences of the global economy. Technical progress, competition and changing consumer preferences will always produce a certain amount of turnover in employment. Every year new "workers" are entering the "market." It seems naive to me to assume that if we sit back and let things sort themselves out, the "market" will provide the best resolution possible. The market is biased towards maximizing profits not fully utilizing resources, and a certain amount of unemployment helps keep wages down in many businesses. No single employer is going to think, "I'll hire more workers and raise my prices or cut my profits in the short term, because if all businesses did that the economy would grow and we'd all be better off." One employer may recognize that widespread unemployment is bad for his business because it means there is less purchasing power out there for his own products or services, but he is not in a position to do anything about it except to vote. If he is persuaded that what is good for General Bullmoose is good for the country,[87] he may vote for the wrong candidate.

Statisticians told us that unemployment in January 2018 was 4.1% and was lower than it had been since 2001. By some standards this indicates that the economy was doing well. I am not at all convinced that a majority of the people in the country would agree with that assessment. Beside the 40 million people living in poverty, there seem to be a lot of people struggling to make ends meet by working multiple jobs or part time jobs. That does not seem like "doing well" to me. Obviously the pandemic in 2020 made things even worse.

One of the obstacles to achieving true full employment is a conviction that there is a trade-off between full employment and inflation. Inflation or even the threat of inflation seems to have nudged out unemployment in terms of the priorities involved in setting monetary and fiscal policy. It seems as though managing levels of unemployment has become a tool for combating inflation.

It is hard to know who suffers most from inflation. Obviously the unemployed person with no income has an even harder time buying the things he needs if prices keep going up, but I have the impression that the most vocal opponents of inflation are wealthier people who are concerned about the declining value of their savings. Does it say something about our values if we are more concerned with protecting the assets of the "haves" than the livelihood of the "have-nots?" Am I the only one who is skeptical of the wisdom of taking a "longer view" in which preventing inflation is more important than feeding and clothing 40 million people? Is it really clear that inflation is inevitable and will make us all worse off? Perhaps the more urgent question is what can be done to eliminate or reduce unemployment.

If voters will not authorize the government to create new jobs with infrastructure projects, what other fiscal or monetary policies can be implemented to create jobs? It can reduce taxes so that people have more money to spend and the increased demand for consumer products will result in the need for more workers to produce them. The problem with this is that increased demand for products may just result in higher prices rather increased production or it may just be met with an increase in productivity of the existing workforce rather than more hiring.

Another angle on cutting taxes in order to boost the economy is the argument that wealthier taxpayers will invest the money thereby earning for themselves the title of "Job Creators." Whether they will invest as venture capitalists rather than simply purchasing less risky financial assets is unspecified. Needless to say I am not convinced that allowing taxpayers to put more money in their investment portfolios rather than turn it over to the government is as effective in boosting the economy as direct government spending on new infrastructure projects. The path from investment in stocks and bonds to reduction of unemployment is circuitous at best and probably depends on rising stock prices and the increased availability of credit. This may be a reason some theorists will say that the best weapon to combat unemployment is monetary policy which makes credit more readily available to businesses.

The problem with using monetary policy to fight unemployment is that businesses will not be interested in borrowing money to expand production unless they have some reason to believe that there is a demand for more of their product than they are currently able to produce. Increasing the supply of money without some corresponding increase in the demand for products does nothing to boost investment and employment.

Ultimately what is needed is more of a bird's eye view of employment and money. Instead of looking at society through the lens of economics, we need to see economics from the perspective of society. There is clearly work that needs to be done. There are large numbers of people who have no job or are not making enough money to live decently. The reason to offer training and employment opportunities is not to further line the pockets of a small number of businessmen, but because we want everyone to have a decent life. If we only want to "reward" people who are productive, we owe everyone the opportunity to be productive.

What are we really saying when we say "We can't afford to pay everyone a decent wage"? Why isn't there enough money circulating in the economy to keep it healthy? From a macro perspective surely the problem is not the amount of money circulating but the distribution and use of that money. With the current system it seems that additional money or credit injected into the economy by whatever method tends to migrate into banks and hedge funds and investment portfolios of the wealthy. Some may find its way into the hands of venture capitalists funding startups or even into small business loans, but not enough to produce full employment.

Most discussions of unemployment are based on the application of supply and demand theory to labor and wages. This can lead to the conclusion that minimum wage requirements are detrimental for employment because they may make labor so expensive that the demand is not sufficient to provide jobs for everyone who wants to work. This seems to me to be a backwards approach to the issue which is really a way of abdicating responsibility for the way we live by hoping that some natural "market forces" can solve our problem better than we can. If decent wages make the cost of a product too great for it to be viable in the marketplace, then we either need to subsidize its production or live without it. If subsidizing the production of necessities requires some form of income redistribution, it is surely worth it.

What could we expect if we restructured finance in the ways outlined above – eliminating financial markets, interest-bearing loans and restrictions on "deficit spending" by the government? Government investment in infrastructure and job training as well as research and development could conceivably generate enough additional jobs to keep everyone employed especially when combined with credit provided by banks to local businesses. The main obstacles seem to be the bugaboo of inflation and perhaps the fear of "statism."

There is another aspect of unemployment, however, which would require some other remedy. Many people lose their jobs because factories where they work are relocated abroad or the production is simply outsourced to a foreign company. If local investment attempted to resurrect the factory, it would be competing with the foreign factory at a great disadvantage unless there is some way to level the playing field in foreign trade.

Foreign Trade

The hopeful myth about foreign trade is that each country has its own unique resources and skill sets so that international trade functions as a kind of division of labor that benefits all. Your climate is conducive to growing cotton; our technology and population density are conducive to textile mills. You sell us cotton; we'll sell you fabrics. We'll all be better off.

An extension of this idea is found in Samuelson and Nordhaus as "the elegant theory of comparative advantage."[88]

> It is only common sense that countries will produce and export goods for which they are uniquely qualified. But there is a deeper principle underlying all trade—in a family, within a nation, and among nations—that goes beyond common sense. The principle of comparative advantage holds that a country can benefit from trade even if it is absolutely more efficient (or absolutely less efficient) than other countries in the production of every good. Indeed, trade according to comparative advantage provides mutual benefits to all countries.[89]

It is initially a little unclear what claims are being made on behalf of this "deeper principle underlying all trade." The principle, which is elsewhere labeled a "law," was first formulated by David Ricardo in the 19th century. He derived it by analyzing a hypothetical situation involving two products and two countries: wine and cloth in Portugal and England. Portugal is more efficient at producing wine than cloth and England is more efficient at producing cloth than wine. In absolute terms Portugal may be more efficient than England in producing both wine and cloth, but the fact that each country is more efficient relatively in producing a different product from the other means that both countries can benefit from trading if they each specialize in the product where they are relatively more efficient. Ricardo's analysis of makes a host of assumptions and is presented in purely verbal logical terms, but others following him were able to express the principle with simple math which lent itself to a neat graphical representation.

Samuelson and Nordhaus use an example based on food and clothing in America and Europe, and they analyze the efficiency of production in terms of "opportunity costs" rather than simply basing it on an "amount of labor." This enables them to incorporate the concept of the "production potential frontier" for each country into their graphical presentation. They also expand it to explain how the world market gravitates towards an equilibrium price for the products. Their presentation, however, seems basically to be an endorsement of Ricardo's original argument.

> The principle of comparative advantage holds that each country will benefit if it specializes in the production and export of those goods that it can produce at relatively low cost. Conversely, each country will benefit if it imports those goods which it produces at relatively high cost.
>
> This simple principle provides the unshakable basis for international trade.[90]

Whether the existence of comparative advantage gives rise to foreign trade in the first place or whether it is discovered after trade has begun for other reasons is perhaps debatable. The real point of the analysis seems to be an argument in favor of free trade and even an argument that "outsourcing" is just another instance of comparative advantage working to everyone's mutual benefit.

Needless to say the concept of comparative advantage has had its critics. Some have pointed out that trade relations between England and Portugal in the 18th century were a great deal more complicated than Ricardo's hypothetical account and others have made arguments undercutting Ricardo's analysis because it is based simply on a labor theory of value with "labor" somehow being completely homogenous. More importantly it has been argued that all of the assumptions about perfect competition or flexible prices and wages make the theory irrelevant to real-world trade. It can also be shown that often international trade involves monopolies and commodities where economies of scale can be exploited to achieve dominance in a world market. Protectionist policies and subsidies or other forms of government intervention can also give a developing economy a chance to build up its own industries to a point where they can compete on the world market.

Most economist will concede that there are circumstances in the real world which may justify "strategic" trade policies if not protectionist policies like tariffs and quotas. Nonetheless the textbook conclusion is that free trade is ultimately best for all:

> Notwithstanding its limitations, the theory of comparative advantage is one of the deepest truths in all of economics. Nations that disregard comparative advantage pay a heavy price in terms of their living standards and economic growth.[91]

When Paul Krugman felt compelled to reassess the case for free trade in 1987, he began:

> If there were an Economist's Creed, it would surely contain the affirmations "I understand the Principle of Comparative Advantage" and "I advocate Free Trade." For one hundred seventy years, the appreciation that international trade benefits a country whether it is "fair" or not has been one of the touchstones of professionalism in economics. Comparative advantage is not just an idea both simple and profound; it is an idea that conflicts directly with both stubborn popular prejudices and powerful interests. This combination makes the defense of free trade as close to a sacred tenet as any idea in economics.[92]

One of the "stubborn popular prejudices" that conflicts with the idea of comparative advantage is the idea that our economy suffers when cheap labor in other countries lets foreign businesses sell products more cheaply in the U.S. than they can be sold by domestic producers. It also encourages U.S. manufacturers to relocate their plants abroad to improve their competitiveness and their profits, regardless of the impact that such a move has on unemployment at home. Our economics textbook tells us that wages are determined by productivity and that outsourcing can in the long run be seen to be just another way in which comparative advantage can benefit both countries.

Samuelson and Nordhaus consider the argument that free trade agreements like NAFTA will harm the U.S. economy by driving down domestic wages and thereby reducing our standard of living.

> This argument sounds plausible, but it is all wrong because it ignores the principle of comparative advantage. The reason American workers have higher wages is that they are on average more productive. If America's wage is 5 times that in Mexico, it is because the marginal product of American workers is on average 5 times that of Mexican workers. Trade flows according to comparative advantage, not wage rates or absolute advantage. ...

The cheap-foreign-labor argument is flawed because it ignores the theory of comparative advantage. A country will benefit from trade even though its wages are far above those of its trading partners. High wages come from high efficiency, not from tariff protection.[93]

They also view outsourcing as a form of trade in services rather than goods and agree with their colleague Alan Blinder's "careful analysis":

> Rich countries such as the United States will have to reorganize the nature of work to exploit their big advantage in non-tradable services: they are close to where the money is. That will mean, in part, specializing more in the delivery of services where personal presence is either imperative or highly beneficial. Thus, the U.S. work force of the future will likely have more divorce lawyers and fewer attorneys who write routine contracts, more internists and fewer radiologists, more salespeople and fewer typists. The market system is very good at making adjustments like these, even massive ones. It has done so before and will do so again. But it takes time and can move in unpredictable ways.[94]

That last caveat is similar to textbook's caveat in its description of how the labor markets adjusts to the needs of comparative advantage:

> Over the long run, labor markets will reallocate workers from declining to advancing industries, but the transition may be costly for many people.[95]

It appears that it may take the labor market a generation or more to adjust to these changes, and obviously that is not an attractive solution politically or even morally. The other caveat one discovers eventually is that there is no guarantee about how the "benefits" of comparative advantage will be distributed. What is good for the bottom line of multinational corporations and their shareholders is not necessarily good for the rest of the population, especially when large numbers of workers are laid off and find their skills are no longer in demand anywhere near where they live.

These are the some of the considerations that lead economists as well as politicians to advocate "strategic trade policies" and lead Paul Krugman to conclude

> free trade is not passé, but it is an idea that has irretrievably lost its innocence. Its status has shifted from optimum to reasonable rule of thumb. There is still a case for free trade

as a good policy, and as a useful target in the practical world of politics, but it can never again be asserted as the policy that economic theory tells us is always right.[96]

Nonetheless Krugman still considers the principle of comparative advantage useful and relevant to the 21st century. The textbook *International Economics: Theory & Policy* that he wrote with Maurice Obstfeld and Marc J. Melitz begins its discussion of international trade theory with a discussion of comparative advantage and says

> In sum, while few economists believe that the Ricardian model is a fully adequate description of the causes and consequences of world trade, its two principal implications—that productivity differences play an important role in international trade and that it is comparative rather than absolute advantage that matters—do seem to be supported by the evidence.[97]

In 1998 Krugman was so frustrated by the way in which "intellectuals who are interested in economic issues so consistently balk at the concept of comparative advantage" that he wrote an essay analyzing the problem.[98] He concluded there were three reasons:

> (i) At the shallowest level, some intellectuals reject comparative advantage simply out of a desire to be intellectually fashionable. Free trade, they are aware, has some sort of iconic status among economists; so, in a culture that always prizes the avant-garde, attacking that icon is seen as a way to seem daring and unconventional.
>
> (ii) At a deeper level, comparative advantage is a harder concept than it seems, because like any scientific concept it is actually part of a dense web of linked ideas. A trained economist looks at the simple Ricardian model and sees a story that can be told in a few minutes; but in fact to tell that story so quickly one must presume that one's audience understands a number of other stories involving how competitive markets work, what determines wages, how the balance of payments adds up, and so on.
>
> (iii) At the deepest level, opposition to comparative advantage -- like opposition to the theory of evolution -- reflects the aversion of many intellectuals to an essentially mathematical way of understanding the world. Both comparative advantage and natural selection are ideas grounded, at base, in mathematical models -- simple models

that can be stated without actually writing down any equations, but mathematical models all the same.

Krugman called his essay "Ricardo's Difficult Idea" in an explicit reference to Daniel Dennett's book *Darwin's Dangerous Idea: Evolution and the Meanings of Life*. Part of his objective is to equate economics with evolutionary biology as forms of scientific thinking based on mathematical modeling. The use of mathematical modeling in economics is to my mind somehow problematic. The principle of comparative advantage is built on a highly simplified imaginary situation similarly to the principle of supply and demand, which is itself eventually incorporated into the fully developed concept of a comparative advantage. Perhaps Krugman's analysis of comparative advantage and the mathematical way of understanding the world can help clarify my hesitations about mathematical modeling and economic thought.

Following Krugman's example in his essay I shall begin my putting all my cards on the table. I believe politics and economics are a form of moral discourse. They are both about values and how we choose to live. Math and science can be useful tools for exploring the consequences of our choices, but they cannot determine what we should choose. No amount of climate science will persuade us to live in a sustainable way if we believe other things are more urgent or important than the longterm survival of life on earth. Moreover mathematical science cannot fully account for human behavior. I have the impression that Daniel Dennett inadvertently provided evidence of this.

A philosophical mentor suggested I try Dennett's book on natural selection after I indicated how impressed I was by volume two of Susanne Langer's *Mind: An Essay on Human Feeling*. Langer is best known for her earlier works on aesthetics (*Philosophy in a New Key* and *Form and Feeling*), but the culmination of her work on symbolic thought is her attempt to examine how the human mind differs from an animal mind using the evidence of evolutionary biology and anthropology. I had never been particularly interested in evolutionary biology and had long since abandoned any idea that science could help me understand the philosophical quandaries the haunted me, but I found Langer's *Mind* to be an extraordinarily illuminating work. The line between philosophy and science dissolved for me in a way that I had never felt with more traditional "philosophy of science." Her interpretation of the scientific evidence was obviously inspired by her sensitivity to the emotional significance of art and music, and her ideas about the significance of language and culture seemed as profound as any philosophy I had read.

Dennett, on the other hand, comes out of the philosophy of mind tradition at Oxford and Harvard, a tradition which I always felt was sterile. His attempt to explain natural selection as an algorithmic process was clear and made sense to me because of my familiarity with computer programming. His attempt to "explain" morality and religion based on evolution and natural selection, however, seemed misguided and based on a narrow view of "mind" as algorithmic decision making. There was none of the appreciation for imagination and feeling that infused Langer's book. In the end I felt his discussions of values and diversity were confused and self-contradictory because his basic argument was unable to incorporate the full significance of language and culture.

Krugman's idea of evolutionary biology is a strain of thought stemming from the work of John Maynard Smith, who pioneered the application of game theory to evolution. Krugman likes Dennett's interpretation of natural selection as an algorithmic process that can be expressed mathematically. He contrasts him and the like-minded Richard Dawkins with Stephen Gould, who he admits is by far the most popular writer on evolutionary biology. He concludes that Gould's popularity is based to some extent on the quality of his writing, but he goes on to cite a deeper reason:

> No, what makes Gould so popular with intellectuals is not merely the quality of his writing but the fact that, unlike Dawkins or Ridley, he is not trying to explain the essentially mathematical logic of modern evolutionary theory. It's not just that there are no equations or simulations in his books; he doesn't even think in terms of the mathematical models that inform the work of writers like Dawkins. That is what makes his work so appealing. The problem, of course, is that evolutionary theory -- the real thing – is based on mathematical models; indeed, increasingly it is based on computer simulation. And so the very aversion to mathematics that makes Gould so appealing to his audience means that his books, while they may seem to his readers to contain deep ideas, seem to people who actually know the field to be mere literary confections with little serious intellectual content, and much of that simply wrong. In

particular, readers whose ideas of evolution are formed by reading Gould's work get no sense of the power and reach of the theory of natural selection -- if anything, they come away with a sense that modern thought has shown that theory to be inadequate.

I have never read anything by Gould, but the little I have read about his work gives me the impression that he never intended to say that natural selection was not an important factor in evolution, only that there were several other factors that needed to be considered as well. If natural selection has been revealed to be "inadequate," it is inadequate in the same way Krugman says the Ricardian model is when he says "few economists believe that the Ricardian model is a fully adequate description of the causes and consequences of world trade, its two principal implications."[99]

Krugman seems to have defined evolutionary biology as a theory based on the mathematical modeling of an algorithm of natural selection, so any theory that does not conform to this model is not "the real thing." Krugman could have chosen another example of mathematical modeling in science. My first choice would have been mathematical modeling and computer simulation in meteorology.

There is a wonderful website summarizing the history of weather forecasting and the development of mathematical models for the weather.[100] Until the 20th century weather was predicted by detailed mapping of atmospheric conditions over time and looking for patterns or trends. The pioneers in "numerical" weather forecasting were a Norwegian mathematician and physicist, Vilhelm Bjerknes, and a British mathematician, Lewis Fry Richardson. Bjerknes applied research in hydrodynamics and thermodynamics to compute the future state of the atmosphere given a set of initial conditions. He realized his equations required an impossible amount of computing power, but he believed that eventually meteorology would be able to predict the weather by solving mathematical equations. Fry simplified Bjerknes' equations to a form that could be solved by arithmetic and yield approximate results. His first attempt in 1916 to calculate a 6 hour forecast retroactively from data that gathered all over Europe in 1910 was completely inaccurate, but he continued to pursue his work, publishing a book in 1921 entitled *Weather Prediction by Numerical Process*. He imagined the amount of computing power it would take in terms of a large facility filled with 64,000 people doing calculations in a way very similar to parallel processing in a super computer. He abandoned his work when it received insufficient recognition, and it was not until the development of the computer that his research was taken up again by team at the Princeton Institute for Advanced Study in the 1940's.

Chaos theory, which Krugman almost seems to equate with deliberate obfuscation for the sake of novelty, was partially developed by a meteorologist, Edward Lorenz, and is part of the reason computational forecasting has achieved the degree of accuracy that it has. It is also the primary reason that meteorologists recognize that it is essentially impossible to predict the weather with any accuracy for more than a 10-day window even using the most powerful super-computers available.

Obviously the mathematical modeling in meteorology is very different from the mathematical modeling involved in the concept of comparative advantage. Meteorology begins with massive amounts of data on the current state of the atmosphere and several very complex equations from hydrodynamics and thermodynamics. The theory of comparative advantage begins with a hypothetical relationship between two countries making two products with differing degrees of productivity, but the simple graphs used to illustrate the implications of trade between these two countries are not the end of the story.

> After all, economists are familiar with a number of reasons why the gains from free trade may not work out quite as easily as in the simplest Ricardian model. External economies may mean underinvestment in import-competing sectors; imperfect competition may lead to a strategic competition over industry rents; because of distortions in domestic labor markets, imports may reduce wages or cause unemployment; and so on. And even if national income rises as a result of trade, the distribution of income within a country may shift in a way that hurts large groups. In short, there are a number of sophisticated extensions to and qualifications of the model introduced in the first few chapters of the undergraduate textbook (typically covered later in the book...).[101]

Starting an examination of international trade with the Ricardian model may be a bit like starting a discussion of weather forecasting with a demonstration that condensation or precipitation in a hermetically sealed terrarium is a function of the temperature of the air inside it. No one would challenge the observed correlation of temperature and precipitation, but the question is how relevant it is in deciding how or where to grow a particular crop or perhaps whether that is even the best starting point for the discussion.

At one point Krugman addresses the idea that too many simplifying assumptions render a model irrelevant to the real world:

> In sum, while the concept of comparative advantage may seem utterly simple to economists, in order to achieve that simplicity one must invoke a number of principles and useful simplifying assumptions that seem natural and reasonable only to someone familiar with economic analysis in general. ("What do you mean, objects fall at the same rate regardless of how heavy they are -- if I drop a cannonball and a feather ... you're assuming away air resistance? Why would you do that?") Those principles and simplifying assumptions are indeed reasonable, but they are not obvious.[102]

Newton's law of gravitation as it applies to free fall in a vacuum may be useful in accounting for phenomena observed by astronomers, but it is not applicable in its simplest form to determining how long a sky diver has before he must open his parachute or how fast he will be going when he hits the ground if he fails to do so. I suspect that the principles and simplifying assumptions involved in the mathematical modeling of trade seem natural and reasonable to economists because they are so familiar and so ingrained in the way economics is taught. As Krugman says, comparative advantage is one of many "stories" the economist understands.

It seems ironically appropriate to me that Krugman refers to the linked ideas as "stories." The fact that these imagined relationships form a coherent whole that can be represented by math and graphs does not guarantee that they can predict how people will behave or how long it will take to achieve the stability implied by the system's tendency to achieve some kind of equilibrium.

The point of beginning the analysis of foreign trade with a discussion of comparative advantage is that is seems to provide an irrefutable argument for the idea that trade between two or more countries is mutually beneficial. What it demonstrates is that trade can be mutually beneficial in certain ways under certain conditions. What we make of that depends on what is deemed beneficial and whether the conditions are in fact satisfied.

By the time the textbook on international economics has added its consideration of other factors affecting trade and of models based on other sets of assumptions, it has changed the model to a "standard trade model" which is general enough for the simpler models to be taken as special cases.

> The standard trade model derives a world relative supply curve from production possibilities and a world relative demand curve from preferences. The price of exports relative to imports, a country's terms of trade, is determined by the intersection of the world relative supply and demand curves. Other things equal, a rise in a country's terms of trade increases its welfare. Conversely, a decline in a country's terms of trade will leave the country worse off.[103]

The primary function of this model seems to be to demonstrate four things:

1) The effect of growth on a country's terms of trade

2) The effect of import tariffs and export subsidies on the terms of trade

3) The effects of changes in terms of trade on a country's welfare.

4) How international finance can be analyzed as a type of trade.

The implications for economic policy derived from this analysis are

> A tariff unambiguously improves the country's terms of trade at the rest of the world's expense. An export subsidy has the reverse effect, increasing the relative supply and reducing the relative demand for the country's export good, and thus worsening the terms of trade. The terms of trade effects of an export subsidy hurt the subsidizing country and benefit the rest of the world, while those of a tariff do the reverse. This suggests that export subsidies do not make sense from a national point of view and that foreign export subsidies should be welcomed rather than countered. Both tariffs and subsidies, however, have strong effects on the distribution of income within countries, and these effects often weigh more heavily on policy than the terms of trade concerns.[104]

The consideration of whether the effects on the distribution of income are detrimental to a country's welfare begins with a caveat that strikes me as peculiar:

> When looking at the actual politics of trade policy, however, it becomes necessary to deal with the reality that there is no such thing as national welfare; there are only the desires of individuals, which get more or less imperfectly reflected in the objectives of government.
>
> How do the preferences of individuals get added up to produce the trade policy we actually see? There is no single, generally accepted answer, but there has been a growing body of economic analysis that explores models in which governments are assumed to be trying to maximize political success rather than an abstract measure of national welfare.[105]

Typically the textbook proceeds to explore various ways economists and political scientists have attempted to model the political process by which trade policies are established. As it does so, however, it continues to oppose irrational policies that benefit a few people with policies that "raise national welfare."[106] Presumably the national welfare is the sum of the satisfied preferences as measured by total consumption without regard to the distribution of that consumption. Before closing the book and looking elsewhere for a more adequate concept of national welfare, it may be worth noting all the assumptions underlying the standard trade model.

The standard trade model again starts with two countries producing two goods. It posits a "production possibility frontier" for each country as a smooth curve. The concept of such a curve is often introduced with the trade-offs available to a society in terms of producing guns and butter given its limited resources. More guns means less butter and vice versa. Such a curve is easy to visualize with two products. It is a bit more difficult to visualize with thousands of products, but I imagine it could be mathematically described as some kind of closed surface in a three dimensional space. I would not want to try to decipher a mathematical account of the effect of outlawing handguns on the consumption of organic butter in such a model.

The standard trade model assumes that "At given market prices, a market economy will choose production levels that maximize the value of its output."[107] That value is expressed in term of the price per unit of each product. The assumption is that if we produce 200 less pounds of butter valued at $3.50 a pound we will then produce one more handgun valued at $700. This would be a completely linear relationship represented by a straight line graph. The standard trade model allows for some complexity in the factors affecting production by making the graph a curve rather than a straight line.

The model then assumes that the consumption decisions of an entire economy "may be represented as if they were based on the tastes of a single representative individual." A footnote points out that this means that the effects of changing income distribution on demand are basically ignored for the model. Using the taste of a representative individual, however, makes possible the use of "indifference curves."

> The tastes of an individual can be represented graphically by a series of indifference curves. An indifference curve traces a set of combinations of cloth (C) and food (F) consumption that leave the individual equally well off.[108]

So we assume if "an individual is offered less food (F), then to be made equally well off, she must be given more cloth (C)."[109] I am not sure in what world a hungry person feels well off if they have more clothing. I can only assume that the authors of the text chose food and cloth as their representative products in order to make sure the reader appreciated the absurdity of a limited model.

The indifference curve enables the model to find the combined consumption of the two products which yields the highest possible welfare, and using this with the analysis of the relative prices of the two products, it can determine how much of each product needs to be imported or exported. Determining the implications of all this for international trade involves two more steps: translating world supply and demand curves into "relative" supply and demand curves for the two products and calculating the "terms of trade" for each country. A relative supply or demand curve for a given product expresses its price in terms of the equivalent price of a second product. Instead of plotting the supply of cloth against the price of cloth it plots the supply of cloth against the amount of food which can be purchased for the same amount. The equilibrium point for the world market for food and cloth is represented by the intersection of the relative supply and relative demand curves.

A country's "terms of trade" is the ratio of its exports to imports. It can refer to a generalized ratio of an index of prices for imported and exported goods, or it can be restricted to two products and two countries as it is in the simplified standard trade model. The analysis of the impact of trade on the welfare of a country starts with the ratio of the domestic prices of the two goods without any foreign trade and proceeds to compare it to what the ratio would be for prices on the world market. An increase in the terms of trade implies an increase in welfare for the domestic economy. Policies for foreign trade can then be evaluated by looking at their effect on the terms of trade. A decrease in the terms of trade would mean a decrease in welfare potentially to the point where trade does nothing to increase the welfare over what it would be without foreign trade. This analysis is essentially another way of demonstrating that comparative advantage is an incentive for foreign trade. To some extent the proposition that a nation is better off when the ratio of exports to imports increases seems like a reframing of the common sense notion that you are better off if you sell more than you buy.

Just as the development of financial institutions is inextricably entwined with the need to raise money for war, trade policy often has been formulated with a view to increasing one nation's wealth and power at the expense of another. Colonization is the extreme example of this, but numerous trade policies like protective tariffs, subsidized exports, and manipulated exchange rates can be used aggressively to maintain a nation's economic dominance. For hundreds of years in Europe a government's intervention in its nation's economy was a weapon in the virtually unending wars between nations. An enemy with a weaker economy was less able to mount armies and build navies. We are still haunted by this view of international trade as a zero sum game in which our national prestige and standard of living are at stake.

Foreign trade rarely takes place on a level playing field. Differences in resources and comparative advantage may be the primary impetus for foreign trade, but differences in standard of living, treatment of workers and government policies can complicate things. It is one thing to import raw materials we do not have or products we cannot make; it is quite another to import cheaper versions of products we already make, especially when the foreign products are made under conditions we consider appalling. The question is whether there is any way to level the playing field short of having one universal currency and equivalent wages and cost of living in all countries.

A positive balance in foreign trade would seem to imply that "we" are accumulating wealth at the expense of "them." This sounds as though it would be a good thing for us and a negative balance would be bad since "they" would be accumulating wealth at "our" expense. I was surprised to learn that many economists dismiss concerns about a negative trade balance because the dollars that other nations accumulate will eventually be invested in our economy. Mark J. Perry offered a concise version of this argument in an op-ed piece about the advantages of free trade in the Los Angeles Times:

> Let's start with two basic economic principles. First, countries don't engage in trade with each other — only businesses and consumers do. Second, when individuals engage in a voluntary market exchange, both parties — the buyer and the seller — are almost always made better off, because both parties get something they want. Trade is win-win, not win-lose as so many politicians these days would have us believe. ...
>
> When American businesses and consumers voluntarily purchase more products from China than Chinese businesses and consumers buy from us, it does lead to a U.S. trade deficit with China. But the trade deficit can't accurately be referred to a "loss," because it's based on millions of mutually agreeable individual exchanges that took place between a willing seller and a willing buyer.
>
> In fact, you could make a strong case that China "lost" last year on trade with America, not vice versa. After all, we acquired $482 billion of merchandise made in China and they acquired only $116 billion of merchandise made in the U.S., for a net merchandise surplus of $366 billion in our favor. China "lost" a net amount of $366 billion of goods that ended up being consumed and enjoyed by Americans.
>
> It would also be accurate to say that China gained a net amount of $366 billion worth of U.S. currency, the exact amount of the trade deficit. But what happened to those dollars? They aren't sitting idly somewhere. On the contrary, they quickly came back into the U.S. as a capital inflow to purchase America's financial assets like corporate stock and bonds, real estate, bank deposits and Treasury securities, and as foreign direct investment in America's factories and businesses.[110]

This is to my mind a perfect example of the how choice of a basic metaphor can lead to what might seem to some a counter-intuitive conclusion. If you stick to the basic idea that all economic activity boils down to transactions between individuals in which each obtains something desired, then you can declare all transactions to be win-win and claim that the more unfettered markets enable transactions the more everyone will win. If on the other hand you assume that a national economy functions like a household, it seems clear that buying more than you sell will eventually get you into hot water. Perry jumps out of the boiling pot by saying that dollars accumulated abroad will inevitably be invested in our economy thereby making us better off. Rather than viewing a negative trade balance as a debt that must eventually be settled, he sees it as simply one column in a bookkeeping system which is balanced by investment in another. An extension of this is the idea that dollars sent to one country will be spent in other countries and eventually work their way around the globe to being used to buy American goods and services.

To be fair Perry does acknowledge in passing that there may be some collateral damage:

> Economists almost universally agree that trade increases our prosperity and standard of living. Certainly there will always be short-run costs to trade — some American businesses may close and some workers may lose their jobs — but the significant benefits of trade always are much greater than the costs, making us stronger economically in the long run.
>
> It follows that restrictions on trade would make us poorer as a nation, not richer. The almost daily proposals to erect trade barriers with double-digit tariffs and the constant misinformed lamenting about America's trade deficit have brought "ignorant nonsense about economics" to new levels.[111]

Needless to say I balk at several points in his argument. I think many American workers might differ in the assessment of how the benefits of trade outweigh the "short-run costs" unless there were a much larger safety net for workers who lose their jobs as businesses close or relocate abroad. If one of the benefits of trade was that it supported social welfare programs rather than simply increased profits to corporations, Perry's argument might find a more receptive audience. The issue here, though, goes beyond free trade vs. protectionism. It is a matter of the overall context within which trade takes place and how the "short-run costs" are handled.

The idea that it is good for foreign investors to own American businesses, real estate and Treasury bonds might also be debated. I like the idea that Honda, Toyota and Mercedes have manufacturing plants in the U.S., but in the abstract it does seem to me that there may be a limit to how much foreign investment is good for a country. At some point, perhaps, it amounts to a kind of colonization given the social and political influence that big business can have. One need only look at some struggling African nations to begin to question the benefits of foreign investment.

Obviously foreign trade can have a positive effect on the economy as it provides sources for raw materials and vast markets for products. I never thought about foreign trade when I was young. Certainly growing up in the '40s and '50s I didn't see "Made In China" stamped on many of the toys or things I owned. Mostly in my youth I associated English and European products with quality. The main reason to buy an imported item was to get something better than what was made in the U.S.. At first Asian goods were regarded as cheap junk, but that began to change with cameras and audio products. Then Japanese technology began to improve exponentially, and before we knew it Americans were scared that Japan was going to conquer the world by economic means. Foreign trade became a hot political issue.

Actually foreign trade had been an issue for at least a decade even though the average citizen may not have been paying any attention to it. The problem was the amount of dollars held abroad. When currencies were based on gold, two nations trading with each other could settle their accounts with gold. A nation that sold us more than we sold them could exchange their surplus dollars for gold from our reserves. Even after currencies were no longer tied to gold for domestic purposes, exchange rates were still more or less fixed relative to gold, and gold was still used to settle international accounts. If we sold a country more than we have bought from them, they would send us gold to settle the account. The problem with this set up of course is that we lose gold if our foreign trade balance is negative. A negative trade balance and years of capitol flowing from the U.S. via loans meant that U.S. gold reserves had been reduced to a point where they could not possibly settle all the foreign accounts. Nixon "temporarily suspended" the convertibility of the dollar to gold, letting the value of the dollar "float" relative to gold. Gold became a commodity like any other whose value fluctuated, and exchange rates between currencies began to be determined by "the market." Surplus dollars in other countries were used to purchase assets other than gold.

Foreign investors have used their dollars to purchase everything from real estate to treasury bonds. If the central bank in a foreign country ends up with a surplus of dollars, the chances are good that they will buy treasury bonds. This creates a situation which many view as the U.S. government being in debt to a foreign country (or its central bank). It's bad enough if foreign investors are buying up houses in the neighborhood or buying companies that seemed like American institutions, but the idea that we as a country are in debt to other nations seems dangerous somehow. What if the Chinese decided to sell all their treasury bonds at once? Whether there would ever be any incentive for them to do so or what the repercussions of such a move would be for the U.S. and China is a very complicated issue. The average voter in me tends not to worry about it simply based on the impression that in addition to whatever havoc it might wreak on the U.S. economy, China would be shooting itself in the foot by undermining its own export business and even its purchasing power in the global economy. Some economists will say, however, that the flood of Chinese held dollars into the market for Treasury bonds was one of the factors contributing to the financial crisis of 2007-2008.

> Because the Chinese were accumulating so much cash and needed a safe place to invest it, they dramatically increased the demand for U.S. Treasury bonds. That pushed interest rates in the United States down to unprecedented lows, which contributed to easy money being available to finance even the riskiest mortgages and, with them, the mortgage-backed securities and their derivatives that eventually drove the economy into the abyss.[112]

This attempt to shift some of the blame for the financial crisis onto foreign trade policies to my mind only underscores the need for better regulation or oversight in the mortgage industry. Obviously if credit for purchasing homes was handled in a different way, "easy money" for risky mortgages and mortgage-backed securities would no longer be an issue.

Another way in which trade deficits may affect the economy, which Perry does not mention, is the impact on the "strength" of the dollar relative to other currencies. Most economists may have accepted that the gold standard is a thing of the past, but Perry's argument does not seem to address the way fluctuations in the value of national currencies can impact the global economy. Foreign currency exchange rates may be the monkey wrench in trade imbalances.

I'm not aware of any concerns about trade imbalances between Alabama and California, even though each has its own unique economic circumstances. Alabama may attract businesses that California would like to have by offering tax and wage incentives, but California is not going to retaliate by imposing tariffs on goods made in Alabama. Californians may view the bankruptcy of a county in Alabama as an alarming sign of the times, but they are not going to vote to send financial aid to the county. Some Californians do worry about businesses relocating to other states with less burdensome wages, taxes and regulations, and sometimes the competition between states for businesses seems to be a race to the bottom in terms of living standards and environmental quality. Of course Alabama and California share more than a common currency. They are both subject to the same federal laws and speak more or less the same language.

When most "average voters" think about economic competition with other countries, most likely they think about jobs being lost because of cheap imports or because of businesses relocating overseas. In many instances it is so much cheaper to make things abroad and ship them here that any American business looking to maximize its profits is bound to consider making its product overseas. One assumes the main reason for this is the cost of labor abroad. Comparing the real cost of labor in one economy to that in another is a complex matter, but deciding whether to pay $2 an hour or $15 an hour for the same amount of labor is a no-brainer for any businessman who learned his multiplication tables in the third grade.

The relocation of a manufacturing plant from Ohio to Mexico or Thailand is motivated by the same things as the relocation of a plant from California to Alabama: lower wages, non-union workers, and various forms of government subsidies. A company may be able to physically move its plant equipment to a new site and train a new workforce for less than the cost of continuing to operate at its current location. Textbooks tell us that wage rates in any country are determined by productivity. Krugman uses the idea of comparative advantage to make the case that trade is always beneficial to a country even if it looks as though workers are being "exploited" because their wages are so much lower than those in the country to which it is exporting its products.

> If one is asking about the desirability of free trade, however, the point is not to ask whether low-wage workers deserve to be paid more but to ask whether they and their country are worse off exporting goods based on low wages than they would be if they refused to enter into such demeaning trade. And in asking this question, one must also ask, What is the alternative?[113]

Let's start with the most extreme example of outsourcing. Suppose a manufacturer in the U.S. shut its factory and shipped all its equipment to Bangladesh and set up shop in an abandoned warehouse. It sends a few managers to train workers and hires workers for a fraction of what it has been paying its American workers. It then ships the products back to the U.S. to sell in the same market that was being served by the plant it closed. Suppose there are no tariffs or trade restrictions involved. Is Bangladesh "exporting" goods to the U.S. in a "free trade" transaction? The goods have always belonged to an American company, and any profit from the sale of the goods accrues to the American company. Bangladesh benefits because more of its workers can find employment in the plant or at the docks. Is this the kind of "win-win" transaction that makes "free trade" so desirable? I doubt that the workers laid off when the American factory shut down would feel that the American economy was benefiting from the increased profits for the company. Presumably the GDP has not been increased by the profits for the company, though "trickle-down" economics might claim that these profits will be used to consume more (than the workers had been consuming?) or invested in ways that will ultimately lead to a greater GDP.

Note that in this case the market value of the goods produced in Bangladesh is the same as the market value of the goods produced in the U.S. before the factory was relocated. Wages paid to the workers in Bangladesh are determined by the labor market in Bangladesh and not by the productivity of the workers as measured by the market value of what they make.

Suppose the alternative that Krugman wonders about is that a non-profit organization helps provide seed money for manufacturing in Bangladesh that produces goods sold in Bangladesh rather than goods for export. Presumably this could gradually increase the GDP and overall standard of living in Bangladesh without causing workers in the U.S. to be laid off. And perhaps what the workers in Bangladesh would be producing would be something more vital to the health and comfort of people in Bangladesh than the disposable clothing or whatever the relocated factory was producing for Americans.

An alternative lying somewhere between these two extremes is the possibility of foreign investors financing growth in industry in Bangladesh. This raises the question of whether money should move between countries as freely as other goods. The textbooks treat capitol as just another good involved in trade. Krugman introduces his analysis of international borrowing and lending with the idea of "intertemporal" trade:

> Any international transaction that occurs over time has a financial aspect, and this aspect is one of the main topics we address in the second half of this book. However, we can also abstract from those financial aspects and think of borrowing and lending as just another kind of trade: Instead of trading one good for another at a point in time, we exchange goods today in return for some goods in the future.[114]

The "price" of capital is, of course, the interest rate, and in this analysis interest rates are determined by preferences for present and future consumption. Krugman presents a curve representing one nation's "intertemporal production possibility frontier." Instead a trade-off between two goods like guns and butter, it presents the trade-off between present and future consumption as a graph with a downward sloping curve: "A country can trade current consumption for future consumption in the same way that it can produce more of one good by producing less of another."[115] Not surprisingly the curve looks identical to the production possibility frontier for two goods, and Krugman builds on it using the concept of comparative advantage to show how differences in the intertemporal production possibility frontiers of two countries can be an incentive for international lending and borrowing. The implication of course is that the free flow of capital between two countries can be beneficial for both.

Currency Exchange

The free flow of capital is often associated with devastating financial crises such as the ones in Mexico in 1994 and Asia in 1997. Some will argue that there is an essential difference between free trade of goods and the free flow of capital.[116] A distinction is also made between direct equity investment in foreign companies and a free flow of capital in the form of loans, especially short term loans. The effect of foreign loans is complicated by the exchange rates between the two currencies involved. Here, for example, is a description of the Asian financial crisis of 1997-1998 precipitated by a collapse in the value of Thai currency which had been pegged at a fixed exchange rate relative to the dollar.

> The financial crisis can be described as having been a "perfect storm": a confluence of various conditions that not only created financial and economic turbulence but also greatly magnified its impact. Among the key conditions were the presence of fixed or semi-fixed exchange rates in countries such as Thailand, Indonesia and South Korea; large current-account deficits that created downward pressure on those countries' currencies, encouraging speculative attacks; and high domestic interest rates that had encouraged companies to borrow heavily offshore (at lower interest rates) in order to fund aggressive and poorly supervised investment. Weak oversight of domestic lending and, in some cases, rising public debt also contributed to the crisis and made its effects worse once the problems had begun.
>
> If factors such as exchange-rate policies had helped to precipitate the financial crisis, above all it was excessive and poorly supervised foreign borrowing that made it so disastrous. As it became too expensive to fend off speculators, currencies were forced to float. This resulted in large falls in the baht, the won and the rupiah against the U.S. dollar. For instance, from an average of Rp2,342 to the U.S. dollar in 1996, the rupiah fell to an average of Rp10,014 in 1998. As a result, companies that had received large unhedged foreign-currency loans now faced impossibly high debt repayments in domestic-currency terms. The panicked capital flight that ensued only exacerbated the currency depreciation, leaving indebted companies in even direr straits. The workout of the bad debts and disposal of the distressed assets created by the

crisis was one of the major tasks for policymakers for several years thereafter.[117]

If you really want to get a sense of how surreal the international financial markets are, read *Traders, Guns and Money: Knowns and Unknowns in the Dazzling World of Derivatives* by Satyajit Das.

In a perfect world one might hope that the equivalent amount of money bought the same amount of labor in every country so that global economic competition would take place on a completely level playing field. It might even be possible to have a single, universally accepted currency. Needless to say we are not likely to live in such a world any time soon. It may even be that the best way to compensate for the terrain of the playing field is to create even more diverse "local currencies" that can isolate an economy from the slings and arrows of international trade.

Theoretically exchange rates are supposed to reflect differences in the cost of goods and services in each country relative to its currency. Economists make a distinction between the "nominal exchange rate," i.e. the actual exchange rate determined by a host of market variables, and a "real exchange rate" adjusted for the relative price of goods and services in the two countries. The problem is that such a real exchange rate is difficult to specify because goods and services in the two countries may be valued differently. It doesn't really make sense to compare the prices of a Big Mac and a pair of blue jeans in the U.S. to their prices in Thailand or Senegal as a way of calculating an appropriate currency exchange rate.[118] Would it even make sense to compare the wages of an apprentice construction worker or a moderately skilled seamstress?

Underneath all these complications is the fact that exchange rates are partially determined by "market" factors and interest rates. When money is a commodity, currency exchange rates are subject to supply and demand for the currencies. Changes in interest rates paid on loans in a specific currency will affect the demand for that currency, and speculators may have as much influence on exchange rates as changes in technology or resources. This means of course that there are psychological factors involved in the determination of exchange rates. If investors believe interest rates are likely to change or inflation is going to undermine the currency of a given country, the demand for the currency will change and its "price" will change. The net result of all this, at least so far as I can see, is that the "money market" for derivatives based on exchange rates has all the logic of global weather patterns and probably the same potential for destruction.

So let's leap out of the box and try to imagine what foreign trade would be like without financial markets and interest bearing loans. Is it possible that some method could be found for setting exchange rates so that they would be stable enough for businesses to plan ahead? What could China do with their dollars if they could not buy Treasury Bills? Would some other method be needed to settle up payment imbalances between countries? How important is all this to national or local economies?

The place to start may be the distinction between international trade in goods and the globalization of "finance." It is the international movement of money in the form loans seeking a better return abroad than they are able to obtain at home that seems to be associated with the precipitation of financial crises like those in Asia and Mexico. The only reason another country should need dollars is to import goods from the US. If finance of businesses in the domestic economy is done with the extension of credit or deferment of payment then there should be no need for loans denominated in a foreign currency. Whether direct foreign investment in the form of equity in a venture is beneficial is another question.

The current system for settling trade imbalances is complicated by the fact that the dollar functions both as an international currency and a national currency. Instead of settling accounts by transferring gold, nations now hold dollars or dollar-denominated bonds. Some economists argue that using one nation's currency as the international currency may bestow some advantage initially on that country, but in the long run it will inevitably cause instability. The "Triffin Dilemma," named after Robert Triffin, the economist who first analyzed it, describes an inevitable conflict between domestic monetary policy and international policy for a nation whose currency is the international reserve currency.[119]

Under the current system a persistent trade deficit is likely to translate into a large amount of our "public debt" held by other countries (or their central banks) in the form of short-term Treasury bonds. These bonds are held largely because of their liquidity. Even though the return on the bonds may be minimal, they are easily converted into cash to settle trade transactions with the U.S. or even other countries which are willing to accept dollars. If for some reason the market for short-term Treasury bonds froze up or there was a precipitous drop in their price, then there would be a ripple effect that could spread around the globe like a wildfire.

Obviously without financial markets and interest-bearing loans this vulnerability would go away. The question then becomes how to handle trade imbalances between nations. The solution favored by Amato and Fantacci is a revival of a proposal that Keynes made at the Bretton Woods conference in 1944: an international clearing union which enables multilateral clearing of trade balances denominated in an international currency which is separate from any national currency. Keynes called the international currency the "bancor," and it was supposed to be purely an unit of account. If international trade balances were ever in a state of complete equilibrium, there would be no bancors in any nation's account with the clearing union. Any given transaction in international trade would result in credit and debit entries in the bancor accounts of the respective nations, and the system was designed to discourage the accumulation of surplus balances as well as deficit balances. Exchange rates between national currencies and the bancor were to be fixed by agreement but subject to adjustment if trade imbalances exceeded a certain limit.

A clearing union along these lines was actually set up in Europe in 1950 when European countries were still struggling to recover from the devastation of the World War II. The numerous bilateral trade agreements between the countries were replaced with the European Payments Union and many obstacles to trade resulting from imbalances were removed. Countries had favored trade with other countries where they had a credit balance and used restrictive policies with countries where they had a negative balance. With the EPU there was no longer any need for separate trade policies. Having it all come out in the wash with multilateral clearing promoted trade between the countries. The Marshall Plan was tied to this agreement since it was also in the interest of the U.S. to have European economies recovering with the help of intra-European trade.

The key to all this is the fact that money is conceived as a scarce resource, a "commodity" with a "price," and "financing" therefore requires the "investment" of reserves of cash in some enterprise. If the financing of enterprises in any country is achieved primarily though the extension of credit by the banking system in that country, how would this affect international trade and exchange rates?

A clearing union using an international currency like the bancor as a unit of account would still need some method of setting exchange rates. It might eliminate the specter of some other nation holding billions of dollars in U.S. debt, but it would not immediately solve the issue of how to set exchange rates for the international currency and all the national or regional currencies. Keynes's proposal contained incentives to prevent both positive and negative Bancor balances for countries in the union, and it acknowledged that periodic adjustments in a country's exchange rate my be required if its balance exceeded a certain limit.

When one nation's currency is used as the de facto international reserve currency it is not possible for that nation to adjust its exchange rate to counter mounting trade imbalances. Any adjustment in the dollar is ineffective if all the other currencies are pegged to the dollar.

It is worth noting that in 2009 Dr Zhou Xiaochuan, Governor of the People's Bank of China wrote a paper entitled "Reform the international monetary system," in which he advocated an implementation of a clearing union based on an international reserve currency:

> The desirable goal of reforming the international monetary system, therefore, is to create an international reserve currency that is disconnected from individual nations and is able to remain stable in the long run, thus removing the inherent deficiencies caused by using credit-based national currencies.
>
> 1. Though the super-sovereign reserve currency has long since been proposed, yet no substantive progress has been achieved to date. Back in the 1940s, Keynes had already proposed to introduce an international currency unit named "Bancor", based on the value of 30 representative commodities. Unfortunately, the proposal was not accepted. The collapse of the Bretton Woods system, which was based on the White approach, indicates that the Keynesian approach may have been more farsighted. The IMF also created the SDR in 1969, when the defects of the Bretton

Woods system initially emerged, to mitigate the inherent risks sovereign reserve currencies caused. Yet, the role of the SDR has not been put into full play due to limitations on its allocation and the scope of its uses. However, it serves as the light in the tunnel for the reform of the international monetary system.

2. A super-sovereign reserve currency not only eliminates the inherent risks of credit-based sovereign currency, but also makes it possible to manage global liquidity. A super-sovereign reserve currency managed by a global institution could be used to both create and control the global liquidity. And when a country's currency is no longer used as the yardstick for global trade and as the benchmark for other currencies, the exchange rate policy of the country would be far more effective in adjusting economic imbalances. This will significantly reduce the risks of a future crisis and enhance crisis management capability.[120]

Perhaps the exchange rates with the international currency could be set so that minimum wages in all countries were equivalent. Surely this would go a long way towards discouraging "outsourcing" or relocation of plants to cut labor costs, even if other measures were required to insure a domestic economy remained prosperous.

Taxes

If the government can "print" all the money it needs to pay for its activities, why do we need taxation? Eliminating taxes would surely be a campaign platform that everyone would love to vote for. Unfortunately, except for libertarians who view all taxation as theft, no one believes it is possible to eliminate taxes. Even Modern Monetary Theory includes a strange justification for taxes. Stephanie Kelton recalls how Warren Mosler explained the need for taxes with a story about a deal he made with his kids.

> Since the U.S. government is the sole source of dollars, it was silly to think of Uncle Sam as needing to get dollars from the rest of us. Obviously, the issuer of the dollar can have all the dollars it could possibly want. "The government doesn't want dollars," Mosler explained. "It wants something else."
>
> "What does it want?" I asked.
>
> "It wants to provision itself," he replied. "The tax isn't there to raise money. It's there to get people working and producing things for the government."
>
> "What kinds of things?" I asked.
>
> "A military, a court system, public parks, hospitals, roads, bridges. That kind of stuff."
>
> To get the population to do all that work, the government imposes taxes, fees, fines, or other obligations. The tax is there to create a demand for the government's currency. Before anyone can pay the tax, someone has to do the work to earn the currency.
>
> My head spun. Then he told me a story.
>
> Mosler had a beautiful beachfront property with a swimming pool and all the luxuries of life anyone could hope to enjoy. He also had a family that included two young kids. To illustrate his point, he told me a story about the time he sat his kids down and told them he wanted them to do their part to help keep the place clean and habitable. He wanted the yard mowed, beds made, dishes done, cars washed, and so on. To compensate them for their time, he offered to pay them for their labor. Three of his business cards if they made their beds. Five for doing the dishes. Ten for washing a car and twenty-five for tending to the yard work. Days turned into weeks, and the house became

increasingly uninhabitable. The grass grew knee high. Dishes piled up in the sink, and the cars were covered in sand and salt from the ocean breeze. "Why aren't you doing any work?" Mosler asked the kids. "I told you would pay you some of my business cards to pitch in around here." "D-a-a-a-a-ad," the kids intoned. "Why would we work for your business cards? They're not worth anything!"

That's when Mosler had his epiphany. The kids hadn't done any chores because they didn't need his cards. So, he told the kids he wasn't requiring them to do any work at all. All he wanted was a payment of thirty of his business cards, each month. Failure to pay would result in a loss of privileges. No more TV, use of the swimming pool, or trips to the mall. It was a stroke of genius. Mosler had imposed a "tax" that could only be paid using his own monogrammed paper. Now the cards were worth something. Within hours, the kids were scurrying around, tidying up their bedrooms, the kitchen, and the yard...

Mosler used this story to illustrate some basic principles about the way sovereign currency issuers actually fund themselves. Taxes are there to create a demand for government currency.[121]

Mosler also cites a project by the economics department at the University of Missouri at Kansas City which created a currency called the Buckeroo. It was used to "pay" students for doing community service volunteer work and established a "tax" requiring each student to submit 20 Buckeroos at the end of the semester in order to receive their grades.[122]

This is a fine example of economic explanation via analogy and narrative of origin. Unfortunately it strikes me as nonsense, and I think it risks discrediting the rest of Modern Monetary Theory. First of all it was absurd to think the kids would regard the business cards by themselves as any kind of motivation to do the work. Presumably they had reached the age where awarding a gold star in recognition of a performance of some task was no longer an effective incentive. Secondly the threat of loss of privilege would probably have sufficed as an incentive without the "currency." All that was needed was some kind of accounting system for keeping track of who had done what. Instead of paying business cards Dad could just make a note in his little book when he was presented with evidence of a job completed. The only thing that the business cards added was perhaps the possibility that the siblings could sell or lend them to each other to cover shortfalls.

The idea that taxes are there to create a demand for government currency seems to an explanation of the origin of taxation and "government currency." Surely various forms of taxation existed long before there was any fiat currency. There is apparently some scholarship which ties the introduction of money in ancient societies to the introduction of taxation, but I am more inclined to believe that taxation began as confiscation by feudal lords as a means of aggrandizement. What makes a government currency work is the legal system enforcing its recognition as "legal tender" for the settlement of any debt.

What Mosler's analogy is really trying to do is reframe the functional analysis of taxation in a system based on a fiat currency that has no "intrinsic" value and to underscore the ability of a government to pay for things by "printing" money. He even defines fiat currency as "a tax credit not backed by any tangible asset."[123]

The key insight of Modern Monetary Theory is that the government of a nation with its own currency is a unique economic entity and should not be viewed like a household or a business in terms of its income and expenses. It does not need income in order to pay expenses, but it does need a form of money which will be accepted as payment for goods and services. Mosler's notion of the government needing to "provision itself" and therefore imposing taxes in order to insure the legitimacy of its money seems to me to put the cart before the horse. It might make sense if a newly issued government currency had to compete with a host of other well established forms of currency used in the nation's economy, but this is hardly the case with any contemporary nation. Kelton, however, seems to find the argument convincing:

> If the British government stopped requiring its people to settle their tax obligations using British pounds, it would rather quickly undermine its provisioning powers. Fewer people would need to earn pounds, and the government would have a harder time finding teachers, nurses, and so on who were willing to work and produce things in exchange for its currency.[124]

Surely all these teachers and nurses would still need to earn pounds to buy food, clothing and shelter, just as people do whose income is so low that they do not have to pay income tax. Modern Monetary Theory does not need this myth to justify its perspective on deficit spending, and in fact Mosler and Kelton also cite other functions served by taxation.

In 1946 Beardsley Ruml, who was chairman of the Federal Reserve Bank of New York, published an article called "Taxes For Revenue Are Obsolete" in which he attempted to explain the real purpose of taxation:

What Taxes Are Really For

> Federal taxes can be made to serve four principal purposes of a social and economic character. These purposes are:
>
> 1. As an instrument of fiscal policy to help stabilize the purchasing power of the dollar;
>
> 2. To express public policy in the distribution of wealth and of income, as in the case of the progressive income and estate taxes;
>
> 3. To express public policy in subsidizing or in penalizing various industries and economic groups;
>
> 4. To isolate and assess directly the costs of certain national benefits, such as highways and social security.
>
> In the recent past, we have used our federal tax program consciously for each of these purposes. In serving these purposes, the tax program is a means to an end. The purposes themselves are matters of basic national policy which should be established, in the first instance, independently of any national tax program.

Kelton's three other justifications for federal taxation are essentially identical with Ruml's first three: inflation, distribution of wealth or income, and encouraging or discouraging certain behaviors and endeavors, although Ruml's concerns about subsidies or penalties was primarily a matter of tariffs and subsidies to industries rather than the sort of excise taxes Kelton may have in mind.

Mainstream economics does not regard taxation as an effective means of controlling inflation because raising taxes is politically difficult, and it thinks inflation can be controlled by monetary policy. Nonetheless the most immediate objection to a simplified notion of Modern Monetary Theory is that "printing money" is a surefire way to undermine the value of the currency and put us on the road to hyperinflation. Inflation prevention is surely the principal justification for taxation in Modern Monetary Theory and is the main caveat overlooked by many critics of the theory. What is involved is a shift in focus from deficit or surplus in the federal budget to inflation or deflation caused by direct changes in the amount of money circulating in the economy.

The use of taxation to redistribute wealth or income and its use as a form of behavior control are both political hot potatoes that many economists shy away from. They are clearly derived from policies that are beyond the scope of economics as such to evaluate – although some economists would argue that the accumulation of wealth in the hands of a minority is a way to promote growth. Excise taxes such as taxes on alcohol or tobacco have been justified by cost benefit analyses given the effect they have on healthcare costs, but I suspect PR campaigns about the dangers posed by both have been more effective in curtailing their use than the economic disincentives represented by a slightly higher cost to the consumer. A more relevant example might be the proposal for a carbon tax as a way to fight climate change.

The textbook explanation of taxation is a bit broader or more general:

> In taxing, government is in reality deciding how to draw the required resources from the nation's households and businesses for public purposes. The money raised through taxation is the vehicle by which real resources are transferred from private goods to collective goods.[125]

This explanation is, of course, based on the assumption that the government must have revenue from taxes or loans in order to have money to spend in the acquisition of goods. The transfer of resources from private to public (collective) occurs when the government spends the money regardless of whether it is fresh off the printing presses or existing money raised by loans or taxation.

It must be emphasized that Modern Monetary Theory applies only to sovereign currency. State and local governments that do not generate their own currency must raise money the old fashioned way i.e. by taxes or loans. One implication of this may be that it would make sense to have state and even local currencies in addition to the national currency. To some extent the introduction of the Euro has backfired because it has become more difficult for countries in the European Union to deal with their own domestic fiscal issues even though the Euro has streamlined international trade within the union.

Taxation is not the only tool for preventing inflation. If money is created by credit extended then the amount of new credit extended to companies or individuals can be tailored to prevent excess money in circulation. Control over money creation is probably a more immediate and effective method for preventing inflation caused by excess money in circulation. It is the equivalent of the monetary policies currently used, but it has the advantage of being a more direct control over the amount of credit available. There is no "pushing on a rope" with lower interest rates.

Relying primarily on money creation rather than taxation to prevent inflation would probably mean that the main justification for taxation is the redistribution of wealth or income. Everyone decries the outrageous imbalance in the distribution of wealth in the US, but few seem to want to vote for a level of taxation that would seriously alter it. Eliminating interest-bearing loans and stock market speculation might go a long way towards reducing income inequality, but it may only be through radical changes in income tax rates and estate taxes that the distribution of wealth can be restored to anything like a reasonable level. Before any of this could happen, though, we need a fundamental change in our understanding of money and finance.

Markets

To market, to market to buy a fat pig.

When a metaphor like "the market" is used to describe something as complex as the institutions and practices associated with the producing and selling of goods in a modern economy, the term will inevitably carry with it the feelings of familiarity and ordinariness associated with the more literal meaning of a market like the one where we buy groceries. Farmers markets which have become so popular in recent years are probably the closest approximation to the village markets which were so central to local economies in the past and which still live in our imaginations thanks to nursery rhymes, songs and stories we heard as kids. Some might want to claim that a shopping mall is the modern equivalent of the village market, but a shopping mall exists on top of a vast network of businesses that have nothing in common with the individuals selling their own produce in an old-fashioned village market.

Adam Smith, who is generally regarded as the father of modern economics, was a moral philosopher and colleague of David Hume. Late in his career he became interested in how nations manage to grow and prosper, partially inspired by the ideas of French physiocrats. He began his analysis by assuming individuals who were each striving to better their own condition through their labor and through barter or trade with others. By comparing the entire economy of an nation to a village market, he was able to conclude that technological progress, division of labor and various forms of infrastructure, made it possible for the total output of everyone's labor to grow and be distributed in a way that benefited everyone. The idea of a market where supply and demand determine prices became the central tenet in almost all economic theory.

In the mid 20th century mathematicians became interested in modeling Adam Smith's idea of a market economy and came up with a general equilibrium theory which gave free market theory a stamp of approval from higher mathematics. Not all economists thought the simplified model was adequate for the task of analyzing a modern economy. Hyman Minsky was among the "post-Keynesian" economists who took the imprimatur of mathematics with a grain of salt:

Arrow and Hahn (1971, pp. vi, vii)[126] rightly emphasized that mainstream economists from Adam Smith to the present "have sought to show that a decentralized economy motivated by self-interest and guided by price signals would be compatible with a coherent disposition of economic resources." Smith's insight of genius was to associate processes that yield a coherent result in a decentralized market economy with the trading that takes place in a village's market square. To this day, formal economic theory makes this demonstration by investigating the characteristics of an abstract trading process. But its validity depends on showing that the "coherence" property demonstrated for the abstract trading process can be preserved when the model is altered to allow for the formalized concepts of production, labor, capital assets, monopoly, and money.

As Arrow and Hahn noted in chapter 14, the proposition that a decentralized market yields a coherent result has not yet been shown to hold for an economy where money is represented by contracts created through banking processes, and capitalist financial practices are required to support the purchase of expensive, long-lived capital assets.[127]

Apparently the math suggests that the nature of money and finance in a modern economy renders the metaphor of a market obsolete.

The textbook definition of a market economy is

An economy in which the what, how, and for whom questions concerning resource allocation are primarily determined by supply and demand in markets. In this form of economic organization, firms, motivated by the desire to maximize profits, buy inputs and produce and sell outputs. Households, armed with their factor incomes, go to markets and determine the demand for commodities. The interaction of firms' supply and households' demand then determines the prices and quantities of goods.[128]

What this implies is that the two things driving this theoretical market are the profit motive and the preferences of individuals. Economics makes no attempt to evaluate either. It assumes that the profit motive is a primary element in human interactions, and it professes to be neutral about the relative merit of individual preferences or what impact they may have on society.

The profit motive is often described as the driving force of capitalism or its life blood. It is the aspect of the individual's self-interested behavior which forms the basis for economic transactions. As an idea the profit motive is subject to extreme interpretations ranging all the way from an almost mystical force which creates society to a moralistic condemnation as a cynical interpretation of human nature which believes "greed is good." Mainstream economics simply accepts it as an obvious component in the way things work.

> In examining the forces determining the supply curve, the fundamental point to grasp is that producers supply commodities for profit and not for fun or charity.[129]

Profits in a market-based economy also serve another function beside lining the pockets of the successful entrepreneur:

> Like a farmer using a carrot and a stick to coax a donkey forward, the market system deals out profits and losses to induce firms to produce desired goods efficiently.[130]

This may seem commonplace and obvious, but somewhere along the way something changes as the desire of individuals to better their condition morphs into profit maximization in large businesses or the focus on shareholder value in publicly held corporations. The most obvious problem is that the profits for successful enterprises are not based on all the costs actually incurred in terms of effects on the environment or society. Supply and demand in a market cannot prevent pollution. As it maximizes profits, corporate agriculture is not only destroying the viability of smaller family-owned farms but also depleting aquifers, destroying the top soil in the Midwest and polluting water as far away as the Gulf of Mexico where polluted runoff has traveled down the Mississippi to create a "dead zone" in the Gulf the size of New Jersey.[131]

Economics addresses such "externalities" by recognizing the need for regulation. In many cases, though, the harm done to the environment or society by a profitable enterprise is questioned in passionate political debate or is simply viewed as less important than the benefits provided by the enterprise. Moreover large corporations often have enough influence in government to prevent regulations that would damage their bottom line.

Markets are also regarded as a key ingredient of the "capitalist" or "free enterprise" system that has proved so effective in improving the "standard of living" for so many people during the last two centuries. Somehow markets and capitalism are responsible for the industrial revolution and the development of the technology that has so enriched our lives. It is not immediately clear to me whether capitalism fosters technology or technology fosters capitalism, but the prevailing belief is that history proves "capitalism works." It may not be perfect, but it is better than any other economic system known to man. Some might be inclined to note that the last two centuries have also brought us war and genocide on an unprecedented scale, working conditions comparable to slavery for masses of people and environmental destruction that threatens the very possibility of human life on the planet. None of this, however, suggests a better mechanism for allocating resources than the market. Marx and others have tried to imagine an economy without profits, but efforts to supplant the profit motive seem to devolve into oppressive re-education.

A market economy is often presented as the only form of social organization that permits individuals to remain autonomous, and any attempt to limit its functioning may be viewed as a threat to individual "liberty" or "freedom." Belief in free markets supports the illusion that we can decide how to live our lives without being subject to some authority. Even if it contributes to the concentration of enormous wealth and power in a tiny portion of the population and forces millions to live in dire poverty, we continue to believe a market economy represents the only form of social organization that fosters individual liberty.

Economists tend to present "the market" as a natural ecosystem that has spontaneously evolved over the centuries. The implication is often that given its spontaneous evolution it is best left alone to function naturally rather that being subject to "interventions." The problem with this assumption is, of course, that the market itself is produced by "interventions" – the social customs and legal framework which permit it to function. A truly "free" market has probably never existed and certainly never existed on any scale other than a small primitive community.

Since mainstream economics aspires to be "scientific" it attempts to understand and model the market as though it were a natural phenomenon using abstractions like supply and demand. Some critics insist that the market can never be understood as a "natural" phenomenon because it involves human choice. The market is an institution based on cultural customs and political choices. The givens that economics uses in modeling such as individual preferences are not fixed givens in the way the behavior of molecules may be. They are influenced by trends, fads, advertising, propaganda, education, religious beliefs and other practices. One might say that molecules are influenced by their context as well such as temperature and the presence of other molecules, but the range of possible behaviors for a molecule seems nowhere near as infinite as the range of behaviors possible for a human being.

The market often seems to be conflated with "democracy" as a form of social organization. In a democracy each citizen theoretically has an equal vote in determining public policies. In a market, however, individuals have radically differing numbers of "votes." The person with more money has more influence over the allocation of resources than his less well-off neighbors, and he is deemed to be entitled to that extra influence due to the fact that he has more money, however he may have come by it. Democracy is theoretically opposed the concentration of power in the hands of a single person or a select group. Revolutions may have eliminated monarchy and an hereditary aristocracy, but market economies foster plutocracy.

Prior to the financial crisis, financial markets were touted as a way of democratizing the market economy. Everyone could become a part-owner of whatever business suited his fancy. Risks and benefits were shared by all. I have the impression that a similar attitude was common in the '20s before the crash. Anyone could get rich by being smart. Apparently most people weren't quite smart enough, and the risks and benefits were not quite equally shared.

Any community or society which recognizes private property and uses money will have some form of market. Perhaps the only real alternative to a market economy is the "gift economy" found in some small primitive societies, but it hardly seems feasible in a large developed economy. Advocates of a society in which all the natural resources, real estate and means of production are owned by "the state" distinguish between "private property" and "personal property" to explain how such a society can still have markets for consumable products. In societies that attempt to control markets too tightly it seems inevitable that "black markets" will emerge. Even in prisons money may take the form of cigarettes in order to permit an orderly market for whatever goods are available. It seems that the whole point of money is to enable markets.

The question then seems to be how to regulate markets and whether there are any limits to the kinds of things sold in markets. There is a more or less universal consensus that human beings are not a suitable "good" to be sold in markets. We don't want "slavery" or "human trafficking." There is, of course, a kind of market for children in that a couple wanting to "adopt" can pay money to the right people and acquire a child legally to raise as their own. Economists also like to talk about "labor markets," but we prefer to think that what is being sold in a labor market is not a person. It is simply – what? – their "services" or some of their time. Wage-earners are not slaves because they can theoretically walk away from the job with the hope of finding another way to earn a living. Whether that hope is groundless will depend on external factors influencing the market.

A market transaction is rarely a negotiation between autonomous individuals on an equal footing. For one thing markets are susceptible to "leverage." A worker with financial reserves can afford to quit while his colleague might not be able to survive while he looked for a better job. Standard Oil could afford to sell gas at a loss in order to bankrupt the competition and eventually acquire a virtual monopoly in some areas. Amazon could lose millions of dollars for years in order to corner the market in book sales and then expand into virtually every other consumer market. Unions can force employers to improve working conditions or pay higher wages. Economies of scale enable Walmart to attract all the customers away from local mom-and-pop businesses.

There is another way in which economists like to tout the market. It is seen increasingly as an information system enabling individual producers and consumers to optimize the use of their resources and maintaining a balance between supply and demand for every conceivable type of "good." Just as the stock market seems to be based on the assumption that investors know more about the value of a company than the company's own managers and accountants, the market at large is seen as an unimpeachable source of knowledge about all kinds of things. The most absurd extreme example of this faith was probably the idea that a futures market in terrorism could be used to help formulate public policy.

> The Pentagon, in defending the program, said such futures trading had proven effective in predicting other events like oil prices, elections and movie ticket sales.
>
> "Research indicates that markets are extremely efficient, effective and timely aggregators of dispersed and even hidden information," the Defense Department said in a statement. "Futures markets have proven themselves to be good at predicting such things as elections results; they are often better than expert opinions."[132]

What exactly is this extremely efficient, effective and timely aggregator of dispersed and even hidden information? Is it simply like Ebay where anyone who has something to sell can make it available and set the price based on what others are charging for similar items or even let the buyers establish a price by bidding? The dispersed information which the market reveals is for the most part simply consumer preferences. Sales are a good indication of the "demand" for a product, and watching the effect of raising and lowering prices can enable a seller to find the sweet spot that maximizes his profit. Market research and polls may help anticipate the demand for a product, but actual sales are the only true measure that reflect all the factors involved in the consumers' decisions.

What is the "demand" that the market reveals. If the price for something goes up and demand for it goes down, does that mean the fewer people really want the product? It means that fewer people can afford the product, but those who would buy it if it were cheaper presumably still would like to have it. So demand is not just an indication of consumer preferences but of consumer preferences tempered by financial resources. That is really the point of market theory, of course, since the measure of the market's effectiveness or efficiency seems to be the extent to which it maximizes producers' profits. It is not to maximize consumer satisfaction.

Suppose you did want to maximize consumer satisfaction. Other than redesigning airliner interiors, how would you do it? Is the satisfaction of owning a 200-ft. yacht greater than the satisfaction of feeding and clothing a child? Is the number of people who own cell phones more or less significant than the number of people who receive proper medical care? Do homeless people count as consumers?

One argument in favor of free markets is that no planner can anticipate the diversity of consumer "demand" as well as individual entrepreneurs who are willing to take a risk to fill a demand that they believe is latent. Or at least it is safer to let individuals take these risks and hope that the ones who are wrong can just go back to their day jobs. No central planner would risk his job betting on a demand for hula hoops, pet rocks or $20,000 handbags. What the market will tell the entrepreneur eventually is whether it is worth his while to sell some product. He may, of course, decide that having a larger customer base is worth more in the long run than maximizing profit in the short run, but he is still hoping to make a profit in the long run.

The individual entrepreneur may say that he really is motivated by a desire to satisfy others, and perhaps his epitaph will be some form of "He provided us with what we wanted." There is undoubtedly satisfaction to be found in giving pleasure to others or providing for their needs, and perhaps economic theory can include that kind of satisfaction under the rubric of "self-interest." Most people would assume, though, that business is about making money. If you want to help others, donate to charity.

I am perfectly happy to let the availability of most consumer products be determined by the supply and demand mechanisms of a market. I am not so sure I feel the same way about things like food, clothing, shelter, healthcare, education and other things which strike me as "necessities." The need for someone to make a profit is not sufficient justification for letting people go hungry.

Minsky puts it nicely at the outset of his analysis in *Stabilizing An Unstable Economy*:

> The general view sustained by the following analysis is that while the market mechanism is a good enough device for making social decisions about unimportant matters such as the mix of colors in the production of frocks, the length of skirts or the flavors of ice cream, it cannot and should not be relied upon for important, big matters such as the distribution of income, the capital development of the economy, and the education and training of the young.[133]

"Market forces" are really just the tip of the iceberg dependent on a host of other institutions and social conventions. The ties that bind us together as a society are not just economic. The nature of our "economic" transactions is an expression of our culture, customs and morality. There is nothing given or inevitable about the functioning of our markets. At some level we have agreed to do things this way, and we could agree to do things differently. We could agree that everyone is entitled to a decent paying job and there are limits to how much "wealth" an individual or company can retain, if our goal was not to maximize profit but to promote the well-being of everyone.

When Minsky attempted to analyze how the economy could be stabilized, he did so with "a recognition that market capitalism is both intrinsically unstable and can lead to distasteful distributions of wealth and power."[134] The key term here is perhaps "distasteful." Most economists seem willing to live with some degree of instability, but if I find the concentration of wealth and power in the hands of a minute percentage of the population "distasteful," what am I really saying? I am pussy-footing around a moral condemnation rooted in values I believe are part of the core foundation of the society in which I want to live.

The economic activity of our society is destroying the viability of life on earth and enabling a minute minority to accumulate vast wealth and power while much of the human race struggles with poverty and insecurity. We have an inhumane economic system which is rooted in ideas propagated either by those who stand to gain from the system or by well-meaning people who have been persuaded that the current system represents centuries of evolutionary progress. Exploring the way we conceive of money is one way to free our minds from the prison cell of dogma to which we have consigned ourselves.

Mainstream economics conflates the creation of surplus goods through technology with the accrual of "profits" to individuals or corporations. It fails to see that money should not be a commodity with a price determined by supply and demand and that the only thing achieved by financial markets is the concentration of money and power in the hands of a few along with an unending series of "crises" that destroy lives. It justifies all this with a simplistic model of human interaction and the pretense of being a science based on mathematical models.

Economic theory is a branch of moral philosophy, and the economic system we live under is an expression of our culture. It is not divinely mandated or the product of inevitable evolution. It is a matter of human choice. The moral arc of history does not bend towards justice unless we are pulling in the right direction with all our might.

Appendix: What About Cryptocurrency

"My hope is that it creates world peace or helps create world peace."[135]

My initial impression of cryptocurrency was that it served two functions: it facilitated money laundering, and it provided a speculative investment. It seemed to me to be an extreme example of the absurdity of having a form of money be a tradable asset. The whole idea that a single Bitcoin, whose value was set at 30¢ in 2011, could have a market value of over $68,000 in 2021 is preposterous.

What exactly is cryptocurrency and why is anyone interested in it other than as a way to hit the jackpot? Theoretically it is a medium of exchange, but paying someone with cryptocurrency is so inconvenient and even expensive that it is not yet a practical way to pay for everyday expenses. I have heard that it is possible to use Bitcoin these days to buy a car, but the main use for cryptocurrency as a medium of exchange has been international transfers of very large amounts of cash where the real benefit seems to be that the transactions are untraceable for all practical purposes.

Bitcoin was not the first cryptocurrency, but it is certainly the most prevalent one at present, and the "Bitcoin White Paper" written by the creator of Bitcoin[136] may be a good place to start in evaluating its potential. To some extent cryptocurrency seems like a solution in search of a problem, but the most important characteristic of Bitcoin is that it is, as the title of the white paper says, "a peer-to-peer electronic cash system." The idea of electronic or digital "cash" is not new, but most forms of electronic cash transactions require an intermediary such as a bank or credit card company not to mention a large infrastructure behind the money and some institution supporting it.

The object of Bitcoin is to enable one individual to pay another in a secure manner without an intermediary. Much of what is written about cryptocurrency focuses on how the transactions can be secure rather than why it is advantageous to eliminate the intermediary. Part of the reason that Bitcoin became so popular after it was introduced in 2009 was the 2007-2008 financial crisis. Many people became convinced that there was something fundamentally wrong with the current financial system, and it seemed natural to blame the government and the large banks that controlled the supply of money. Cryptocurrency offered a way to take the monetary system out of their hands.

One way to understand the point of cryptocurrency is to view it in the context of how money has evolved. When money consisted of coins made from "precious" metals, it was possible when someone paid you to verify that you had in fact been paid. The metal used for the coins was considered valuable in itself and its weight and purity could be tested. The term "acid test" derives from one method of testing the purity of gold. Gold is also soft enough that one can test a coin by biting it.

Once paper currency replaced precious metal coins, an element of trust was required for transactions. Paper currency may have unique serial numbers and elaborate engraving techniques to make it difficult to counterfeit, but the institution issuing the currency must be trustworthy and have the means to enforce the use of the bills as "legal tender."

With cryptocurrency the object is to make the currency self-verifying by having it contain a record of its provenance and transaction history. This would prevent someone from using the same Bitcoin in different transaction or just generating counterfeit Bitcoins, and it is achieved with blockchain technology and a network of computers. This is not the place (nor am I the person) to explain blockchain technology. Suffice it to say, blockchain is a method of encrypting data which requires a lot of computing power distributed over a network of computers. Elements of the theory had been available for 25 years, but Bitcoin was the first application of it to a decentralized network. The network is an essential element in the security of Bitcoin, and the number of computer processors verifying the validity of a transaction needs to be greater than the number of computers trying to hack the system.

The creation of a new Bitcoin is the first transaction stored in it and requires similar computing power to the verification of later transactions. Anyone with sufficient resources can create Bitcoins which they then own, although there is an algorithm embedded in the scheme which limits how fast the number of Bitcoins can grow. Anyone who puts their computers on the network to verify transactions may also received transaction fees in Bitcoin. Both creation and verification are referred to as "mining" in a comparison to gold mining where anyone who extracts gold from the ground or a stream is the owner of a form of money. The resources required for Bitcoin mining are computer hardware and enough electrical energy not only to run the computers but to keep them cool. Computer installations devoted to Bitcoin mining can consume enormous amounts of electricity, and, even though computer processors are always becoming more efficient, the difficulty of verifying a cryptocurrency transaction grows as the cryptocurrency becomes more widely adopted.

If we ignore any technical obstacles, what are the reasons for adopting a self-verifying digital currency? It seems to me that the only conceivable reason is that it severs any connection between the currency and a government or some other centralized authority. Whether this is advantageous is a matter of debate. The main argument against having a government issue and regulate money is that the government cannot be trusted to maintain the value of the money rather than simply increasing its supply to pay for wars or for institutions designed to subjugate the population. Control over money gives the government too much power, and individuals in the government can use monetary policy to increase their own power.

Cryptocurrency involves what is called a "decentralized autonomous organization" (DAO). Verification of transactions is not done by a centralized process but requires the involvement of many computers on a network operating independently of any human intervention. It is difficult to appreciate the significance of this. A credit or debit card authorization also involves a large network of computers and any given transaction is authorized without any human intervention. I can easily imagine that no human hand touches anything between the time I swipe or insert or tap my card at the grocery store checkout counter and the time when I receive my monthly statement. It is certainly hard enough to speak with a human being when questioning a transaction on a statement.

Does the fact that every Bitcoin contains a unique record of its provenance make a given transaction any more secure than one using a credit card or debit card? It prevents "double spending" of the Bitcoin. In fact the prevention of "double spending" seems to be the principal justification for Bitcoin.

> A purely peer-to-peer version of electronic cash would allow online payments to be sent directly from one party

> to another without going through a financial institution. Digital signatures provide part of the solution, but the main benefits are lost if a trusted third party is still required to prevent double-spending. We propose a solution to the double-spending problem using a peer-to-peer network.[137]

I suspect that trying to eliminate trust from social interactions is as self-defeating as the attempt to eliminate risk from investing. I can understand why individuals do not trust large institutions that use their power to benefit a small group of people, but perhaps the solution is to regulate the institutions rather than eliminate the need for trust. This of course requires trust in the government that must enforce the regulations.

I actually do not understand why one would trust the security of a cryptocurrency transaction more than a credit or debit card transaction. The problem with banks and credit card companies is not that their involvement in transactions makes them less secure, but that their other activities can have devastating effects on the economy and often benefit only the extremely wealthy. If cryptography can provide a way to securely embed the provenance of a given amount of cryptocurrency, surely it can provide an equally effective method for insuring the security of credit and debit card transactions and bank accounts. The issue of "double spending" is a problem introduced by a digital currency for peer-to-peer transactions. Solving that problem is not a justification for adopting a digital currency capable of peer-to-peer transactions. The critical lack of trust lies in the method for creating and regulating the currency itself.

Cryptocurrency is created by "mining," and the system design includes some method for limiting the rate at which the amount of currency in circulation can grow. Someone or some group has to determine the appropriate rate for the currency to grow if its purchasing power is to be stable.

When Satoshi Nakamoto created Bitcoin, he installed a strict limit on the number of Bitcoin that could ever exist. There will never be more than 21 million bitcoin. This limit, known as the hard cap, is encoded in Bitcoin's source code and enforced by nodes on the network.

> Bitcoin's hard cap is central to its value proposition, both as a money and an investment. Like gold and real estate, Bitcoin is a successful store of value because it is difficult to increase its supply. Thanks to the halving, bitcoin becomes

more difficult to produce every four years, and eventually, it will become impossible.[138]

According to coinmarketcap.com there were 19,013,687 units of Bitcoin circulating on April 16, 2020. The limit on the number of Bitcoins in circulation may be an essential element in its value as an asset, but it does not means that its purchasing power can be stabilized. Bitcoin rapidly became an extremely speculative asset for investors. Apparently the earliest use of Bitcoin to purchase something was in 2010 when an early adapter persuaded his local Papa Johns pizzeria to sell him two pizzas for 10,000 Bitcoins, which he regarded as worth $40. By 2021 those Bitcoins would have been worth $680,000,000. On the other hand an investor who watched the trading value of Bitcoin rocket from $1 in April 2011 to $29.60 in June could have bought it only to see its value plummet to $2.05 in about five months. Some advocates of cryptocurrency, of course, say that it will gradually stabilize, but it is worth noting that the investors in Bitcoin who have made fantastic amounts of money have done so by selling the cryptocurrency for dollars or some other established currency. The idea that a cryptocurrency can function as a store of value because it is a scarce resource seems undermined by the fact that it is a tradable asset whose value is determined simply by a market created by speculators. The success of Bitcoin seems also to have given rise to the "nonfungible token" (NFT) which uses the same technology to create a unique digital object whose only value is that it is a tradable on a market comparable to the market for collectibles like baseball cards.

The number of Bitcoin in circulation may be limited, but there is nothing to stop other cryptocurrencies from being created.

Since the 2008 invention of the first cryptocurrency, Bitcoin, cryptocurrencies have proliferated. In recent years, they experienced a rapid increase and subsequent decrease in value. One estimate found that, as of March 2020, there were more than 5,100 different cryptocurrencies worth about $231 billion.[139]

Wikipedia lists only 180 currencies recognized at legal tender by nations or their dependencies. Bitcoin is one of these since it has been recognized as legal tender by El Salvador. Wikipedia also says there are another 300 "complementary" local or regional currencies. One has to wonder what the economic impact would be if there were 5,000 different currencies used globally.

Among the commonly cited benefits of cryptocurrency are

1. Transaction speed
2. Transaction costs
3. Accessibility
4. Security
5. Privacy
6. Transparency
7. Inflation protection

Transaction speed. Comparisons of the speed of a cryptocurrency transaction are often made to the speed of a wire transfer, which can sometimes take several days to go through. Often a check issued electronically by Quicken can take three or four days to be fully processed as well. Other forms of electronic payment, however, seem virtually instantaneous to the payer. If I buy something online using a credit card, I only have to wait few seconds for the payment to be verified, and, if I authorize a bill to be paid by supplying my bank account information to the payee, it seems to be credited the same day.

It seems as though the verification of a Bitcoin transaction can take anywhere from 10 minutes to 7 days, depending on how many other transactions are waiting to be verified and how much of a transaction fee the sender is willing to pay. The computational difficulty of the verification of a Bitcoin transactions is systematically modified with a view to keeping the time required around 10 minutes.

Transaction costs. Transactions costs are paid by the spender, and generally someone initiating a cryptocurrency transfer has the option of increasing the transaction fee to secure a higher priority in the cue of transactions waiting to be processed by the computer network. Transactions costs for Bitcoin transfers have varied dramatically over the years, rising as high as $54 in 2017 and an all time high of $62 in April 2021. As of April 18, 2022, the Bitcoin average transaction fee was $1.04.

Transaction costs in other forms of electronic payment are often paid by the merchant rather than the customer, though the cost of the transaction may affect the retail price of the good. The Dodd-Frank Act included a provision for limiting the transaction fees charged to vendors when a purchase is made with a credit card. Generally these fees range between 1.5% to 3.5% of the purchase amount. Banks charge the sender for wire transfers, and they may charge a monthly fee for processing electronic checks from Quicken, but they do not seem to charge a transaction fee for bill-paying when it is done directly with the bank.

With cryptocurrency the transaction fee is the incentive for "miners" to put their computers on the network to verify transactions. According to Statista.com "The average energy consumption for one single Bitcoin transaction in 2022 could equal several hundreds of thousands of VISA card transactions." Another source estimates the average amount of electrical power required to verify each Bitcoin transaction as 1,173 kilowatt hours, an amount comparable to the power consumed in about 6 weeks by an average household. It is difficult to see how earning a transaction fee of $1.04 every ten minutes provides sufficient incentive. Other forms of cryptocurrency require significantly less power to verify transactions. Ethereum is said to require 87.29 kilowatts per transaction, and its average transaction fee as of March 10, 2022, was $15.

Accessibility. Motley Fool describes the accessibility of cryptocurrency as an advantage for people who do not or cannot deal with a traditional bank in managing their money:

> Anyone can use cryptocurrency. All you need is a computer or smartphone and an internet connection. The process of setting up a cryptocurrency wallet is extremely fast compared to opening an account at a traditional financial institution. There's no ID verification. There's no background or credit check.
>
> Cryptocurrency offers a way for the unbanked to access financial services without having to go through a centralized authority. There are many reasons a person may be unable or unwilling to get a traditional bank account. Using cryptocurrency can allow people who don't use traditional banking services to easily make online transactions or send money to loved ones.[140]

Sending money to loved ones conjures up an image of refugees or undocumented workers sending money back home to support their family, and in fact there is some indication that this is a growing use of Bitcoin.

Security. There are two aspects to the security of a cryptocurrency. One is the difficulty of generating false transactions because of the nature of the network involved in verifying transactions. The larger the network becomes, the more difficult it is to hack it and the more secure the currency transactions are. The other factor affecting the security of a cryptocurrency is how the owner of the currency stores it in his digital "wallet." He has a private "key" which gives him access to his own currency and which is distinct from the public key employed when the currency is involved in a transfer. If someone else discovers what your private key is, he or she can access your currency as easily as you can. If you lose or forget you private key, you lose your money. Some people apparently write their private key down somewhere rather than store it on a digital device.

Privacy & Transparency. There is something incongruous and ironic about the way in which proponents of cryptocurrency tout both its privacy and its transparency. Cryptocurrency transactions are said to be transparent because anyone can see all of the transactions for a given currency. For example, there is a website called blockchain.com which updates information about Bitcoin transactions in real time. As I write I can see there is a transfer of $76,724,684.46 initiated a couple of minutes ago and still waiting for verification. During the time it has been waiting to be confirmed the value of the Bitcoin involved has apparently increased by $45,667.51. I can see the "address" of the sender (a 64-character string) , but I cannot see any real information about the person or company behind that address. This is because of the main source of privacy with cryptocurrency: the sender is always using a pseudonym and may in fact use a different pseudonym for every transaction.

Inflation Protection. The design of Bitcoin includes a hard clip limiting the number of Bitcoin that can be created to 21 million. While there is a convoluted process by which this limit could be altered, the prevailing attitude at present seems to be that it will not because having a fixed limit on the amount of Bitcoin in circulation is protection against inflation. Most economists will say that excessive supply of money is a major cause of inflation. One the other hand if productivity increases while the supply of money remains constant, the money becomes more valuable in terms of its purchasing power. Ideally, of course, the supply of money should somehow track with fluctuations in productivity so that the purchasing power of the money remains constant.

Apparently not all cryptocurrencies are designed with this type of limit on the supply of currency, and obviously the main appeal of cryptocurrencies so far is not that they are form of money whose value is stable, but rather that they are a type of financial asset whose market value is highly volatile.

Any argument that cryptocurrencies are better at preventing inflation would also have to factor in the way in which any number competing currencies can be created.

To my mind, the only coherent justifications for cryptocurrency are the separation of money from government or large banks and the supposed elimination of the need for trust in financial transactions. It is unclear to me that current forms of cryptocurrency can even achieve these goals. Their use depends on the ability to exchange the cryptocurrency for whatever currency is regarded as legal tender and accepted in the society in which one lives. One might even say that the elimination of a trusted intermediary is an illusion since the currency seems to rely on large installations of dedicated computers mostly owned, operated and maintained by a relatively small number of individuals or companies seeking to make a profit off mining and transaction fees.

Some advocates of cryptocurrency are very enthusiastic about the concept of decentralized autonomous organizations in general and the descriptions of how such organizations function sounds very much like the functioning of a cooperative or even a democratic or representative form of government. For some reason it seems to be easier to put ones trust in an anonymous "node" of computer processors than in the person owning it. There may be a lot to be said in favor of decentralizing many aspects of how a society is organized and, as the example of Sardex illustrates, there are clearly some advantages to localized currencies. The problem with cryptocurrencies, though, is that they designed to be global and are not in any way connected to a local economy.

Aside from the waste of energy resources involved in supporting a cryptocurrency, the biggest objection I have to the concept is that is repeats the mistake of assuming that money itself can be an asset that trades on an open market. While there may be nothing inherent in the concept of a cryptocurrency that requires it to be a tradable asset whose value is determined by a market, all of the current implementations seemed to be designed to encourage that. Money can function as a store of value without being a tradable commodity. The techniques involved in cryptocurrency could conceivably used to facilitate international transfers of money without having the currency itself be an "asset" whose value fluctuated according to the expectations of speculators. Whether the degree of secrecy (aka "privacy") currently possible with cryptocurrency transactions is desirable is another matter.

Endnotes

1   When James Carville was a strategist for Bill Clinton's presidential campaign in 1992, he hung a sign in his campaign headquarters that included three points: 1. Change vs more of the same, 2. The economy, stupid and 3. Don't forget health care.

2   Patterson, Richard G, *Understanding Thomas Sowell,* Los Angeles: Royal Garden Press, 2011.

3   "Remarks on The Squam Lake Report: Fixing the Financial System" https://www.federalreserve.gov/newsevents/speech/bernanke20100616a.htm

4   "Chapter 9. Credit Default Swaps, Clearinghouses, and Exchanges". The Squam Lake Report: Fixing the Financial System, Princeton: Princeton University Press, 2010, pp. 109-121. https://doi.org/10.1515/9781400835805-011

5   Ecclesiastes 10:19

6   Rothbard, *The Mystery of Banking* p. 8

7   Samuelson and Nordhaus, Economics, p. 458

8   Pettifor, *Just Money*, p.16

9   Edward Posnett, "The Sardex Factor" Financial Times 9/18/2015

10 For a database of complementary currency systems worldwide see https://www.complementarycurrency.org/ccDatabase/les_public.html

11 Ingham. "Money is a Social Relation."

12 Samuelson and Nordhaus, Economics, p. 453

13 Samuelson and Nordhaus, Economics, p. 420

14 Greider, *Secrets of the Temple* p. 496f

15 Keynes, "Economic Possibilities for our Grandchildren"

16 cf. Greider on usury: Certain principles of money were not subject to alteration by the modern technocratic managers. They might be ignored or forgotten for a time, but they could not be repealed. One of these principles was the ancient biblical injunction against usury. The particular definitions of usury had changed over the centuries, but the

moral meaning had not. Usury was present when lenders insisted on terms that were sure to ruin the borrowers.

Like most moral principles, the sin of usury was grounded in practical necessity. It was more than a social plea for fairness or generosity on the part of the wealthy. No social system could tolerate usury, not as a permanent condition, because it led to an economic life that was self-devouring. The rentier collected his due until he owned all the property and the peasants had nothing. But who would buy the rentier's grain if he had all the money? And how would the peasants survive?

Modern capitalism, less obviously, was subject to the same pathology. The miracle of compound interest, celebrated for its power to stimulate new ventures and generate new wealth, contained a malevolent potential. The process could not function indefinitely if the creditors got most all of the rewards – the new wealth that was derived from their lending – and the enterprising borrowers got little or none. Interest rates set the terms on which the rewards of capitalism would be divided and interest was usurious when the borrower's rightful share of profit was confiscated by the lender.

Capitalism could not long function in that condition. The creative powers of capital were reversed and the compounding interest became destructive. Instead of distributing the bounty widely, the rewards were steadily concentrated in fewer and fewer hands. The process might go on for quite a long time, but eventually it had to fail, either from social upheaval or economic exhaustion.
Greider, *Secrets of the Temple* p. 707

17 Amato & Fantacci *Saving The Market* p. 6

18 Amato & Fantacci *Saving The Market* p. 8f

19 Samuelson and Nordhaus, *Economics*, p.461

20 Keynes, "Economic Possibilities for our Grandchildren"

21 Ibid."

22 Samuelson and Nordhaus, *Economics*, p. 291

23 Samuelson and Nordhaus, *Economics*, p.293

24 Gardner, Jonathan, "When it comes to wealth creation there is no pie." http://www.forbes.com/sites/objectivist/2011/06/14

25 Samuelson and Nordhaus, *Economics*, p.508f

26 Samuelson and Nordhaus, *Economics*, p. 509

27 Ibid.

28 Samuelson and Nordhaus, *Economics*, p. 504

29 Davis and Kim, "Fincialization of the Economy" https://webuser.bus.umich.edu/gfdavis/Papers/Davis_Kim_financialization_revised.pdf p.4

30 Ibid. p 11f

31 Keynes *General Theory* chpt 12

32 "How to hedge a bet for guaranteed profit" https://www.pinnacle.com/en/betting-articles/Betting-Strategy/how-to-hedge- a-sports-bet/T3N2JT3CPUKG78TG

33 Keynes *General Theory* chpt 12

34 One exception may be Justin Fox, a columnist for Bloomberg Opinion. See his"Financial capitalism, what is it good for?" By Justin Fox. Time; January 19, 2010 https://business.time.com/2010/01/19/financial-capitalism-what-is-it-good-for/ and his book *The Myth of the Rational Market: A History of Risk, Reward and Delusion on Wall Street*. New York : Collins Business, 2009|

35 Creating A Sovereign Monetary System Ben Dyson, Andrew Jackson, Graham Hodgson see also Sovereign Money: An Introduction by Ben Dyson, Graham Hodgson & Frank van Lerven http://positivemoney.org/wp-content/uploads/ 2016/12/SovereignMoney-AnIntroduction-20161214.pdf

36 Ibid.

37 cf. Yunus, Muhammad with Karl Weber. *A World of Three Zeros: The New Economics of Zero Poverty, Zero Unemployment, and Zero New Carbon Emissions*. New York: Public Affairs, 2017.

38 Locke, *Second Treatise of Goverment*.

39 Locke, *Second Treatise of Goverment*.

40 Rothbard *For A New Liberty* p. 45

41 https://www.margaretthatcher.org/document/106689

42 Rothbard For A New Liberty p. 47

43 Samuelson and Nordhaus, *Economics*, p. 33

44 Samuelson and Nordhaus, *Economics*, p. 34

45 see for example Bradsher, Greg "How the West Was Settled: The 150-Year-Old Homestead Act Lured Americans Looking for a New Life and New Opportunities" https://www.archives.gov/files/publications/prologue/2012/winter/homestead.pdf

46 Samuelson and Nordhaus, *Economics*, p. 34

47 Samuelson and Nordhaus, *Economics*, p.255

48 Ibid.

49 Shell, Ellen Ruppel. "College May Not Be Worth It Anymore" NY Times, May 16, 2018 https://www.nytimes.com/2018/05/16/opinion/college-useful-cost-jobs.html

50 Samuelson and, *Economics*, p. 33

51 Samuelson and Nordhaus, *Economics*, p. 34

52 Coolidge https://coolidgefoundation.org/resources/essays-papers-addresses-35/

53 Personal email

54 https://www.statista.com/statistics/268356/ratio-of-government-expenditure-to-gross-domestic-product-gdp-in-the-united-states/

55 Mitchell, "Monetary Sovereignty"

56 Roche "Understanding The Modern Monetary System."

57 Amato & Fantacci End Of Finance p. 6

58 Amato & Fantacci End Of Finance p. 89

59 Lerner "Functional Finance and the Federal Debt"

60 cf. http://www.forbes.com/sites/objectivist/2011/06/14/when-it-comes-to-wealth-creation-there-is-no-pie/ where Jonathan Gardner says:
    "All governments act by force when they act.
    Acting by force destroys wealth.
    Therefore, all governments destroy wealth when they act."

61 Thatcher https://www.margaretthatcher.org/document/106689

62 Kelton, Stephanie, *The Deficit Myth*.

63 Samuelson and Nordhaus, *Economics*, p. 617

64 Friedman "The Counter-Revolution in Monetary Theory"

65 Samuelson and Nordhaus, *Economics*, p. 617

66 Samuelson and Nordhaus, *Economics*, p.46

67 Samuelson and Nordhaus, *Economics*, p.47

68 Samuelson and Nordhaus, *Economics*, p. 656

69 Rekhi, Samia "Empirical Estimation of Demand: Top 10 Techniques" https://www.economicsdiscussion.net/demand/empirical-estimation-of-demand-top-10-techniques/19772

70 Samuelson and Nordhaus, *Economics*, p. 654

71 Samuelson and Nordhaus, *Economics*, p. 51

72 Samuelson and Nordhaus, *Economics*, p.52

73 Samuelson and Nordhaus, *Economics*, p.654

74 Samuelson and Nordhaus, *Economics*, p.594

75 Ibid.

76 Samuelson and Nordhaus, *Economics*, p.54

77 https://www.magnifymoney.com/news/us-credit-card-debt-by-the-numbers/

78 https://www.bls.gov/opub/hom/cpi/calculation.htm

79 https://www.investopedia.com/articles/investing/052913/inflations-impact-stock-returns.asp

80 Samuelson and Nordhaus, *Economics*, p 621

81 Phillips. A. W. "A Simple Model of Employment, Money and Prices in a Growing Economy"

82 Samuelson and Solow. "'Analytical Aspects of Anti-Inflation Policy"

83 Samuelson and Nordhaus, *Economics*, p 620

84 Ibid.

85 Samuelson and Nordhaus, *Economics*, p 619

86 United Nations. "Universal Declaration of Human Rights."

87 Readers who are too young to remember Li'l Abner can see Wikipedia: "Created by Al Capp in June 1953, Bashington T. Bullmoose was the epitome of a mercenary, cold-blooded capitalist tyrant tycoon. Bullmoose's bombastic motto...was adapted by Capp from a statement made by Charles E. Wilson, the former head of General Motors when it was America's largest corporation. In 1952, Wilson told a Senate subcommittee, "What is good for the country is good for General Motors, and vice-versa."

88 Samuelson and Nordhaus, *Economics*, p 348

89 Samuelson and Nordhaus, *Economics*, p. 341

90 Samuelson and Nordhaus, *Economics*, p. 342

91 Samuelson and Nordhaus, *Economics*, p. 349

92 Krugman, "Is Free Trade Passé?"

93 Samuelson and Nordhaus, *Economics*, p. 356

94 Samuelson and Nordhaus, *Economics*, p. 344

95 Samuelson and Nordhaus, *Economics*, p. 356

96 Krugman."Is Free Trade Passé?"

97 Krugman, Obstfeld and Melitz. International Economics. p. 47

98 Krugman, "Ricardo's Difficult Idea"

99 Krugman, Obstfeld and Melitz. International Economics. p. 47

100 https://mathshistory.st-andrews.ac.uk/HistTopics/Weather_forecasts/]

101 Krugman, "Ricardo's Difficult Idea"

102 Ibid.

103 Krugman, Obstfeld and Melitz. International Economics. p. 130

104 Krugman, Obstfeld and Melitz. International Economics. p. 130f

105 Krugman, Obstfeld and Melitz. International Economics. p. 229

106 Krugman, Obstfeld and Melitz. International Economics. p. 234

107 Krugman, Obstfeld and Melitz. International Economics. p. 112f

108 Krugman, Obstfeld and Melitz. International Economics. p. 114

109 Ibid

110 Perry, Mark. "Trumpis completely wrong about the U.S. trade deficit." Los Angeles Times, March 16, 2016.

111 Ibid.

112 Brill, *Tailspin* p. 157

113 Krugman, Obstfeld and Melitz. International Economics. p. 39

114 Krugman, Obstfeld and Melitz. International Economics. p. 127

115 Krugman, Obstfeld and Melitz. International Economics. p. 128

116 Bhagwati, Jardish. "The Capital Myth"

117 The Ecnomist "Ten years on: How Asia shrugged off its economic crisis" July 4,2007 https://www.economist.com/news/2007/07/04/ten-years-on

118 Since the 19th century there have been various proposals for basing not just exchange rates but money itself on baskets of goods similar to the basket used to determine the consumer price index. One proposal for a commodity backed international currency used a basket consisting simply of ammonium nitrate, copper, aluminum and plywood, which apparently tracked closely with the U.S. consumer price index for 30 years. Others involved as many as 60 different commodities.]

119 Triffin, R. *Gold and the Dollar Crisis.* New Heaven, CT: Yale University Press 1960

120 Xiaochuan, Zhou. "Reform of the International Monetary System." https://www.bis.org/review/r090402c.pdf.

121 Kelton, Stephanie. *The Deficit Myth p.* 24 ff

122 "The UMKC Buckaroo - A Currency Model for World Prosperity" http://moslereconomics.com/2011/09/19/the-umkc-buckaroo-a-curreny-model-for-world-prosperity/

123 Mosler "Soft Currency Economics"]

124 Kelton, Stephanie. *The Deficit Myth* p. 32

125 Samuelson and Nordhaus, *Economics*, p. 312

126 Arrow, K. J., and Hahn, F. H. General Competitive Analysis. San Francisco: Holden-Day, 1971.

127 Minsky "Money, Financial Markets, and the Coherence of a Market Economy"

128 Samuelson and Nordhaus, Economics, p. 667

129 Samuelson and Nordhaus, Economics, p.52

130 Samuelson and Nordhaus, Economics, p.28

131 Frazier, Ian. "Grim Reapers" The New York Review of Books, February 9, 2023.

132 http://www.nytimes.com/2003/07/29/us/threats-responses-plans-criticisms-pentagon-prepares-futures-market-terror.html

133 Minsky *Stabilizing An Unstable Economy* p.112

134 Minsky *Stabilizing An Unstable Economy* p.112

135 Jack Dorsey in an interview: https://www.cnbc.com/2021/07/21/jack-dorsey-hopes-bitcoin-will-help-bring-about-world-peace.html

136 Nakamoto, "Bitcoin"

137 Ibid.

138 "Can Bitcoin's Hard Cap of 21 Million Be Changed?" https://river.com/learn/can-bitcoins-hard-cap-of-21-million-be-changed/

139 Congressional Research Service. "Cryptocurrency: The Economics of Money and Selected Policy Issues" Updated April 9, 2020 https://sgp.fas.org/crs/misc/R45427.pdf

140 Frankel, Matthew. "Could Bitcoin Help Bring Banking to the Underserved?" Apr 6, 2021. https://www.fool.com/investing/2021/04/06/could-bitcoin-help-bring-banking-to-the-underserve/

Bibliography

Abdur-Rahman, Pavel. "What are the assumptions behind Neo-Classical Economics?" Pavel's Thought Wave, June 24, 2011. https://prahman.wordpress.com/2011/06/24/what-are-the-assumptions-behind-neo-classical-economics/.

Abrahamian, Atossa Araxia. "The Rock-Star Appeal of Modern Monetary Theory: The Sanders generation and a new economic idea. The Nation, May 8, 2017.

Aggarwal, Rajesh K. and Tarik Yousef. "Islamic Banks and Investment Financing." Journal of Money, Credit and Banking. Vol. 32, No. 1 (Feb., 2000), pp. 93-120.

Akhtar, M. A. "Understanding Open Market Operations." https://files.stlouisfed.org/files/htdocs/aggreg/meeks.pdf.

Allen, Franklin and Anthony M. Santomero. "The Theory of Financial Intermediation." Wharton Financial Institutions Center Working Paper 96-32. https://ideas.repec.org/p/wop/pennin/96-32.html.

Amato, Massimo and Luca Fantacci. Saving the Market from Capitalism: Ideas for an Alternative Finance, trans Graham Sells. Cambridge: Polity, 2014.

Amato, Massimo and Luca Fantacci. The End of Finance. Cambridge: Polity, 2012.

Anderson, Spencer. "A History of the Past 40 Years in Financial Crises." International Financing Review, 2000 Issue Supplement, http://www.ifre.com/a-history-of-the-past-40-years-in-financial-crises/21102949.fullarticle.

Athanasoulis, Stefano, Robert Shiller and Eric van Wincoop. "Marcro Markets and Financial Security." FRBNY Economic Policy Review, April 1999.

Atkinson, Anthony B. Inequality: What Can Be Done? Cambridge: Harvard University Press, 2015

Baker, Dean. Rigged: How Globalization and the Rules of the Modern Economy Were Structured to Make the Rich Richer. Washington: The Center for Economic and Policy Research, 2016.

Barron, Patrick. "Why We Need Private Property to Deal with Scarce Resources." Mises Daily, Nov. 2, 2015. https://mises.org/library/why-we-need-private-property-deal-scarce-resources.

Barrott, Cheryl, Cllr Matthew Brown, Andrew Cumbers, Christopher Hope, Les Huckfield, Rob Calvert Jump, Neil McInroy, Linda Shaw, et al. "Alternative Models of Ownership: Report to teh Shadow Chancellor of the Exchequer and Shadow Secretary of State for Business, Energy and Industrial Strategy." https://labour.org.uk/wp-content/uploads/2017/10/Alternative-Models-of-Ownership.pdf

Basel Committee on Banking Supervision. "Consultative Document: Strengthening the resilience of the banking sector." Bank for International Settlements, December 2009.

Bator, Francis M. "The Anatomy of Market Failure." The Quarterly Journal of Economics, Vol. 72, No. 3 (Aug., 1958), pp. 351-379.

Bator, Francis M. "The Simple Analytics of Welfare Maximization." The American Economic Review, Vol. 47, No. 1 (Mar., 1957), pp. 22-59

Bell, Stephanie. "Causes and Cures for Unemployment: Assessing the Mainstream View." Center for Full Employment and Price Stability Working Paper No. 8, Jul. 2000. https://pdfs.semanticscholar.org/48bb/ee893b78e8fa6423decf1f66805d6758c5b6.pdf.

Bentham, Jeremy. Defence of Usury. http://oll.libertyfund.org/titles/bentham-defence-of-usury.

Bernanke, Ben S. "Remarks on The Squam Lake Report: Fixing the Financial System." June 26, 2010. https://www.federalreserve.gov/newsevents/speech/bernanke20100616a.htm.

Bhagwati, Jardish. "The Capital Myth: The Difference between Trade in Widgets and Dollars." Foreign Affairs, May/June 1998 pp. 7-12

Bibow, Jörg. "Bretton Woods 2 Is Dead, Long Live Bretton Woods 3?" Levy Economics Institute of Bard, Working Paper No. 597, May 2010.

Block, Walter. "The Negative Interest Rate: Toward a Taxonomic Critique." Journal of Libertarian Studies, Vol. 2, No. 2, pp. 121-124.

Boettke, Peter J. "On reading Hayek: Choice, consequences and The Road to Serfdom." European Journal of Political Economy, 21 (2005), pp. 1042-1053.

Bordo, Michael D. "A Brief History of Central Banks" https://www.clevelandfed.org/newsroom-and-events/publications/economic-commentary/economic-commentary-archives/2007-economic-commentaries/ec-20071201-a-brief-history-of-central-banks.aspx.

Bordo, Michael D. "Gold Standard." Library of Economics and Liberty, http://www.econlib.org/library/Enc/GoldStandard.html.

Brill, Steven. Tailspin: The People and Forces Behind America's Fifty-Year Fall – and Those Fighting to Reverse It. New York: Knopf, 2015

Brown, Brendan. "The case for negative interest rate now." Financial Times, Nov. 20, 2008.

Brown, Norman O. Love's Body. Berkeley: University of California Press, 1966.

Caramazza, Francesco and Jahangir Aziz. "Fixed or Flexible? Getting the Exchange Rate Right in the 1990s." International Monetary Fund: Economic Issues, No. 13, April 1998.

Carlson, Allan. "The Problem of Karl Polanyi." The Intercollegiate Review, Spring 2006, pp. 32-39.

Carruthers, Bruce G. and Arthur L. Stinchcombe. "The Social Structure of Liquidity: Flexibility, Markets and States." Theory and Society, Vol. 28, No. 3 (Jun., 1999), pp. 353-382.

Carsey, William. "Capital Mobility and Comparative Advantage," Economics Colloquium 12/9/14, www2.gcc.edu/dept/econ/assc/.../ASSC%202015%20-%20Carsey,%20William.docx.

Cashell, Brian W. "Inflation and Unemployment: What is the Connection?" Washington, D.C.: Congressional Research Service, 2004.

Cassidy, John. How Markets Fail: The Logic of Economic Calamities. New York: Picador, 2010.

Cassidy, John. "The Minsky Moment." The New Yorker, Feb. 4, 2008.

Catão, Luis A. V. "Why Real Exchange Rates." Finance & Development, September 2007.

Chodorov, Frank. "Taxation Is Robbery." Mises Daily. https://mises.org/library/taxation-robbery.

Choudhury, Masudul Alam. "Princiiples of Islamic Economics." Middle Eastern Studies, Vol. 19, No. 1 (Jan. 1983), pp. 93-103.

Chung, Hun, and Brian Kogelmann. "Enough and as Good: Modeling First Appropriation of Property under Right and Left Libertarianism." http://as.nyu.edu/content/dam/nyu-as/econ/documents/2017-fall/papers_fall-2017/colloquium/Kogelmann%20and%20Ogden%20Paper.pdf.

Clews, Henry. "Money and Usury." The North American Review, Vol. 154, No. 425 (Apr., 1892), pp. 480-488.

Coyne, Edward J., "Mr. Belloc on Usury." Studies: An Irish Quarterly Review, Vol. 21, No. 82 (Jun., 1932), pp. 283-297.

Das, Satyajit .Traders, Guns and Money: Knowns and Unknowns in the Dazzling World of Derivatives. New York: Prentice Hall, 2006.

Davidson, Paul. "A Modest Set of Proposals for Resolving the International Debt Problem." Journal of Post Keynesian Economics, Vol. 10, N. 2 (Winter, 1987-1988) pp. 323-338.

Davidson, Paul. "Efficiency and Fragile Speculative Financial Markets: Against the Tobin Tax and for a Creditable Market Maker." American Journal of Economics and Sociology, Vol. 57, No. 4 (Oct., 1998), pp. 639-662.

Davidson, Paul. "Money and the Real World." The Economic Journal, Vol. 82, No. 325 (Mar. 1972) pp. 101-115.

Davidson, Paul. "Reforming the World's Money" Journal of Post Keynesian Economics, Vol. 15, No. 2 (Winter, 1992-1993), pp. 153-179.

Davis, Gerald F. & Suntae Kim. "Financialization of the Economy." Annual Review of Sociology, Vol 41, No. 1, (2015) pp. 203-221, https://webuser.bus.umich.edu/gfdavis/Papers/Davis_Kim_financialization_revised.pdf

Defila, Heidi. "60 Years WIR Business Circle Cooperative: Origins and Ideology." Frederika Almstedt, trans., https://reinventingmoney.com/almstedt-60_years_wir/.

Dempsey, Gary. "Hayek's Terra Incognita of the Mind." Cato Institute White Paper, March 1, 1996, http://www.cato.org/pub_display.php?pub_id=5101&full=1.

Dillard, Dudley. "Keynes and

Marx: A Centennial Appraisal." Journal of Post Keynesian Economics, Vol. 6, No. 3 (Spring. 1984), pp. 421-432.

Dillard, Dudley. "The Barter Illusion in Classical and Neoclassical Economics." Eastern Economic Journal, Vol. 14, No. 4 (Oct.-Dec. 1988), pp. 229-318.

Dougherty, Ann and Robert Van Order. "Inflation, Housing Costs, and the Consumer Price Index." The American Economic Revue, Vol. 72, No. 1 (Mar., 1982), pp. 145-164.

Dowd, Kevin. "Lessons from the Financial Crisis: A Libertarian Perspective." Libertarian Alliance Economic Notes, No. 111. http://www.libertarian.co.uk/lapubs/econn/econn111.htm.

Duffie, Darrell and Hugo Sonnenschein. "Arrow and General Equilibrium Theory." Journal of Economic Literature, Vol. XXVII (June 1989) pp. 565-598.

Duttagupta, R., R. Goyal, P. Khandelwal, I. Mateos y Lago, A Piris, and N. Raman. "Reserve Accumulation and International Monetary Stability." https://www.imf.org/external/np/pp/eng/2010/041310.pdf.

Dyson, Ben, Andrew Jackson and Graham Hodgson. "Creating A Sovereign Monetary System." Positive Money, July 15, 2014. www.positivemoney.org.

Dyson, Ben, Andrew Jackson and Graham Hodgson. "Would a sovereign money system be flexible enough?." Positive Money, www.positivemoney.org.

Dyson, Ben. "Why We Disagree with Ann Pettifor." Positive Money, June 27, 2014. http://positivemoney.org/2014/06/disagree-ann-pettifor/.

Farooq, Mohammad Omar. "Partnership, Equity-Financing and Islamic Finance: Whither Profit-Loss Sharing." Review of Islamic Economics, Vol. 11, Special Issue 2007, pp. 67-88.

Feser, Edward. "Hayek on Tradition." The Journal of Libertarian Studies, Vol. 17, No. 1 (Winter 2003), pp. 17-55.

Fiebiger, Brett and Scott Fullwiler, Stephanie Kelton and L. Randall Wray. "Modern Monetary Theory: A Debate." Practical Economy Research Institute Working Paper Series, No. 279, January 2012.

Financial Crisis Inquiry Commission. "March 2008: The Fall of Bear Stearns." Financial Crisis Inquiry Report, Chapter 15, Jan. 2011.

Fleming, Michael J. and Kenneth D. Garbade. "Repurchase Agreements with Negative Interest Rates." Current Issues in Economics and Finance, Vol. 10, No. 5, April 2004.

French, Kenneth R., Martin N. Baily, John Y. Campbell, John H. Cochrane, Douglas W. Diamond, Darrell Duffie, Anil K Kashyap, Frederic S. Mishkin, Raghuram G. Rajan, David S. Scharfstein, Robert J. Shiller, Hyun Song Shin, Matthew J. Slaughter, Jeremy C. Stein, René M. Stu. The Squam Lake Report: Fixing the Financial System. Princeton: Princeton University Press, May 2010.

Friedman, Milton. "The Counter-Revolution in Monetary Theory." Institute of Economic Affairs Occasional Paper, No. 33, 1970.

Gardner, Jonathan, "When it comes to wealth creation there is no pie." http://www.forbes.com/sites/objectivist/2011/06/14

Gibson, Michael S. "Credit Derivatives and Risk Management." Finance and Economics Discussion Series, Division of Research & Statistics and Monetary Affairs, Federal Reserve Board, Washington, D.C., 2007-47

Gnos, Claude and Louis-Philippe Rochon. "Reforming the International Financial and Monetary System: From Keynes to Davidson and Stiglitz." Journal of Post Keynesian Economics, Vol. 26, No. 4 (Summer 2004) pp. 613-629.

Goodfriend, Marvin. "Overcoming the Zero Bound on Interest Rate Policy." Federal Reserve Bank of Richmond Working Paper Series, WP 00-03, August 2000. http://www.richmondfed.org/publications/.

Gordon, Barry J. "Aristotle, Schumpeter, and the Metalist Tradition." The Quarterly Journal of Economics, Vol. 75, No. 4 (Nov., 1961), pp. 608-614.

Graeber, David. Debt: The First 5,000 Years. Brooklyn, NY: Melville House, 2011.

Gray, John N. "F. A. Hayek on Liberty and Tradition." The Journal of Libertarian Studies, Vol. IV, No. 2 (Spring 1980), pp. 119-137.

Greco, Thomas H, Jr. Money and Debt: A Solution to the Global Crisis. (Second Edition). Tucson, AZ: Thomas H. Greco, Jr., 1990.

Greco, Thomas H., Jr. and Theo Megalli. "An Annotated Précis, Review, and Critique of WIR and the Swiss National Economy by Prof. Tobias Studer." http://monetary-freedom.net/reinventingmoney/Studer-precis_critique_review_of_wir.pdf.

Greco, Thomas H., Jr., "Sardex, a brief report." https://beyondmoney.files.wordpress.com/2015/08/2015-sardexreport.pdf.

Greenspan, Alan. "Gold and Economic Freedom." http://www.constitution.org/mon/greenspan_gold.htm.

Greenwal, Bruce and Jospeh Stiglitz. "A Modest Proposal for International Money Reform." Jan. 4, 2006. https://www.ofce.sciences-po.fr/pdf/documents/international_monetary_reform.pdf.

Greider, William. Secrets of the Temple: How the Federal Reserve Runs the Country. Greider.New York: Simon and Schuster, 1987.

Griffin, Edward G. The Creature from Jekyll Island: A Second Look at the Federal Reserve Third Edition. Westlake Village, CA: American Media, 1998.

Grignon, Paul. "Is it "Money" or is it "Credit"? What is the Difference?" www.moneyasdebt.net.

Griswold, Daniel T. "Stop Worrying about the U.S. Trade Deficit." Georgetown Journal of International Affairs, Vol. 1, No. 1 (Winter/Spring 2000), pp. 67-72.

Haas, Armin, Leanne J. Ussher, Klaus Töpfer, and Carlo C. Jaeger. "Currencies, Commodities, and Keynes." http://www.sandelman.ca/tmp/earthreserve.pdf.

Hacker, Jacob S. "Universal Insurance: Providing Economic Security to Expand Economic Opportunity." https://www.brookings.edu/research/universal-insurance-enhancing-economic-security-to-promote-opportunity/.

Harari, Yuval Noah. Sapiens: A Brief History of Humankind. New York: Harper Collins, 2015.

Harvey, John T. "What Actually Causes Inflation (and who gains from it)." Forbes, May 30, 2011, https://www.forbes.com/sites/johntharvey/2011/05/30/what-actually-causes-inflation/#1ca73828f9a9.

Hatsopoulos, George N., Paul R. Krugman and Lawrence H. Summers. "U.S. Competitiveness: Beyond the Trade Deficit." Science, New Series, Vol. 241, No. 4863 (Jul. 15, 1988), pp. 299-307.

Hayek, Friedrich A. "A Rejoinder to Mr. Keynes." Economics, No. 34 (Nov. 1931) pp. 398-403.

Hayek, Friedrich A. "Reflections on the Pure Theory of Money of Mr. J. M. Keynes (continued)." Economics, No. 35 (Feb. 1932) pp. 22-44.

Hayek, Friedrich A. "Reflections on the Pure Theory of Money of Mr. J. M. Keynes." Economics, No. 33 (Aug. 1931) pp. 270-295.

Hayek, Friedrich A. "The Pretence of Knowledge." Lecture to the memory of Alfred Nobel, December 11, 1974, http://nobelprize.org/nobel_prizes/economics/laureates/1974/hayek-lecture.html?print=1.

Hayek, Friedrich A. Denationalisation of Money: The Argument Refined (Third Edition). London: The Institute of Economic Affairs, 1990.

Hayek, Friedrich A. The Constitution of Liberty. Chicago:University of Chicago Press, 1978.

Hayek, Friedrich A. The Road to Serfdom with The Intellectuals and Socialsim. London: The Institute of Economic Affairs, 2005.

Hayes, M. G. "Ingham and Keynes on the Nature of Money." Post Keynesian Economics Study Group: Working Paper 1209, https://www.postkeynesian.net/downloads/wpaper/PKWP1209.pdf.

Hazlitt, Henry. Economics in One Lesson. Auburn, AL: Ludwig von Mises Institute, 2008

Hewes, Amy. "Russian Wage Systems under Communism." Journal of Political Economy, Vol. 30, No. 2 (Apr., 1922), pp. 274-278.

Heyne, Paul. The Economic Way of Thinking: Sixth Edition. NewYork: Macmillan, 1991.

Holt, Richard P.F., J. Barkley Rosser, Jr. and L. Randall Wray. "Paul Davidson: The Truest Keynesian?" Eastern Economic Journal, Vol. 24, No. 4 Fall 1998.

Hopper, Gregory P. "What Determines the Exchange Rate: Economic Factors or Market Sentiment?" Business Review, September/October 1997.

Horsefield, J. Keith, ed. The International Monetary Fund 1945 - 1965: Twenty Years of International Monetary Cooperation, Volume III: Documents. Washington: International Monetary Fund: 1969. http://digitalcommons.bard.edu/hm_archive/24

Ingham, Geoffrey. "Further reflections on the ontology of money: responses to Lapavitsas and Dodd." Economy and Society, Vol. 35, No. 2, (May 2006) pp. 259-278.

Ingham, Geoffrey. "Money is a Social Relation." Review of Social Economy, Vol. LIV, No. 4, (Winter 1996) pp. 507-529.

Ingham, Geoffrey. "The Specificity of Money." European Journal of Sociology, Vol. 48, No. 2, (2007) pp. 265–272.

Ingham, Geoffrey. The Nature of Money. Cambridge: Polity, 2004.

Innes, A. Mitchell. "What Is Money?" The Banking Law Journal, May 1913.

Jadlow, Joseph M. "Smith on Usury Laws." The Journal of Finance, Vol. 32, No. 4 (Sep., 1977), pp. 1195-1200.

Jensen, Michael C. "Eclipse of the Public Corporation." Harvard Business Review, September-October 1989, Revised 1997.

Jones, Mark. "Spiritual Capitalism: Wordsworth and Usury." The Journal of English and Germanic Philology, Vol. 92, No. 1 (Jan., 1993), pp. 37-56.

Karabell, Zachary. "The Case for Derivatives: Economist Robert Shiller believes they could help solve the crisis." The Daily Beast, Jan. 23, 2009

Kelton, Stephanie. The Deficit Myth: Modern Monetary Theory and the Birth of the People's Economy. New York: Public Affairs, 2020.

Keynes, J. M. "The Pure Theory of Money: A Reply to Dr. Hayek." Economics, No. 34 (Nov. 1931) pp. 387-397.

Keynes, John M. "Proposals for an International Currency Union: Second Draft, November 18, 1941." http://la.utexas.edu/users/hcleaver/368/368keynesoncutable.pdf.

Keynes, John Maynard. "Economic Possibilities for our Grandchildren" Essays in Persuasion, New York: W. W. Norton & Co., 1963, pp. 358-373.

Keynes, John Maynard. The General Theory of Employment, Interest and Money. https://www.marxists.org/reference/subject/economics/keynes/general-theory/.

Klein, Steven. "Fictitious Freedom: A Polanyian Critique of the Republican Revival." American Journal of Political Science, Vol. 61, No. 4, October 2017, Pp. 852–863.

Kopf, Edwin W. "The Early History of the Annuity." https://www.casact.org/sites/default/files/database/proceed_proceed26_26225.pdf

Kregel, Jan. "Minsky's Cushions of Safety: Systemic Risk and the Crisis in the U.S. Subprime Mortgage Market." Levy Economics Institute Public Policy Brief, No. 93, 2008.

Krugman, Paul R. "Equilibrium Exchange Rates." http://www.nber.org/chapters/c6948

Krugman, Paul. "Deficits and the Printing Press (Somewhat Wonkish." The New York Times, March 25, 2011.

Krugman, Paul R., Maurice Obstfeld and Marc J. Melitz. International Economics: Theory & Policy, Ninth Edition. Boston: Addison-Wesley, 2012.

Krugman, Paul. R. "Is Free Trade Passé?" The Journal of Economic Perspectives, Autumn, 1987, Vol. 1 No. 2, pp. 131-144

Krugman, Paul. "MMT, Again." The New York Times, August 15, 2011.

Krugman, Paul. R. "Ricardo's Difficult Idea" https://web.mit.edu/krugman/www/ricardo.htm

Ladler, David and Nicholas Rowe. "George Simmel's Philosophy of Money: A Review Article for Economists." Journal of Economic Literature, Vol. 18, No. 1 (Mar., 1980), pp. 97-105.

Lavoie, Marc. "The monetary and fiscal nexus of neo-charalism: A friendly critical look." Journal of Economic Issues, Vol. 47, No. 1, pp.1-32.

LeFevre, Robert. "Autarchy Versus Anarchy." Rampart Journal of Individualist Thought, Vol. 1, No. 4(Winter 1965).

Lerner, Abba P. "Functional Finance and the Federal Debt." in Readings In Fiscal Policy. Homewood, IL: Richard D. Irwin, 1955.

Lerner, Abba P. "Money as a Creature of the State." The American Economic Review, Vol. 37, No. 2 (May, 1947). pp. 312-317.

Lewis, Michael. The Big Short: Inside the Doomsday Machine. New York: W. W. Norton, 2011.

Lewison, Martin. "Conflicts of Interest" The Ethics of Usury." Journal of Business Ethics, Vol. 22, No. 4, (Dec., 1999), pp. 327-339.

Lieberman, Marc. "How Budget Deficits Cause Trade Deficits: The Simple Analytics." The Journal of Economic Education, Vol. 21, No. 4 (Autumn, 1990), pp. 388-394.

Little, Jeffrey B. and Lucien Rhodes. Understanding Wall Street: 2nd Edition. Blue Ridge Summit, PA,: Liberty House, 1987.

Locke, John. Second Treatise of Government. https://www.gutenberg.org/files/7370/7370-h/7370-h.htm

Long, Heather. "Why America's return to $1 trillion deficits is a big problem for you." The Washington Post, Apr. 9, 2018.

Lucarelli, Bill. "A New International Bretton Woods System?" Real-World Economics Review, Issue No. 58.

MacKenzie, Donald. "Physics and Finance: S-Terms and Modern Finance as a Topic for Science Studies." Science, Technology, & Human Values, Vol. 26, No. 2 Spring 2001, pp. 115-144.

Maloney, Robert P. "Usury in Greek, Roman and Rabbinic Thought." Traditio. Vol. 27 (1971), pp. 79-109.

Mankiw, N. Gregory. "It May Be Time for the Fed to Go Negative." The New York Times, April 18, 2009.

Matkovic´, Aleksandar, Mark Losoncz and Igor Krtolica ed., Thinking Beyond Capitalism. Belgrade: Institute for Philosophy and Social Theory, University of Belgrade, 2016.

Maurer, Bill. "Forget Locke? From Proprietor to Risk-Bearer in New Logics of Finance." Public Culture Vol. 11 No. 2 (1999) pp. 365-385.

Maurer, Bill. "The Anthropology of Money." Annual Review of Anthropology, Vol. 35 (2006), pp. 15-36.

Mauss, Marcel. The Gift: Forms and Functions of Exchange in Archaic Societies. New York: Norton Library, 1967.

McCulley, Paul A. "The Liquidity Conundrum." CFA Institute Conference Proceedings Quarterly, March 2008.

McTeer, Bob and Pamela Villarreal. "How the Fed Creates Money." National Center for Policy Analysis No. 611, Feb. 28, 2008.

Meikle, Scott. "Aristotle on Money." Phronesis, Vol. 39, No. 1 (1994), pp. 26-44.
Mews, Constant U. and Ibrahim Abraham. "Usury and Just Compensation: Religious and Financial Ethics in Historical Perspective." Journal of Business Ethics, Vol. 72, No. 1 (Apr., 2007), pp. 1-15.
Minozzi, Pietro and Umberto Parisi, "The integration of the stamped money issue into the general equilibrium models." http://sdocument.ish-lyon.cnrs.fr/cc-conf/conferences.ish-lyon.cnrs.fr/index.php/cc-conf/2011/paper/viewFile/51/24.pdf.
Minsky, Hyman P. "Capitalist Financial Processes and the Instability of Capitalism." Journal of Economic Issues, Vol. 14, No. 2 (Jun.., 1980), pp. 505-523.
Minsky, Hyman P. "Money, Financial Markets, and the Coherence of a Market Economy." Journal of Post Keynesian Economics, Vol. 3, No. 1 (Autumn, 1980), pp. 21-31.
Minsky, Hyman P. "The Financial Instability Hypothesis." Levy Economics Institute Working Paper, No. 74, May 1992.
Minsky, Hyman P. and Charles J. Whalen. "Economic Insecurity and the Institutional Prerequisites for Successful Capitalism." Journal of Post Keynesian Economics, Vol. 19, No. 2 (Winter., 1996-1997), pp. 155-170.
Minsky, Hyman P. Ph.D., "Central Banking and Money Market Changes" (1957). Hyman P. Minsky Archive. Paper 194. http://digitalcommons.bard.edu/hm_archive/194
Minsky, Hyman P. Stabilizing an Unstable Economy. New York: McGraw Hill, 2008.
Minsky, Hyman P., "A Positive Program for Successful Capitalism" (1995). Hyman P. Minsky Archive. Paper 74. http://digitalcommons.bard.edu/hm_archive/74
Minsky, Hyman P., "Marxian Economics: A Centenary Appraisal" (1994). Hyman P. Minsky Archive. Paper 170. http://digitalcommons.bard.edu/hm_archive/170.
Minsky, Hyman P., "Reforming Banking in 1995: Repeal of the Glass Steagall Act, Some Basic Issues" (1995). Hyman P. Minsky Archive. Paper 59. http://digitalcommons.bard.edu/hm_archive/59.

Minsky, Hyman P., "Uncertainty And The Institutional Structure Of Capitalist Economies" (1996). Hyman P. Minsky Archive. Paper 24.

Mises, Ludwig von. Human Action: A Treatise On Economics (Fourth Revised Edition). San Francisco: Fox & Wilkes, 1963.

Mises, Ludwig von. The Causes of the Economic Crisis: And Other Essays Before and After the Great Depression. Percy L. Greaves, Jr. ed., Auburn, AL: Ludwig von Mises Institute, 2006.

Mises, Ludwig von. The Theory of Money and Credit. H.E. Batson, trans., Indianapolis: Liberty Fund, 1981.

Mishkin, Frederic S. "Over the Cliff: From the Subprime to the Global Financial Crisis." National Bureau of Economic Research Working Paper No. 16609, Dec. 2010. http://www.nber.org/papers/w16609.

Mishkin, Frederic S. "Systemic Risk and the International Lender of Last Resort." Sep. 28, 2007. https://www.federalreserve.gov/newsevents/speech/mishkin20070928a.htm.

Mishra, Girish. "Karl Polanyi and Globalization." ZNet, Oct. 20, 2008. https://zcomm.org/znetarticle/karl-polanyi-and-globalization-by-girish-mishra/.

Mitchell, Rodger Malcolm. "Monetary Sovereignty: The key to understanding economics." https://mythfighter.com/2010/08/13/monetarily-sovereign-the-key-to-understanding-economics/.

Mitchell, William, L. Randall Wray and Martin Watts. Modern Monetary Theory and Practice: An Introductory Text. Callaghan, NSW: Centre of Full Employment and Equity, 2016.

Mosler, Warren B. "Soft Currency Economics" http://econwpa.repec.org/eps/mac/papers/9502/9502007.txt.

Mosler, Warren B. Seven Deadly Innocent Frauds of Economic Policy. Valence: 2010. www.moslereconomics.com.

Muller, Jerry Z. "The Philosopher of Money." The Wilson Quarterly (1976-), Vol. 26, No. 4 (Autumn, 2002), pp. 52-60.

Murphy, Robert P. "Did Deregulated Derivatives Cause the Financial Crisis?" The Freeman, Vol. 59, Issue 2 March 2009.

Nadeau, Robert. "The Economist Has No Clothes: Unscientific assumptions in economic theory are undermining efforts to solve environmental problems." Scientific American, April 1, 2008. https://www.scientificamerican.com/article/the-economist-has-no-clothes/.

Nakamoto, Satoshi. "Bitcoin: A Peer-to-Peer Electronic Cash System" satoshin@gmx.com www.bitcoin.org

Naughton, Shahnaz and Tony Naughton. "Ethics and Stock Trading: The Case of an Islamic Equities Market." Journal of Business Ethics, Vol. 23, No. 2, (Jan., 2000), pp. 145-159.

Packer, George. "A Dirty Business: New York City's top prosecutor takes on Wall Street crime." The New Yorker, June 27, 2011.

Palley, Thomas I. " Financialization: What It Is and Why It Matters." The Levy Economics Institute Working Paper #525 (December 2007). https://www.levyinstitute.org/pubs/wp_525.pdf

Perry, Mark J. "Trump is completely wrong about the U.S. trade deficit." Los Angeles Times, March 16, 2016.

Persky, Joseph. "Retrospectives: From Usury to Interest." The Journal of Economic Perspectives. Vol. 21, No. 1 (Winter, 2007). pp. 227-236.

Pervez, Imtiaz A. "Islamic Finance." Arab Law Quarterly, Vol. 5, No. 4, (Nov., 1990), pp. 259-281.

Pettifor, Ann. "Islamic Finance: Money, credit and the rate of interest: how today's global financial architecture blocks Islamic Finance." Prime, 2014. http://www.primeeconomics.org.

Pettifor, Ann. "The Power to Create Money 'Out of Thin Air': A review of Geoffrey Ingham's Capitalism." Prime, January 2013. http://www.primeeconomics.org.

Pettifor, Ann. "Why I disagree with Positive Money and Martin Wolf." www.opendemocracy.net /ourkingdom/ann-pettifor/why-i-disagree-with-positive-money-and-martin-wolf.

Pettifor, Ann. Just Money: How Society Can Break the Despotic Power of Finance. Commonwealth Publishing, 2014.

Pettinger, Tejvan. "The link between Money Supply and Inflation." https://www.economicshelp.org/blog/111/inflation/money-supply-inflation/.

Phillips. A. W. "A Simple Model of Employment, Money and Prices in a Growing Economy" Economica Vol. 28, No. 112 (Nov., 1961), pp. 360-370. https://www.jstor.org/stable/2601407

Pierce, Dale. "What is Modern Monetary Theory, or "MMT"?" http://neweconomicperspectives.org/2013/03/what-is-modern-monetary-theory-or-mmt.html.

Pinchot, Gifford. "The Gift Economy" In Context, No. 41, Summer, 1995.

Polanyi, Karl. The Great Transformation. Boston: Beacon Press, 1944.

Posnett, Edward. "The Sardex factor." Financial Times, Sep. 18, 2015. https://www.ft.com/content/cf875d9a-5be6-11e5-a28b-50226830d644.

Prasso, Sheridan T. "The Riel Value of Money: How the World's Only Attempt to Abolish Money Has Hindered Cambodia's Economic Development" Asia Pacific Issues, Analysis from the East-West Center, N. 49, Jan. 2001.

Quirk,William J. "Too Big to Fail and Too Risky to Exist." The American Scholar, Autumn 2012. https://theamericanscholar.org/too-big-to-fail-and-too-risky-to-exist/#.Wwhhay-ZPDY.

Rajan, Raghuram. "The Paranoid Style in Economics." Project Syndicate August 8, 2013. https://www.project-syndicate.org/commentary/the-declining-quality-of-public-economic-debate-by-raghuram-rajan?barrier=accesspaylog.

Roche, Cullen O. "Understanding The Modern Monetary System." http://ssrn.com/abstract=1905625. See also updated version at : https://ssrn.com/abstract=1905625 or http://dx.doi.org/10.2139/ssrn.1905625.

Rojas, Pierre-Hernan. "Triffin Dilemma and Regional Monetary Approach: An appraisal." March 1, 2016. https://hal.archives-ouvertes.fr/hal-01298999.

Rothbard, Murray N. Man, Economy, and State: A Treatise on Economic Principles. Volume 1. Los Angeles: Nash Publishing. 1970.

Rothbard, Murray N. "Praxeology: The Methodology of Austrian Economics." https://mises.org/library/praxeology-methodology-austrian-economics.

Rothbard, Murray N. For a New Liberty: The Libertarian Manifesto. 2nd edition. Auburn, AL: Ludwig von Mises Institute. 1978.

Rothbard, Murray N. The Case Against the Fed. Auburn, AL: Ludwig von Mises Institute. 1994.

Rothbard, Murray N. The Mystery of Banking. 2nd edition. Auburn, AL: Ludwig von Mises Institute. 2008.

Rothbard, Murray N. What Has Government Done to Our Money?. 5th edition. Auburn, AL: Ludwig von Mises Institute. 2005.

Roy, Delwin A. "Islamic Banking." Middle Eastern Studies, Vol. 27, No. 3 (Jul., 1991), pp. 427-456.

Ruml, Beardsley. "Taxes for Revenue Are Obsolete." American Affairs, Jan. 1946.

Samuelson, Paul A. and William D. Nordhaus. Economics: Nineteenth Edition, New York: McGraw-Hill/Irwin. 2010

Samuelson Paul A. and Robert M. Solow. "'Analytical Aspects of Anti-Inflation Policy" The American Economic Review, Vol. 50, No. 2, Papers and Proceedings of the Seventy-second Annual Meeting of the American Economic Association (May, 1960), https://www.jstor.org/stable/1815021

Sandel, Michael J. "What Money Can't Buy: The Moral Limits of Markets." https://tannerlectures.utah.edu/_documents/a-to-z/s/sandel00.pdf.

Sen, Amartya. "Capitalism Beyond the Crisis." The New York Review of Books. March 26, 2009.

Shiller, Robert J. "Derivatives Markets for Home Prices." Cowles Foundation Discussion Paper, No. 1648, March 2008. http://ssrn.com/abstract=1114102.

Shiller, Robert J. "Financial Markets and Risk: Solving Social Problems." Challenge, Vol. 46, No. 3 (MAY-JUNE 2003), pp. 124-134.

Shiller, Robert J. "In Search of a Stable Electronic Currency." The New York Times, March 1, 2014.

Shiller, Robert J. "Indexed Units of Account: Theory and Assessment of Historical Experience." Cowles Foundation Discussion Paper, No. 1171, Feb. 1998. http://ssrn.com/abstract=1114102. http://www.nber.org/papers/w6356.

Shiller, Robert J. "Reviving Real Estate Requires Collective Action." The New York Times, June 23, 2012.

Shiller, Robert J. "Whatever Happened to Wage Insurance." Project Syndicate, March 21, 2006. https://www.project-syndicate.org/commentary/whatever-happened-to-wage-insurance?barrier=accesspaylog.

Shiller, Robert J. and Stefano Athanasoulis. "World Income Components: Measuring and Exploiting International Risk Sharing Opportunities." http://www.nber.org/papers/w5095.

Siems, Thomas F. "10 Myths About Financial Derivatives." Cato Policy Analysis, No. 283, September 11, 1997.

Sill, Keith. "The Economic Benefits and Risks Of Derivative Securities." Business Review, January/February 1997.

Sizemore, Charles Lewis, CFA. "Milton Friedman was Wrong. Inflation is Not Always a Monetary Phenomenon." Demographics, November 30, 2014.

Smith, Adam. An Inquiry into the Wealth and Causes of the Wealth of Nations. http://worldlibrary.org/eBooks/WPLBN0003164422-An-Inquiry-Into-the-Nature-and-Causes-of-the-Wealth-of-Nations-by-Smith-Adam-1723-1790.aspx?&Words=Smith%20Adam%201723-1790.

Speth, James Gustave. "The Joyful Economy: A Next System Possibility." https://thenextsystem.org/the-joyful-economy.

Squam Lake Working Group on Financial Regulation "Credit Default Swaps, Clearinghouses, and Exchanges." Forgien Affairs. Council on Foreign Relations, Center for Geoeconomic Studies, July 2009.

Stiglitz, D. Joseph. "Moving Beyond Market Fundamentalism to a More Balanced Economy." https://www8.gsb.columbia.edu/faculty/jstiglitz/sites/jstiglitz/files/2009_Moving_Beyond_Market_Fundamentalism.pdf.

Stiglitz, Joseph E. "The Current Economic Crisis and Lessons for Economic Theory." Eastern Economic Journal (2009) 35, 281–296.

Stiglitz, Joseph E. "The Ethical Economist." Foreign Affairs, Nov./Dec. 2005, pp. 128-134.

Stiglitz, Joseph E. "Towards a General Theory of Consumerism: Reflections on Keynes' Economic Possibilities for our Grandchildren." https://www.researchgate.net/publication/302984729_Toward_a_general_ theory_of_consumerism_reflections_on_Keynes%27_economic_possibilities_for_our_grandchildren.

Stiglitz, Joseph E. Freefall: America, Free Markets, and the Sinking of the World Economy. New York: W.W. Norton, 2010.

Striner, Richard. "How to Pay for What We Need." The American Scholar, Winter 2012, https://theamericanscholar.org/how-to-pay-for-what-we-need/#.

Taeusch, Carl. F. "The Concept of Usury: The History of an Idea." Journal of the History of Ideas, Vol. 3, No. 3 (Jun., 1942), pp. 291-318.

Tame, Chris R. "Taxation Is Theft." Libertarian Alliance Political Notes No. 44. http://www.libertarian.co.uk/lapubs/polin/polin044.pdf.

Tobin, James. "A General Equilibrium Approach to Monetary Theory." Journal of Money,Credit and Banking, Vol. 1, No. 1 (Feb. 1969), pp. 15-29.

Tobin, James. "Inflation and Unemployment." The American Economic Review, Vol. 62, No. 1/2 (Mar. 1, 1972), pp. 1-18.

Tobin, James. "Money and Finance in the Macro-Economic Process." Nobel Memorial Lecture, Dec. 8, 1981. https://www.nobelprize.org/nobel_prizes/economic-sciences/laureates/1981/tobin-lecture.pdf.

Tutino, Antonella and Carlow E. J. M. Zarazaga. "Inflation Is Not Always and Everywhere a Monetary Phenomenon." DallasFed Economic Letter,Vol. 9 No. 6, (June 2014).

Tymoigne, Éric. "Keynes and Commons on Money." Journal or Economic Issues, Vol. 37, No.3 (Sep., 2003) pp. 527-545.

Tymoigne, Eric. "The U.S. Mortgage Crisis: Subprime or Systemic?" https://www.pdx.edu/sites/www.pdx.edu.econ/files/Tymoigne/Mortgage/Crisis/and/Minsky.pdf.

United Nations. "Universal Declaration of Human Rights." 2015. http://www.un.org/en/universal-declaration-human-rights/.

Ussher, Leanne J. "Combining International Monetary Reform with Commodity Buffer Stocks Keynes, Graham and Kaldor." https://www.ineteconomics.org/uploads/papers/BWpaper_USSHER_040811_EDIT.pdf.

Ussher, Leanne J. "Kaldor's Commodity Reserve Currency." http://www.qc-econ-bba.com/seminarpapers/leanne_figss.pdf.

Whalen, Charles J. "Integrating Schumpeter and Keynes: Hyman Minsky's Theory of Capitalist Development." Journal of Economic Issues, Vol. 35, No. 4 (Dec., 2001), pp. 805-823.

Williamsen, Kurt. "So I'm Told Trade Deficits Are Good." The New American, March 11, 2015. https://www.thenewamerican.com/economy/economics/item/20341-so-i-m-told-trade-deficits-are-good.

Wray, L. Randall. "A Comparison of the Evolution of the Positions of Hyman Minsky and Abba Lerner." Levy Economics Institute Working Paper, No. 900, Jan. 2018.

Wray, L. Randall. "An Irreverent Overview of the History of Money from the Beginning of the Beginning through to the Present." Journal of Post Keynesian Economics, Vol. 21, No. 4 (Summer, 1999), pp. 679-687.

Wray, L. Randall. "Keynes's Approach to Money: An Assesssment After 70 Years." Levy Economics Institute Working Paper No. 438. https://papers.ssrn.com/sol3/papers.cfm?abstract_id=880440&rec=1&srcabs=1639844&alg = 7&pos=7.

Wray, L. Randall. "State Money." International Journal of Political Economy, Vol. 32, No. 3, Heterodox Perspectives on Money and the State (Fall, 2002), pp. 23-40.

Wray, L. Randall. "The Monetary Macroeconomics of Dudley Dillard." Journal of Economic Issues, Vol. 27, No. 2 (Jun, 1993), pp. 547-560.

Wray, L. Randall. "What Happened to Goldilocks? A Minskian Framework." Journal of Economic Issues, Vol. 36, No. 2 (Jun., 2002), pp. 383-391.

Xiaochuan, Zhou. "Reform of the International Monetary System." https://www.bis.org/review/r090402c.pdf.

Yunus, Muhammad with Karl Weber. A World of Three Zeros: The New Economics of Zero Poverty, Zero Unemployment, and Zero New Carbon Emissions. New York: Public Affairs, 2017.

Name Index

A
Amato, Massimo 4, 35, 99, 162
Aristotle 34

B
Bailey, George 75
Bernanke, Ben 3
Branson, Richard 51
Bullmoose, General 133

C
Cassidy, John 2
Cornfeld, Bernard 59
Crusoe, Robinson 50, 51

D
Das, Satyajit 160

E
Einstein, Albert 106
Elliott, T.S. 128

F
Fantacci, Luca 4, 35, 99, 162
Friday 50, 51
Friedman, Milton 110

G
Getty, J. Paul 34
Greenspan, Alan 8

H
Hefner, Hugh 128

K
Kelton, Stephanie 101, 109, 165, 167, 168
Keynes, John Maynard 16, 37, 40, 72, 162, 163

L
Lerner, Abba 100
Lewis, Michael 2, 144
Locke, John 86, 89

M
Madoff, Bernie 69
McDuck, Scrooge 8
Minsky, Hyman P. 64, 171, 178, 179
Mises, Ludwig von 9, 10, 53
Mitchell, Rodger Malcolm 97
Mosler, Warren 97, 165, 166, 167, 168

N
Nakamoto, Satoshi 183
Nixon, Richard 59, 100, 154
Nordhaus, William 57, 110, 112, 115, 122, 137, 139

P
Parker, Dorothy 128
Perry, Mark J. 151, 152, 155
Pettifor, Ann 16, 130
Phillips. A. W. 121, 123
Posnett, Edward 19

R

Rand, Ayn 50, 57
Roche, Cullen O 98
Rothbard, Murray 12, 89, 91
Ruml, Beardsley 168

S

Samuelson, Paul A 57, 110, 112, 115, 122, 123, 137, 139
Sanders, Bernie 101
Smith, Adam 2, 48, 50, 143
Soros, George 59, 78
Stevens, Wallace 128
Stewart, Jimmy 75

T

Tarkovsky, Andrei 86
Thatcher, Margaret 90
Triffin, Robert 161

Y

Yunus, Muhammad 81, 130

www.ingramcontent.com/pod-product-compliance
Lightning Source LLC
Chambersburg PA
CBHW031618210526
45464CB00004B/1637